LOOKING BACKWARD AND LOOKING FORWARD

Looking Backward and Looking Forward

Perspectives on Social Science History

edited by

HARVEY J. GRAFF

LESLIE PAGE MOCH

PHILIP McMICHAEL

with JULIA WOESTHOFF

THE UNIVERSITY OF WISCONSIN PRESS

The University of Wisconsin Press
1930 Monroe Street
Madison, Wisconsin 53711

www.wisc.edu/wisconsinpress/

3 Henrietta Street
London WC2E 8LU, England

Library of Congress Cataloging-in-Publication Data
Looking backward and looking forward : perspectives on social science history / edited
by Harvey J. Graff . . . [et al.].
p. cm.
Includes papers originally presented at the Social Science History Association's annual
meeting in Pittsburgh, 26–29 October 2000, marking its 25th anniversary. The program
was dedicated to the theme: "Looking backward and looking Forward: perspectives on
social science history."
Includes bibliographical references and index.
ISBN 0-299-20340-9 (hardcover : alk. paper) — ISBN 0-299-20344-1 (pbk. : alk. paper)
1. Social sciences—United States—History—Congresses. I. Graff, Harvey J. II. Social
Science History Association.
H53.U5L66   2004
300'.973—dc22   2004012826

CONTENTS

Contents

PREFACE

At its annual meeting in Pittsburgh 26–29 October 2000, the Social Science History Association celebrated its twenty-fifth anniversary. To mark the occasion, the program for the meeting was dedicated to the theme "Looking Backward and Looking Forward: Perspectives on Social Science History." The SSHA departed from convention in order to shape a substantial portion of the program around this broad perspective. This book reflects that special program: it explores the intellectual history of interdisciplinary social science and history, and their relationships within the contexts of the changing structures and organization of knowledge in the second half of the twentieth century.

ACKNOWLEDGMENTS

For major assistance in preparing this volume for publication, we wish to thank:

The Social Science History Association and its officers and executive committee for their support, endorsement, and financial assistance to meet the costs of transcribing the recordings of the Presidential Sessions; and especially, Erik Austin, Executive Director, for untold depths of generosity and help. The SSHA's generous subvention enormously eased and speeded the book's preparation and production.

Laurie McClain, Historical and Legal Transcription, Nashville, for expertly transcribing the tape recordings

Julia Woesthoff, a recent Ph.D. in history at Michigan State University, who assisted with both the original conference program and the preparation of the copy for this book. Julia has worked so long and well on this project that she has earned a place in the SSHA 2000 team

The Program Committee for the 2000 Social Science History Annual Meeting in Pittsburgh, chaired by Leslie Page Moch and Philip McMichael

Judy Warner, Conference Coordinator, Indiana University Conferences

Robert A. Mandel of the University of Wisconsin Press, who immediately understood the value of this book and helped to turn it into print

Raphael Allen, Duke University Press, for valuable conversations about the book and alternative visions for its development.

ABBREVIATIONS

AHA   American History Association
APSA   American Political Science Association
ASA   American Sociological Association
EAP   EurAsian Project in Population and Family History
ESSHC   European Social Science History Conference
HDFH   Historical Demography and Family History
ICPSR   Inter-University Consortium for Political and Social
          Research
INED   Institut National d'Etudes Demographiques
IPUMS   Integrated Public Use Microdata Series project
IUSSP   International Union for the Scientific Study of
          Population
PAA   Population Association of America

LOOKING BACKWARD AND

LOOKING FORWARD

INTRODUCTION

HARVEY J. GRAFF, PHILIP McMICHAEL,

AND LESLIE PAGE MOCH

The Social Science History Association celebrated its twenty-fifth anniversary with its annual meeting in Pittsburgh, 26–29 October 2000. To mark the occasion, we dedicated the program for this annual meeting to the theme "Looking Backward and Looking Forward: Perspectives on Social Science History" and departed from convention in order to shape a substantial portion of the program around this broad perspective. A collection of selected presentations in a variety of formats, this book is one major outcome from an unusually rich program of intellectual celebration and critical stocktaking of what is known collectively as social science history.

To celebrate the foundational and the continuing achievements of the SSHA and social science history more generally *and* to critically review the organization's course and take stock of the interdisciplinary/multidisciplinary fields that we embrace, a substantial number of special sessions took place. These included ten presidential sessions on the founding of SSHA, social science history's prospects for the future, new scholarly communications, philosophy of social science history, and teaching social science history, and seventeen "retrospective" assessments from most of SSHA's networks. The contents of this book are among the products of that rich harvest.

The special sessions made good use of a variety of modes of presentation, from relatively formal presentations of wide-ranging perspectives as well as highly focused critiques and proposed reorientations. Some of the most exciting took the form of panel discussions that fostered a good deal of give-and-take. The contents of this retrospective/prospective volume purposefully reflect that diversity and offer, within the limits of our record of the meeting and of the medium, what one perceptive reviewer referred to as a sense of "being there" and of "scholarship in process" when dialogue and exchange among participants is represented.

Two presidential sessions were conducted as early evening plenaries, with large audiences: "Twenty-Five Years Later: SSHA in the Eyes of Its Founding Spirits" and "Looking Backward and Looking Forward: Social Science History at 2000, Critical Perspectives." The "founders' session" brought together four of SSHA's earlier presidents, in some cases, perhaps, for their final major contribution to the organization. "Looking Backward" included another former president and brought together historians, political scientists, sociologists (among them future presidents). Both are included in this book.

The special sessions combined contributions from senior scholars and younger social science historians; scholars from a number of disciplines and areas of specialization with long histories of active participation in the SSHA shared the podium with junior and senior persons new to the organization. Many of the organization's early leaders were among the distinguished scholars from a wide range of social science and humanities disciplines who participated. Their long and active associations mark social science history.

The ten presidential sessions were audiotaped and transcribed. Together, they constitute a permanent record of the discussions and debates that each of these forums stimulated. They form an exciting part of the record of this special annual meeting, an important resource that we wish to make more accessible in a book drawn from the collective critical stocktaking that formed the core of the twenty-fifth anniversary celebration. This book includes selections from four presidential sessions as well as four of the network reassessments.

Drawing from both presidential and retrospective network sessions, 1999–2000 president Harvey J. Graff and 2000 program chairs Leslie Page Moch (2001–2 president) and Philip McMichael offer in this volume a set of the most current and cogent presentations from the conference. When possible, highlights from the transcribed discussions join with the texts of those presentations to expand on major themes and raise key questions. Enhancing the intellectual importance and excitement of the presentations, the discussions explore ideas in different historical and theoretical contexts; highlight collegial exchanges, often across geographic, chronological, and disciplinary boundaries; and evidence a collective search for new relationships and new modes of understanding across historical social science and social science history. The book captures but also goes beyond the celebration of the SSHA's anniversary and its major components. It is not a "souvenir book." As mentioned above, we strive to present at least a partial sense of "being there" with the variety of formats and modes of presentation included in this collective volume.

In addition to critical reappraisal, the volume also addresses key questions in the history and sociology of knowledge; theory and method across historical social science and social science history; the organization of research; matters of disciplines, multidisciplines, and interdisciplines; and issues of communication across boundaries of disciplines and specializations. The contributors place a very important scholarly and cultural era in historical contexts; they demonstrate and criticize a variety of approaches and interpretations that derive from the intellectual and institutional development of historical social science and social science history.

In making selections for inclusion, our goal is a creative, experimental mix of topics and themes, with presentations and discussions, formal and informal, arranged to promote linkages and contrasts. Taken together, the selections exemplify the past twenty-five and more years of social science history: its achievements and limits, and directions for the future. The volume offers new perspectives on disciplines (and the academy itself), inter- and multidisciplinarity, and movements within or across key dimensions of social science history(ies). We aim at a different kind of collection and an intellectual contribution that develops from efforts to explore modes of interdisciplinarity and multidisciplinarity; and past, present, and future questions about "knowledge" and "history." The Social Science History Association is treated substantively, but it is also a core case study within the recent history of innovations in the intellectual, organizational, and institutional foundations of scholarship.

The twenty-fifth anniversary of an avowedly interdisciplinary scholarly association like the Social Science History Association, which incorporates and privileges (rather than downplays or disparages) differences among scholars with respect, say, to approach, method, or discipline, is in itself grounds for a volume of critical celebration and stocktaking. But the SSHA also represents one critical element and exemplar of fundamental changes in the organized formal pursuit of knowledge that transformed higher education and its disciplinary foundations since World War II.

The circumstances that led to the emergence of social science history within the academy were part and parcel of larger, more thoroughgoing patterns of development that included the enormous expansion of higher education. Over a period of several decades, that expansion embraced the substantial growth of many disciplines *and*—both within and across a number of them—multi- and interdisciplinary challenges to modern universities' organization by discipline. Those challenges or searches for alternative organization or structures of knowledge included area studies, urban studies, human development, race- and ethnic-based studies, and women's or gender studies, for example. To a considerable degree, the inclusion of a number of previously excluded social groups into the modern university propelled much of that change.

The postwar era also saw the rise of whole new realms of expertise within and also across disciplines. Modern specialized research grew in tandem with increased private and especially public support, for example, from the National Science Foundation, the National Institutes of Health, and the National Endowment for the Humanities, for whose grants and awards disciplines and their scholars competed.

While there were some moves in the direction of new departments and disciplines, many important developments seldom led toward new departmental foundations, but stimulated other kinds of connections, communications, and association. The Social Science History Association developed in the interstices between the modern social sciences and the humanities (and certain aspects of the sciences).

The SSHA is important as a significant manifestation of critical transformations that struggled to remake institutional and intellectual structures and relationships both within and across major disciplines. Social science history stands as a compelling study of scholars from a number of specialties and disciplines coming together—regardless of their own differences—in order to search for new, different, and better paths to develop and test new knowledge with new and different theories, hypotheses, sources, approaches, and methods. The critique of the "old" ways was inseparable from the search for "new" ways. These are significant chapters in the intellectual history of the past half-century.

Looking Backward and Looking Forward: Perspectives on Social Science History tells the story of the Social Science History Association in itself and also in terms of the transformation of higher education and academic knowledge. This is the instructive example of a rare but not unique professional society that has searched for ways to develop interdisciplinarily, sometimes as part of an effort to transform disciplines but at other times to provide alternatives to them. The book critically reviews the SSHA's own history as it also evaluates its accomplishments and its limits—new and old—in the year 2000, after twenty-five years as an independent association. Key chapters also raise questions about social science history's future in historical and institutional contexts.

Looking Backward and Looking Forward: Perspectives on Social Science History addresses these questions. Its distinguished contributors speak to these and related themes. To do that, they draw on a variety of modes of presentation, communication, and exchange that constitute one of the book's highlights: from formal papers to shorter statements prepared for panel discussions and aimed at stimulating responses, and summaries of discussions and exchanges. The volume is organized topically, across a set of linked or connected topics. Specifically, the book focuses on an interrelated set of major themes: the SSHA and social science history at 2000; teaching social science history; major fields and networks of social science history past and present; and the future of social science history.

The publication of *Looking Backward and Looking Forward: Perspectives on Social Science History* is very timely. It appears at a moment at which there is an unusual amount of interest in a number of its central issues across a wide range of disciplines in the social sciences and the humanities. The turn from the twentieth to the twenty-first century has been marked by intense interest in and repeated attention to the condition and future of the disciplines as we have known them and the organization of knowledge in the modern university. Simultaneously, the place and the possible futures of interdisciplinarity capture sustained commentary and proposals within disciplines as normatively constructed and, increasingly, across them.

There are many signposts to this stimulating moment. Consider, for example, on the one hand, Sander Gilman's *The Fortunes of the Humanities: Thoughts for After the Year 2000* (2000) with its sustained call within the humanities for interdisciplinary and the transdisciplinary teaching and research. On the other hand, from the social sciences come Immanuel Wallerstein's *The End of the World as We Know It: Social Science for the Twenty-First Century* (1999) and Wallerstein, ed., *Open the Social Sciences: Report of the Gulbenkian Commission on the Restructuring of the Social Sciences* (1996). Within the discipline of history comes Victoria Bonnell and Lynn Hunt, ed., *Beyond the Cultural Turn* (1999) and Terrence McDonald, ed., *The Historic Turn in the Human Sciences* (1996). And from social sciences, normatively construed, there is George Steinmetz, ed., *State/Culture: State Formation after the Cultural Turn* (1999). These are examples from a growing if sometimes very uneven stack of articles, books, and special issues of journals. Their production and consumption by scholars and their students show no sign of decline.

Looking Backward and Looking Forward: Perspectives on Social Science History takes its place among and speaks to these rising currents within and across the disciplines that Europeans usefully call "the human sciences" today. Its appearance, as well as its contents, mark the important place of social science history/historical social science within the changing landscape of the humanities and social sciences in general, and, more specifically, major disciplines that sometimes cross that line itself (history or anthropology, for example).

Looking Backward and Looking Forward's central topics and themes all

8

speak to wider questions about intellectual challenges, innovations, and resistance among and across the fields that constitute the "higher learning" of the modern university.

There are at least four major audiences to whom this book speaks. First are the members and active participants of the Social Science History Association and also the Historical Sociology section of the American Sociological Association and their peers. Their numbers include scholars from history, the social sciences (prominent representatives from economics, political science, sociology, geography, anthropology, including demography, methodology and statistics, theory, comparative studies), a scattering across the humanities (linguistics, philosophy, literature), and graduate students. For them, there is a close fit between very common professional concerns, and the topics, themes, and major examples from the book's essays, panels, and transcriptions. Singly and together, these scholars and their colleagues in several disciplines have followed closely or been involved with the "new currents" of the past thirty to forty years: from quantitative and theoretical turns to those of language, history, culture, and beyond. A number of the intense debates about the present state and possible futures at a time of many promised and threatened changes—*within disciplines and interdisciplinarily*—that occupy many practitioners of the social sciences and the humanities are reflected in the contribution to *Looking Backward and Looking Forward: from qualitative research to new narratives and beyond the cultural turn.*

A larger audience is found more generally among other historians and social scientists interested in general in contemporary issues and debates in their own disciplines and others across their universities. For them, the book is useful with respect to historiography, methods, and approaches; the historical roots of major issues; and the contemporary scene.

Potentially the largest audience is comprised of scholars, advanced students, and a non- or trans-academic readership among those who follow the major debates that have raged widely across all the disciplines of the humanities and social sciences for some years now. The disciplines and interdisciplinary developments, and their organization, locations, and interrelationships—past, present, and future—continue to attract major, probably increasing, attention. The contents of many journals, the titles of conferences, and other professional markers repeatedly attest to this. So do the pages of both general and specialized scholarly journals—such as *Critical Inquiry, Cultural Studies, Social Text, History & Theory, New Literary History, Theory and Society, Politics and Society, Dialectical Anthropology, Reconstructing History, Radical History Review*—in their regular numbers and their special issues.

A fourth audience may be the most important: graduate students in history, the social sciences, and social science history. For them, the book will serve as an introduction to the field and some of its best-known and respected scholars. Other books present important essays in social science history; but the strength of this collection lies in its provision of a valuable means by which to view scholarship as process, providing readers a sense of "being there" as dialogue between and among scholars takes place.

Harvey J. Graff's presidential address, "The Shock of the '"New" (Histories)': Social Science Histories and Historical Literacies" sets the stage and presents an agenda for much of the following discourse. He places the SSHA and social science history in the contexts of changing disciplines and institutions of higher education in the second half of the twentieth century. In part he tells the story of his own generation. He relates disciplinary and intellectual change to perceptions of "crisis" within the discipline of history, and rising interest in history among social scientists. In reviewing critically this history, he takes up the challenge of evaluation—has the SSHA and social science history succeeded or not—and presents examples from his own scholarship in the history of literacy, ending by posing the challenge of "historical literacies."

The two plenary sessions whose presentations follow—"Twenty-Five Years Later: SSHA in the Eyes of Its Founding Spirits," with a roster of earlier presidents and longtime active members, and "Looking Backward and Looking Forward: Social Science History at 2000, Critical Perspectives"—elaborate many of these issues and also examine the continuing promises and problems of interdisciplinary social science history in the late twentieth and early twenty-first centuries.

Closely related issues occupy an original examination of teaching social science history, "Worlding History" by anthropologist Daniel Segal. Segal's paper is followed by excerpts from discussion in the second part of the book.

The third portion of the book considers "Social Science History Past and Present." Shorter essays evaluate major SSHA fields or networks. Richard Steckel overviews major trends in SSHA annual meetings and then focuses on economic history; James Lee considers the history of the family and demography; and Michael Brown the history of race and ethnicity: all centers of longtime interest for social science historians. In the different format of a focused panel discussion on another longstanding interest—literacy—Chad Gaffield, Harvey J. Graff, David Mitch, Anders Nilsson, and David Vincent review the history of literacy as social science history.

Harvey J. Graff, Philip McMichael, Leslie Page Moch

The future of social science history comprises the final section. Sociologist Richard Biernacki's "The Event of Place in Historical Sociology" is followed by discussion from two sessions that focused on these themes: "Southern Perspectives on Historical Social Science" and "New Directions in Historical Social Science."

Part One

THE SSHA AND SOCIAL SCIENCE HISTORY AT 2000

PRESIDENTIAL ADDRESS 2000

THE SHOCK OF THE "'NEW'

(HISTORIES)": SOCIAL SCIENCE

HISTORIES AND HISTORICAL

LITERACIES

HARVEY J. GRAFF

In memoriam: Allan Sharlin (1950–1983),
Social Science Historian

At this meeting, we celebrate twenty-five years of the Social Science History Association, the SSHA. With appreciation from all of us, I acknowledge the achievements of our founders and our long-time members. We stand on their shoulders metaphorically and historically. We mark this anniversary with a plenary president's "founder's session," a variety of retrospective and prospective panels, and the conference theme "looking backward and looking forward."[1] We also commemorate more than twenty-five years of groundbreaking research and recognition of the presence and practice of social science historians along the hallowed halls of history and social science departments—even if it has not always been accompanied by a ready welcome or complete acceptance. (We mark no fewer years of controversy.)[2]

Twenty-five years is a long time in the history of academic disciplines and interdisciplines, a professional association, and professional life courses. The past quarter century has seen the rise, and sometimes the fall, of numerous "'new' histories." Some of the passages have been unusually boisterous. A cry, a refrain of history as a discipline in "crisis" has often accompanied them (see Bogue 1986, 1987; also Fox-Genovese and Lasch-Quinn 1999; Higham 1989; Novick 1988; Ross 1995, 1998, among the literature). For me, these years also embrace my graduate education, my professional vocation as an interdisciplinary and comparative social historian, and my practice as a social science historian.

Despite the recognized achievements of the fields that constitute the SSHA, the status of contemporary social science history is clouded by criticism that risks misconception and distortion. In her recent presidential address to the American Historical Association, Joyce Appleby (1998, 5, 6) complimented social historians but then silenced them: "The new social history swept all before it for a decade or more"—despite its failure to move from data to understanding. By the late 1970s, she said, "social history settled into middle age, its disruptive potential spent."[3] Acknowledging "the rich contribution of much of what was once called the 'new social history,'" Eugene Genovese (1999, 6–7) condemned "much of the history now practiced in the academy [for] becoming increasingly specialized, careerist, bureaucratized, and politically conformist.... Contemporary academic history is being systematically gutted of the breadth, the drama, and, most dangerously, the tragedy that have accounted for its abiding hold over the public imagination." Ironically (to choose a word), Genovese's Historical Society may reflect the historical moment of its founding much like the SSHA reflected its time. Each presented itself as new, in opposition to established or mainstream practice, general and open, and restorative. For the SSHA, the problem was "traditional" or "narrative" history; for Genovese's Historical Society, it was the "new histories," like social science history, that came of age in the decades after the 1960s. Their ideals and agendas differ accordingly.[4] More sympathetic to social science history, Dorothy Ross (1998, 93) observed that "those involved in SSHA's original aims tend to be disappointed" with the outcomes.

SSHA's twenty-fifth anniversary provides an appropriate—perhaps a necessary—occasion to review our own history: to reconsider social science history and the SSHA in their historical contexts. As the terms of criticism old and new illustrate, certain fundamental misconceptions plague the field and promote misunderstanding, at times widely. I seek to clarify that understanding by returning to the historical grounds of our origins and development. By renewing that connection, I propose alternative perspectives on several major issues about which misconstruals are common.

Toward that reconceptualization, I offer a set of intersecting reflections. First, perceptions of a discipline of history in crisis are inseparable from considerations of the rise of new histories, such as social science history. Notions of disciplinary crises and reconstructions of conceptions and practices within disciplines intricately interrelate and powerfully influence each other. That recognition aids efforts to understand crises, new histories, and disciplinary change. Second, despite many images to the contrary, the history of social science history reveals not one but many social science histories. Third, especially when taken together, those histories contradict many claims of declension—of social science history in decline—claims that do violence to social science history and the SSHA. Fourth, at its best social science history transforms the organization and practice of historical research by fostering collaboration. Fifth, social science history makes crucial contributions to important questions in social science, theory, and public discourse, as well as to history. The historical study of literacy provides a rich case in point.[5] Finally, social science histories may help advance special modes of understanding that I call historical literacies.

I present these arguments selectively and briefly. Together they counter common complaints about social science history and offer a different perspective on a vital, ongoing enterprise. Portions of four intersecting stories provide our ground: the history of social science history, the history of the SSHA, the history of the study of literacy, and my own history in social science history.

My predecessors have addressed many of the relevant threads and themes. (See Appendix A for a listing of all the presidential addresses to date.) Lee Benson urged us to "change social science to change the world"; Louise Tilly sought to unite social science history with people's history. Allan Bogue taught us about the SSHA's early history and our "data's dilemmas." William Aydelotte searched for ideas, and William Flanigan queried the conduct of our inquiries. Deirdre McCloskey located the historical squabbles of our times within the battles of "ancients and moderns." Barbara Hanawalt listened to the "voices of social history records" and Barbara Laslett to those of gender. Later, Eric Monkkonen taught lessons from social science history's history, and Susan Watkins explored social networks in history and the social networks of social science history. Tamara Hareven asked, "What difference does it make?" and emphasized the significance of the life course. Theda Skocpol and Ira Katznelson discussed historical problems and promises of democracy, while Roger Schofield and Michael Haines addressed those in demography. All these speak to important chapters in the story of social science history, and they appear in varying combinations of the programmatic, perspectival, promotional, polemical, and personal. As the anniversary moment dictates, my task differs, although I build on their contributions.

Join me as I reflect on our histories past and future. We historians know how tricky this can be. William Taylor's (1992, xviii) comment on his own writings across the 1970s and 1980s about New York City urban culture capture the spirit: "They are shots . . . at a moving target."[6] For us, the historical and the social science disciplines have changed, raising questions about the definitions and practices of both social science history and history. So, too, have the university environments in which most of us labor, along with the world that surrounds us (see Pescosolido and Aminzade 1999). There is also the impact of our own aging, individually and collectively—the life course and generations of social science history—and our patterns of reproduction and production.

Professional Biography and Collective Experience

Temporally, my education and professional life overlap almost completely with the emergence and institutionalization of social science history. Historical, social, and individual times merge and blur. As an undergraduate history major at Northwestern University in the last years of the 1960s, I was generally unaware explicitly that "new histories" were forming. Among assigned course readings, I encountered many new, but now classic works of a historiographic age dawning. The new histories also had the power to shock, we soon learned. (Younger social science historians may not comprehend how exciting this could be, or the strong passions provoked, pro and con.[7])

In a senior honors seminar and a few other courses, I first met Stephan Thernstrom's *Poverty and Progress: Social Mobility in a Nineteenth-Century City* (1964), Peter Laslett's *The World We Have Lost* (1965), Charles Tilly's *The Vendée* (1964), Lawrence Stone's *The Crisis of the Aristocracy, 1558–1641* (1965), Thomas Kuhn's *The Structure of Scientific Revolutions* (1962), E. P. Thompson's *The Making of the English Working Class* (1963), and Barrington Moore Jr.'s *Social Origins of Dictatorship and Democracy: Lord and Peasant in the Making of the Modern World* (1966) among the ur-texts and exemplars of the "new" that was beginning to rock some of the pillars of the mainstream historical and social science professions. All had been published very recently. I met most of these texts again in graduate seminars. I first heard about counterfactuals and canals, slavery's possible profitability, counting occupational and geographic movements, and the early "hyphenated" histories. An avowedly interdisciplinary orientation and a renewed, sometimes passionate sense of the new breadth, the new possibilities for studying the past, and novel uses of history accompanied the presentation and reception of these books.

The new histories that would bloom like a thousand flowers (and some weeds) during the next two decades were only partly visible, but my professors' excitement and the new works themselves were infectious.[8] When we sang "the times they are a-changin'," sometimes we referred to times past. The social and political excitement of the mid-1960s contributed to the aura.

I entered graduate school in 1970. That was a special time. In that one year, John Demos (*A Little Commonwealth: Family Life in Plymouth Colony;* 1970), Philip Greven Jr. (*Four Generations: Population, Land, and Family in Colonial Andover, Massachusetts;* 1970), and Kenneth Lockridge (*A New England Town, The First Hundred Years: Dedham, Massachusetts, 1636–1736;* 1970) published books that changed the terms of American social history. Regardless of differences, each of these works was radically shaped by working on the boundaries of social science and history and by influences outside the borders of American history. The fundamental journals *Comparative Studies in Society and History, Journal of Social History, Historical Methods,* and *Journal of Interdisciplinary History* all began to publish within a few years before or after 1970. Another wave of new history and social science history journals (including *Social Science History, Journal of Family History, Social History, Journal of Historical Sociology, Studies in American Political Development, Journal of the History of Sexuality,* and three journals in women's history, among others), anthologies, and book series soon joined them.[9]

The ICPSR (Inter-University Consortium for Political and Social Research) and the Newberry Library offered the needed grounds for learning methods and techniques, primarily but not exclusively quantitative methods, one badge of the "new" of this era. Those research practices became inseparably associated with social science history, like identification or membership cards.[10] Small conferences and special sessions at annual meetings contributed directly to making personal connections, sparking incipient networks, and forming community(ies) within and across major areas of new histories. They forged links in the chains of historical practices and disciplinary changes that underlay the diffusion of new histories and new historians. In some cases, they led to more formal associations and research groups.[11]

Unaware of perceptions of an impending crisis of the historical discipline as threatened by the new histories, I journeyed north to the University of Toronto to pursue graduate work in history. (I was only a bit more aware of the impending job crisis.) I expected to concentrate in modern British and European history. During my first year, on the recommendation of another student, I met Michael B. Katz, already known for pioneering research in the "new social history" of education, who became my mentor. He introduced me to the practice of social science history and the new social history (see Katz 1968, 1969).

In 1970 Katz was in the early stages of a long-term quantitative study of urban social structure that centered on industrializing Hamilton, Ontario. Around this research he built a group of faculty, graduate students, and staff. The project's collective, collaborative, and continuing dimensions contrasted markedly with the individualism and isolation of traditional historical practice, which represented concrete embodiments of social science history. Katz's study blurred some of the boundaries between graduate research assistant work and serious involvement in empirical research. It promoted shared access to research materials; constructive collective responses to work in progress (in regular seminar meetings); collaborative searches for conceptual approaches and learning methods; and students and faculty working, sometimes publishing, together. The project also helped support some of the direct and indirect costs of student research. A multilayered intellectual and personal support group, the project team was also self-consciously and purposefully interdisciplinary.[12]

For some students, the social organization of social science history was different. As a mode of doctoral-level training, its collective and collaborative dimensions have great advantages.[13] At its best, social science history is a real boost to graduate education and the conduct of research—especially, but not only, large-scale social science historical research. It can be exhilarating, both demanding and supportive, and it can cushion some of the shock of the new. For me, the Toronto experience was formative. I became a new social historian and a quantitative social science historian. I acquired a professional identity, one that was beginning to be recognized, along with knowledge and skills.[14] No less significant, my long involvement with the historical study of literacy began in Katz's seminar (see Graff 1979, 1987, 1995b, and the following discussion).[15]

True to the times, and the fervor of early practitioners, the organization and conduct of social science history constituted a kind of counterculture (or subculture) for new historians—or so they may be viewed historically, with all the ambiguities that the term conveys. This was part of its shock effect—and its appeal. Among the relevant signs—some exaggerated beyond recognition—I identify the collective mode of social organization with principles of sharing and exchange highly praised, method as a membership card (mainly but not only quantitative method), conceptual obsessiveness, numerical biases, and materialist foundations for group maintenance. Specialized professional language (discourse or jargon, depending on one's point of view, or observer bias)—also new to historians—bound many of us, while it distinguished and separated us from others. And, of course, there was an obsession with the "new." These characteristics could take on an aura of cultishness with secret signs; special kinds of behavior and appearance; or in-groupiness, performative elements (distributing and reviewing tables, certain patterns of speech), and intellection. Many of us were seldom seen without an armload of printout or stacks of IBM cards to feed the mainframe. While that might distinguish us from humanities grad students, that we also carried piles of books separated us from social science and science grads. A certain blend of historical and social science rhetoric and attempts at requisite humor characterized our talk. In this construction, the SSHA, especially its early meetings, resembled, if not a rock festival, then perhaps a teach-in (more than, say, a cockfight or a love-in).

By the early to mid-1970s, social science and other new histories' shock of the new redounded loudly of divisions throughout the profession. Doubts expressed by Arthur Schlesinger Jr. (1962) a decade earlier—among other "humanistic" objections to "history by the numbers" and other deviations from master narratives and normative expectations—reverberated and were amplified. Brash overstatements by some new historians about the quality of their history did not lessen the often shrill, (but not always) ill-informed denunciations and wails of woe.

The case against the new mixed and confused a lengthy list of ingredients, including the following: history's supposed loss of identity and humanity in the stain of social science, the fear of subordinating quality to quantity, conceptual and technical fallacies, violation of the literary character and biographical base of "good" history (rhetorical and aesthetic concern), loss of audiences, derogation of history rooted in "great men" and "great events," trivialization in general, a hodgepodge of ideological objections from all directions, and a fear that new historians were reaping research funds that might otherwise come to their detractors. To defenders of history as they knew it, the discipline was in crisis, and the pursuit of the new was a major cause. "Crisis" embraced an extraordinarily wide range of indications, as the preceding list illustrates; it also impinged on issues of identity and confidence. The sins of the sons and daughters seemed without end (see Schlesinger 1962; Himmelfarb 1987; Handlin 1979; Barzun 1974; Stone 1977, 1979, 1987; see also Novick 1988; Higham 1989; Ross 1998).[16]

"New Histories" and "Crisis in History" as History (and as Historical Phenomenon)

Despite its self-proclaimed novelty, what was identified by the 1970s as social science history (in today's cant, for historians, the "social science" or the "quantitative turn"; for social scientists, the "historical turn") was neither as new nor as shocking as outcries suggested. Nor was there one "new history." Important precedents of new histories span the history of history writing. A number have used the New History label. From the mid-to-late nineteenth through the early twentieth centuries, the professionalization of academic disciplines and their institutionalization in universities magnified the importance of claims for novelty and the counterclaims against novelty that they sparked. With other academic disciplines, history's discourse privileges claims of novelty about important aspects of the discipline and its practices (while also privileging certain opposing claims in favor of tradition, trusted "old ways"): discovery, invention, revision, renaissance, and reformation.

Not coincidentally, history also displays a discourse of crisis. Claims about new histories, including recent social science history, bear complicated connections with concerns about academic disciplines that are perceived to be in crisis. Observers differ dramatically, sometimes famously, in their diagnoses about whether disciplinary crises give rise to new histories or whether the new histories themselves precipitate or accompany crises. Those who favor the pursuit of the new tend to see novelty as forged in response to alleged crisis conditions in a field of inquiry. Those opposed to the new view it as cause, accompaniment, or symptom of a dire crisis. I lean more on the side of new histories as responses to perceived problems than as causes of alleged crises. Others disagree (see Hamerow 1987; Higham 1989; Novick 1988; Ross 1998). Over the long term, the rises and falls of new histories are inseparable from perceptions of history in crisis. Grasping their connection, in conjunction with seeing both new histories and crises as multiple and as arising from differing historical contexts, leads us toward a new understanding of what we might call historical change.[17]

Contests over the origins of various new histories (social science history in particular) and the "origin myths" that they stimulate, nicely exhibit these historiographic (and cultural) phenomena. Are they the work of "great male" researchers? solitary work in the laboratory or collective action? results of "scientific method"? work within or at the boundaries of "normal science" because of perceived "breakdowns" in normal practice? knowledge-, problem-, or data-driven? shaped primarily by internal or external factors? actions of historians struggling to save their discipline from the threat of social scientists? Are the origins located or were they found early in regional political and social history research of the 1890s by Frederick Jackson Turner or A. Laurence Lowell, or by the Progressive New Historians led by J. H. Robinson and Charles Beard? New Economic Historians point to Alfred Conrad's and John Meyer's seminal papers on slavery's economics and the early cliometrics meetings. New Political and New Social Historians have their parallels and parables. With respect to cliometrics, Fogel (1983, 8) relates: "Placing a specific date on the birth of cliometrics is quite arbitrary. . . . The difficulty is with the metaphor. Cliometrics was not 'born.' It gradually emerged from a complex set of developments in the social sciences, in history, and in applied mathematics, much of which had already taken place before World War II" (see also Jensen 1969; Bogue 1987; cf. Hamerow 1987). These "complex set[s] of developments" differ for different new histories and different components of social science history. That qualification supports the conclusion that new histories, including social science history, have long had many rooms. They embrace a variety of interests and approaches, theories and methods, regardless of expectations of homogeneity. There are subcultures within the counterculture of social science history's congregants.

Over the long term, we can construe modern history as a succession of one new history after another. Successive proclamations of crises punctuate the landscape: the many threatened deaths of history (see Megill 1985, 1995; White 1966, 1978, 1987; Cohen 1986, 1998). The new histories of the last half-century took root over a longer span. According to I. Olábarri (1995, 4, 6), they derive from historicism, "the 'new way' of understanding history [that] goes back to the first part of the nineteenth century," and from "diverse proposals" for new historical approaches at the turn of the twentieth century. From that genealogy came "the chief 'new histories' which in the last fifty years have . . . brought about a real revolution in historical practice": the Annales school; Marxist historiography; the historians centered around *Past and Present*; American "social scientific" history; and German *Gesellschaftsgeschichte* (or the "Bielefeld school") (ibid., 5–6).[18] Olábarri (ibid., 11) observes, bracingly: "Today it seems that all the 'new histories' which . . . are 'modern histories,' are in crisis."

Many (if not all) of history's periodic crises and contested new waves, especially in the recent era, revolve around relationships with social science disciplines, theories, and methods. History's variable location between the arts and humanities on the one hand and the social sciences on the other has long been a source of ambiguity, ambivalence, and conflict. "Beginning early in the century . . . there has been a succession of 'new histories' based on alliances with the social sciences," observes Ross (1998, 85). After World War II American social scientists and historians "joined again, this time around a more structural analytic model of historiography" (ibid., 89; see also Higham 1989; Novick 1988). "Historians who look to the other social sciences tend to be dissatisfied with

Harvey J. Graff

what they see as their own discipline's conceptual sloppiness, its reliance on anecdotal evidence, its happy privileging of certain stories over others," explains Eric Monkkonen (1994b, 4); "the seeming 'hardness' of the other social sciences, hardness in the sense of rigor, conceptual precision, and the explicit prior stipulation of what constitutes an adequate explanation," attracts them (see also Bogue 1986, 137; Katz et al. 1982, ix–xiii). Those attributes constitute core elements in the crucible from which social science history and the SSHA emerged.

The explosion of new histories after the mid-twentieth century stemmed from the more or less simultaneous remaking of global relationships and social orders within the Western democracies; shifting and conflicting intellectual, cultural, and ideological currents; developments in universities, disciplines, and academic professions; and the promises and problems of seemingly ceaseless transformations. Numerous social groups cried out for recognition of their voices and their histories. They defined themselves by race or ethnicity, class or gender, age or associations, and geography or common historical experiences. These new histories were forged in a world in which overarching hopes and fears proved difficult to separate. A sense of one crisis after another inside and outside the academy closely accompanied the proliferation of one new history after another. Scholars struggled to respond, maintain, or redefine themselves. These were expansive, heady times; they were also tense with challenges, competition, insecurity, and "troubles" (to use Higham's word).

These phenomena combined to create the outlines of social science history among the many new histories and the many crises. Eric Hobsbawm (1972a, 4) finds a first factor in the linkage of global social change to a "general historicization of the social sciences." Revolutions and struggles for emancipation around the world captured the attention of governments, research organizations, and social scientists "to what are essentially problems of historic transformations. These were subjects which had hitherto been outside, or at best on the margins of, academic orthodoxy in the social sciences and had increasingly been neglected by historians" (ibid.; see also Eley 1996; C. Tilly 1981; Ross 1998; and recent issues of *Daedalus*).

In Hobsbawm's view, "the progressive infiltration of history" went farthest fastest in economics with "the deliberate specialization of economic history to fit in with the requirements of the rapidly developing economic theory and analysis." Economics was joined by "the remarkable and world-wide growth of sociology as an academic subject and fashion." In turn, both economics and sociology influenced the stunning rise of historical demography (Hobsbawm 1972a, 4; C. Tilly 1981; Fogel

1975, 1983; Higham 1989). Internal and external forces, pushes and pulls, reinforced each other. On the one hand, as Fogel (1983, 8–9) recounts in the case of economics: by the 1950s "as historians and historically minded social scientists became familiar with [statistical methods developed to study group behavior in biology and physical anthropology, and later to estimate social scientific models] they began to experiment with their applicability to historical issues." On the other hand, as Charles Tilly (1981, 38) tells for other disciplines: "History began to matter." Social science disciplines such as anthropology, sociology, and political science "reached out to reestablish their historical connections," with particular interest in industrialization, rebellion, and family structure: "First, the social-scientific work that had been proceeding in history doubled back on the social sciences. The success of historical demography provided a model. . . . Historical studies of crime, of voting, of urban structure, of social mobility were sufficiently fruitful or provocative. . . . Second (and more important), disillusion with models of modernization and development turned students of large-scale social change toward history" (ibid., 37–38).

Within a global context, social upheavals at home stimulated interests in new histories and social science history. "The political conflict of the 1960s created new historiographical energies and directions," Ross (1998, 91) emphasizes. The civil rights movement, the Vietnam war, youth and women's movements, and changes in higher education shattered the "American Moment" and its faith in the virtues of consensus. The post–World War II democratization of higher education opened the historical profession to men and increasingly to women, making it more representative of American society. From the New Left, the profession gained a wider range of radical views that embraced liberal democratic, populist, Marxist, feminist, and contemporary radical traditions. "It produced a social-cultural history that focused on the 'inarticulate,' the working class, racial minorities, and women, those who had been marginalized in American history and left out of its historiography" (ibid.). These new social histories "from the bottom up" were also influenced by the achievements of European historiography.

"Many varieties of historiography flowed from these influences," Ross (ibid.) rightly states. They include the social science history that cohered in the mid-1970s around the SSHA. Significantly, that new history overlapped with two others: a historical literature that was allied with modernization theories, and the cultural history of marginalized groups that were encouraged by the activism of the 1960s (ibid.).[19]

Almost every one of the many topics generated its own new history, with increasing participation of scholars from groups that were new to academic professions. Almost all the topics found their way into the emerging social science history, and into the SSHA, despite important differences in approaches and emphases. Research that is influenced by modernization theory, the "organizational synthesis," and sociocultural histories of race, gender, class, and ethnicity has always been present (if not dominating or at a consistent level).[20] Absence of such research from many images of the SSHA and social science history is striking (see Ross 1998; Higham 1989; Monkkonen 1994a; see also Bogue 1983, 1986, 1987, and Baker 1999; on differences, see the following discussion). Overly narrow, usually (but not always) denigrating images of social science history exaggerate the omnipresence of quantification; they caricature social science abstractness, obtuseness, and abstruseness—and prose; and they overemphasize homogeneity among researchers and results. They sometimes also brand the approach as ideologically conservative (although for other critics it is ideologically liberal or radical). And they miss the overlap and interplay of interests among proliferating new histories, which I consider to be one of the most interesting dimensions.

The SSHA's principal objective, drafted by Allan Bogue and enshrined in the constitution, declares: "The major purpose of the Social Science History Association is to improve the quality of historical explanation in every manner possible, but particularly by encouraging the selective use and adaptation in historical teaching and research of relevant theories and methods from related disciplines, particularly the social sciences." Bogue's (1986) own construction of "systematic revisionism" captures this nicely (better, for example, than QUASSH; see Kousser 1980). Perhaps greater clarity is found in a conception of social science histories than in a singular social science history. Questions about social science history as theory or practice also arise (see the SSHA presidential addresses, especially those of Benson [1978], Aydelotte [1981], and L. Tilly [1983]; see also Bogue, Floud, and C. Tilly; for critiques, see Handlin 1971, 1975, 1979; Himmelfarb 1975, 1984, 1987; Genovese and Fox-Genovese 1982). (Excerpts from the SSHA constitution and mission statements of purpose from the journal appear in Appendix B.)

Social science history and new history are not synonymous or interchangeable. Neither are they fixed categories. They are dynamic historical constructions. They share a great deal (although this fact is neglected by common images or shorthand descriptions). We find their often-rich interplay more common in practice (at the SSHA but elsewhere, too) than in proclamations. The "new social history" is probably the best example of this tangled web. It is joined by other fields that overflow boundaries that sag and blur under efforts to construct them more rigidly than research practices and agendas merit: from cultural or family history to race, gender, immigration, labor, and various hyphenated histories, and many SSHA networks, for example.[21]

With the cumulative effects of the new histories and the social science histories, history changed. And it was a shock. Theodore Rabb (1982, 316–17) reflected: "Starting in the decade after 1945, however, when an exponential increase in the number of new directions for historical research began to develop, confidence about subject matter became less and less attainable." Beset with growth in volume of publications and numbers of Ph.D.s, "assimilating all of this newness—whether it be the use of computers and psychoanalysis, the borrowing from demography and dendrochronology, or the study of hitherto non-subjects, such as fertility and festivals, madness and magic . . . dazzles and dismays, because it appears to have ruptured the traditional bounds of the discipline beyond repair" (ibid.).[22]

Societal transformations—Charles Tilly's (1984) "big structures, large processes"—challenged disciplines that were divided between factions in support of the "new" or the "old," opportunity or crisis, and "correct" positions on the conception and value of history in structures of inquiry and pursuits of knowledge. Historians and social scientists (others, too) reacted contradictorily. Responses to circumstances declared to be "crises" stimulated "new histories" and resistance to them. "Probably the most important of all [historian's reactions in the 1950s] was a general defensiveness and fear of the new and strange," avers Peter Novick (1988, 385). The ascending social sciences attracted historians "who saw an alliance with sociology or political science as a strategy for checking history's relative decline vis-à-vis those disciplines" (ibid., 384). Others responded to the same situation as "a mortal challenge, mandating intransigent resistance." Some scorned new methods; others greeted findings with skepticism or ridicule. To Eugene Genovese and Elizabeth Fox-Genovese (1982, 183), "the social scientist or social historian, in full retreat from the last vestiges of anthropomorphism, scrambles for a theory to consecrate the obscurantism of some seamless abstraction immune to the vagaries of the human will." That there were social scientists who believed and said that historians "would be most usefully employed in supplying them with reliable data" provoked some of the historical discipline's shrillest defensive stances. Differences widened capaciously. The multiple shocks of the new rippled outward (Novick 1988, 384; see also Higham 1989; Ross 1998; C. Tilly 1981; Bogue 1986, 1987). No wonder that in his history Higham (1989) surveys the postwar era as "a time of troubles." However problematic for understanding new histories as historical phenomena, these labels reflect contemporary clashes.[23]

Harvey J. Graff

Conceptual, theoretical, and interpretive elements cut in different directions. As status, material support, intellectual authority, and theoretical foundations all appeared to grow, post–World War II American social science attracted historians who sought to understand a nation that was seemingly disabled by its own success. At the same time, the social sciences "promised relief from historians' epistemological problems" (Ross 1998, 90). For some historians, this relief meant the explicit influence of social science theory (often supporting "ironic" interpretations); for others, it meant more formal use of social science concepts (status anxiety, for example); and for others again, it meant the use of scientific methods. A growing number enlisted in the move toward (social) science, although conceptions of "science" and "social science" (and "history") varied widely. Some social scientists turned toward history as empirical social scientists but also in efforts to redefine their own epistemology and identity (Ross 1998, 92; see also Higham 1989; Monkkonen 1994a; Ross 1991, 1995, 1998; Sewell 1992, 1996; cf. Bogue 1983, 1986, 1987; Aydelotte 1971; C. Tilly 1981; Kousser 1980; and both "hard" and "soft" visions in the SSHA presidential addresses).

In the 1950s and 1960s, an increasing number of political and economic historians argued that "it was scientific method that produced novel findings and reliable generalizations, not borrowed concepts" (Ross 1998, 91). They used theory, but increasingly they urged historians to adopt scientific methods, especially quantitative methods. A new social history "from the bottom up" aimed to correct impressionistic and overgeneralized stories by using large data sets and statistical techniques (Ross 1998, 91). They launched the Social Science History Association (best account is Bogue 1987).

The Social Science History Association as History

This was not the first time that new historians made, or responded to, such claims and advanced such agendas. But this time their effect was greatest, both quantitatively and qualitatively. Never more than a substantial minority, their influence has been significant. History changed, albeit within certain broad limits. Bogue's 1986 (157) conclusion holds: founding social science historians "had a vision of a new era in which different approaches and better tools would bring them closer to a definitive resolution of long-standing historiographic controversies. . . . Their influence is found today in rows of books, substantial runs of new periodicals, recently founded organizations and great changes in old professional institutions and their programs. Some old historiographic controversies have indeed been closed and many unforeseen ones begun." He stopped short of "a verdict," beyond a conviction that their dream's "influence will long be felt."

Neither the historical profession (and its mainstream practices) nor its departments and other institutions, writ large, were transformed or remade. Nor were the social sciences (see Bogue 1986, 1987; Kousser 1989; Reynolds 1998; see also Baker 1999, Burke 1992; Higham 1989; Kammen 1980; Novick 1988; Ross 1998; Stearns 1980; Stone 1977, 1979, 1987; and presidential addresses, especially by Clausen [1988], Hareven [1996], and Monkkonen [1994a]). Social science history changed (Sewell 1992; Maynes 1992; Monkkonen 1994b; McDonald 1996a; Hunt 1989; Bonnell and Hunt 1999; Steinmetz 1999). Fewer and less frequent, newer new histories have changed, too (McDonald 1996a; Hunt 1989; Bonnell and Hunt 1999; Steinmetz 1999). The shocks of the new and their impact were disruptive at times. Nevertheless, Bogue's (1986, 147) riposte to those who complained that new histories "hopelessly splintered the discipline" stands: "Is the degree of scatteration within the profession unreasonable or deleterious? Given the increase in numbers . . . much of the broadening of interest and endeavor appears to be reasonable." Not all agreed (Bogue 1986, 1987; cf. AHR Forum 1989; Hamerow 1987; Handlin 1979; Himmelfarb 1987).

Among the most important of those results is the SSHA. Incorporated in Michigan in 1974, SSHA represented the shared interests of a group of historians and historically minded social scientists who began to develop and promote a "new political history" amid other "new histories." Their common experience at a 1957 Social Science Research Council conference on early American political behavior, and service on the American Historical Association's Ad Hoc Committee on the Use of Quantitative Data in History led them to seek professional change in the form of a new scholarly organization. Bringing historians together with social scientists and developing a historical foundation for political and social research, the ICPSR helped move SSHA's founders toward action.[24]

"New economic historians" contributed another influence, constituent group, and "new history." Adding "new social historians" rapidly expanded the circle of scholars likely to associate with and benefit from a group of other "new historians." Motives ranged widely, from Lee Benson's desire to "change social science to change the world"—establishing general laws of human behavior along the way—to William Aydelotte's goal of improving the practice of historical generalization and explanation, with others in between. Many new historians felt the need for an intellectual and collegial home in their search for new ways "to improve the quality of historical explanation in every manner possible" (SSHA Constitution; see Appendix B). Distinguished by an impressively wide range of interests, they were also marked by an exceptional presence of new Ph.D.s (like myself) and graduate students. Planning took place from 1972 to 1974. A regional conference met in Madison in 1975. Under the umbrella of SSHA's broad objectives, the memorable founding and first annual meeting took place at the University of Pennsylvania in the fall of 1976 (see Bogue 1986, 1987; Monkkonen 1994a and other presidential addresses).[25]

The SSHA began with great expectations: "The early meetings . . . were characterized by an intellectual élan and a sense of being on the cutting edge of scholarship that was most remarkable," recalled Bogue (1987, 338).[26] "In its earliest years a good proportion of the group represented the feeling that quantification equaled social science and that social science history was going to conquer the world," Monkkonen (1994a, 162) remembered.[27] Never disappearing, that spirit has ebbed and flowed over the years. From the first, the SSHA embraced an array of new histories and new historians. Despite contrary images and caricatures, SSHA was never the province mainly of quantitative political or economic historians.[28] Benson, Fogel, and others had proselytized for some years, trumpeting the transformative powers of a social science history that would rewrite history, settle long-standing questions, and resolve uncertainties with its better methods and increased explanatory power. Winning support, paving SSHA's way, they also sparked a varied—sometimes vociferous—opposition. A number of historians, some of them prominent, disagreed, loudly (and famously, led by Bridenbaugh's [1963] notorious "bitch-goddess QUANTIFICATION" slur during his American History Association presidential address (see also Schlesinger 1962; Hexter 1971a, 1971b; Handlin 1979; Himmelfarb 1987; Barzun 1974). Lines immediately formed behind the banners of social science history: pro or con, followed by a parade of dichotomies. SSHA inherited a mixed genealogy, based at least as much on myths, images, and exaggerations as on actual historical practices.

Great expectations inescapably lead to disappointment. For Bogue (1986, 338), "once organized, SSHA drifted rapidly into the pattern of activities found in most small learned societies. Association leaders devoted their attention mainly to sponsoring an annual meeting and publishing a society journal. These functions were in no way reprehensible or trivial," but they lacked the early "élan." They marked a "drift toward conventionality" and accommodation with changing circumstances inside and outside the academy (see also Monkkonen 1994a).

At the same time, SSHA innovated in developing a structure of networks that represent members' major interests—and rise and fall with the fate of those interests, draw members together, plan the annual meeting program, and attract new recruits. They play instrumental roles in maintaining and sustaining the organization, mandating and undergirding multiple "new" social science histories. Network activity— "an unexpected bonus"—became a hallmark or signature of the association, an essential ingredient in SSHA's success (Bogue 1987, 338).[29] As I learned as a graduate student, and occasionally thereafter, social science history can be organizationally innovative.

The question of social science history's legacy does not stop here. A sense of declension is not hard to find: "Those involved in SSHA's original aims tend to be disappointed," surmises Ross (1998, 93), "whether historians devoted to the original quantitative scientific program or social scientists who wanted to transform the social sciences into genuinely historicist disciplines." Despite her awareness of social science history's multiple "theoretical strains," for Ross "quantitative American social science predominated" (ibid.).[30] She writes in a trope of (satirical) declension: "During the 1980s, the scientific fervor of the social science history program receded, the victim of powerful critiques of the results of quantitative history and the broad attack on positivism" (ibid., 92–93). Equating a (relative) decline of science in the form of quantification with disappointment in social science history, she (ibid.) also senses a balance shifting toward social scientists. Her conclusion is muted and ambiguous: "The SSHA nonetheless remains one of the few forums where historians, sociologists, political scientists, and historical economists can listen to one another . . . but it is a long way from the original efforts to reconstitute American historiography" (ibid.).[31]

Ross's unusually sensitive view is incomplete and misleading. She defines social science history too narrowly. She also neglects the significance of the many and changing social science histories; the SSHA's and, more generally, social science history's organizational advances (and organizational culture); and the historical contexts of social science history's "life and times." "Scientific fervor receded" from the founding years. With that shift, the qualities that Bogue subsumes under "élan" faded. This is neither surprising nor exceptional. "Scientific fervor" also receded across the social sciences, and views of science changed. A "drift toward conventionality" may constitute possible grounds for disappointment on one level. Yet all these shifts and drifts are signs of SSHA's establishment, institutionalization, maturation, even a "routinization of charisma."[32] Echoing others, Ross's (partial) misreading raises important questions about SSHA's identity. They include the roles

Harvey J. Graff

of quantification and science; the varieties of social science histories; standards for evaluation (and expectations); and relationships among intellectual currents, professional patterns, and organizational embodiments in the final quarter of the twentieth century and the first years of the twenty-first.

SSHA began amid perceptions of crisis. From its origins the SSHA was attached to certain ideals within historical and social scientific scholarship around which there existed great divisions. Despite changes within disciplines since the 1960s, opposing intellectual currents and their myths persist. This is an ambivalent historical legacy. SSHA's own history provides important clarification. Let us review.

First, consider definitions of social science history and the role of quantification. If the SSHA and social science history have one identifying image, it is quantitative methods. They are a powerful symbol and image. As central as quantification is to social science history and to research in many major branches, it is neither requirement nor test. To presume greater equivalence or synonymy risks erring epistemologically and methodologically (and descriptively), and confusing the two.

Useful definitions of social science history make greater claims for social science history than primarily identifying with the quantitative. These definitions distinguish or at least avoid equating the two.[33] In their 1971 report, *History as Social Science*, David Landes and Charles Tilly (1971, 71–73) list three characteristics of "most (though not all) work in social-scientific history." First is collective history (some call it collective biography). Second is the use of theoretical concepts and models to understand patterns of collective behavior.[34] Third is extensive reliance on comparison.[35] Landes and Tilly (1971, 73) deem quantification one of the "secondary shibboleths of history as social science," while Tilly (1981) notes that quantification is not "the essence." For Bogue (1987, 341), quantification was "never a sine qua non of social science history."[36]

An adequate conception of social science history reflects its preeminent place among the new histories: the expansion of historians' subjects and questions to embrace "virtually every human activity"; a widened range of sources, methods, and conceptual tools to study them; analysis of structures and processes prized over events; and a strong if not exclusive interest in "history from below," rather than identification with a particular set of methods (see Burke 1992; Sewell 1992; Baker 1999).

Second, social science history is more accurately conceptualized and understood in terms of plural or multiple social science histories. Although at times, certain approaches—"empirical, behaviorist, quantitative social science practiced in the United States"—appear to dominate, there has never been one form or formula. The presumption of a single or predominating social science history camouflages important differences among scholars who follow its paths. The SSHA's networks reflect the blending of similarities and differences in practice, along with their changes, topically, methodologically, conceptually, and theoretically. Recognizing SSHA's diversity enhances our appreciation of its achievements (and limits). From the first, students of the working class, women, culture, and other areas shared physical and intellectual space with "hardcore" quantifiers. Where there were once networks in intellectual history and psychohistory, there is now strong interest in narrative and culture. Over the years, the mix but not the fact of diversity has changed.[37]

Varied paths distinguish the journeys that bring different scholars to the SSHA, and then differentiate practitioners across its networks. In the early years, as later, "scientific fervor" had a range of meanings and applications. Participants found different alternatives to normal science. "Some of the social scientists who joined the SSHA in the mid-1970s shared the historians' scientific aspirations," reports Ross (1998, 93); "But most had a very different agenda: while retaining the goal of a generalizing science, they wanted to move beyond a narrow positivism in social science and import some of the hermeneutic understanding and contextual richness of historiography." Monkkonen (1994b, 6–7) quips: "As characterized by Abbott, the issue of quantification in the 1970s worked this way: some historians ran toward it, seeking in quantitative methods the rigor and precision which they felt history lacked, while simultaneously some sociologists (and by extension, other social scientists) ran away from it for what they saw as its false promise of scientificity."[38]

Third, expectations about the course of social science history's development and questions about appropriate standards for its evaluation are complicated problems. Circumstances at the time of SSHA's founding have long influenced the terms and tenor of evaluations. Images of social science history, new histories, and quantification continue to serve as symbols of crisis and division. Too often, the question of numbers becomes a single standard for failure or success; examples taken out of context are turned into hyperbole.[39]

In contrast, expectations were sometimes so high that they were unlikely to be met. The danger of "great expectations" supplies the foundation for the "disappointment" perceived by Ross. History was not "remade." The social sciences were not "transformed into genuinely historical disciplines." Social science history did not "conquer the world" (Ross 1998). Unattainable great expectations were used in arguments that denied significance to social science histories. For promoters,

32

Harvey J. Graff

expectations were spurs to action, modes of recruitment, and ways to attract interest (up to a point). For the faithful, disappointment most often was a temporary condition that faded in the continuing challenge of a "new" past, buoyed by the progress that had been made. Although it was more moderate, that progress was also cumulative, as my predecessors Tamara Hareven and Michael Haines illustrate for the life course and the mortality transition. "A drift toward conventionality"; a recession of "scientific fervor"; a "broadened . . . array of interests represented in the SSHA": Those qualities speak to the intellectual and institutional processes by which new subjects and approaches become part of the academy (see Ross 1998, 93). The SSHA is one major product and symbol of that negotiation (see Bogue 1986, 1987; Higham 1989; Ross 1998; Monkkonen 1994b; Abbott 1991, 1999).[40]

Change accompanies development. The SSHA has grown substantially. Its influence is acknowledged widely, and it is honored with imitation by the European Social Science History Association. The membership embraces impressive numbers of graduate students and international scholars. The networks spread quantitatively and qualitatively into areas that were not even contemplated in the 1960s and 1970s. Conceptions of method and theory grow beyond the boundaries of the early years. From "new political" and "new economic" histories to "new social," then "new cultural" histories, "turns" historical and linguistic and beyond [the cultural turn]—new histories and social science histories continue to intermingle and interchange (Bonnell and Hunt 1999; Steinmetz 1999).[41] *Social Science History* publishes critiques from the vantage of changing science and changing humanities, as well as changing social science, as those domains cross each other, blurring boundaries.[42]

With aging and growth also come challenges.[43] Within the SSHA interests shift. Narrative, culture, gender, the state, certain aspects of religion, labor, race/ethnicity, and attendant theory and methods lately attract renewed attention (Baker 1999; Sewell et al. 1992). Cultural and anthropological topics, including discourse, appeared on early SSHA programs but were not major currents. Interest in them grew in accord with larger intellectual trends. Narrative, for example, became a more abiding interest by the mid-to-late 1980s. SSHA seems to have come late to certain rising intellectual currents; it has had implicit limits and exclusions. Conceptions (often implicit) of both social science and history were sometimes narrow, but at other times or with other topics, they were expansive. Topics and themes that were not ordinarily associated, at least rhetorically, with SSHA were present as a kind of "cultural underground." SSHA has changed over its quarter century (changes over which practitioners conflict) (see Abbott 1991; Baker 1999; Bonnell and Hunt 1999; Hunt 1989; McDonald 1996).

Introducing a special section on narratives and social identities in *Social Science History* in 1992, William H. Sewell Jr. (1992, 479), emphasized a "departure" from the usual contents of *Social Science History* and the vision of "social-scientifically informed historical study that has dominated the SSHA since its founding." He argues that the articles on narrative mark "a global change" in the relationship of history to the humanities. Sewell (ibid., 481) speaks to the dynamism, potential, and limits of a maturing social science history that no longer saw the humanities as "an atheoretical backwash." During the 1970s and 1980s, he narrates, the humanities disciplines were transformed. They became "at least as theoretically self-conscious as the social sciences." At the same time, "many social science historians became dissatisfied with the intrinsic limitations of quantification, which proved of only slight value in reconstructing the life worlds of the past populations it enumerated so precisely." In the 1970s, a number of social science historians turned to cultural anthropology for "inspiration." In the 1980s, some also turned to literary theory and poststructuralist philosophy. Among a "significant subset" of historically minded social scientists, Sewell claims, narrative is "one of the emerging points of intersection" in a developing intellectual collaboration with the humanities (ibid., 480; see also Hunt 1989; Bonnell and Hunt 1999; Steinmetz 1999; McDonald 1996).[44] Therein lay one form of reorientation and renewal for social science historians.

Responding to the same limitations of social science history—"leav[ing] the experiences of identifiable people as historical agents by the wayside as it reconstructed the powerful historical processes that contextualized individual lives . . . losing sight of the larger agenda aimed at understanding and explaining social relations in transformation"— M. J. Maynes (1992, 518; 1995) identifies a related course for reorientation. While Sewell turned to cultural anthropology, literary theory, and contemporary philosophy, Maynes's path lay in interpreting personal documents through feminist theory.

That two sophisticated quantitative social science historians follow new paths within the SSHA attests to the ability to probe, grow, and, much of the time, tolerate difference. That they rub against boundaries, meet resistance, and challenge "traditions," themselves not so old, is unsurprising and potentially constructive. Despite social science history's real achievements, it has had limits, even blinders and biases, along the lines of theory and methods, disciplines, and constellations of fields of inquiry. This, I think, is inescapable. It teaches lessons that are practical and theoretical.[45]

Harvey J. Graff

Social Science Histories and Historical Literacies

With other social science historians whose interests span a wide spectrum, Sewell and Maynes sketch possible "new" social science histories for the twenty-first century. Constituting a part of what I call, collectively, social science histories, they look not only to the social sciences but also to the humanities, the sciences, and developing interdisciplines. Many paths and practices in social science history constitute distinct social science histories. Many of us have known this (almost) all along but have not embraced our differences within commonality publicly and proudly. The number of social science histories, and their breadth, grows. Under a shared umbrella, pluralism—consciously and consistently rigorous, systematic, theoretical, interdisciplinary, and comparative—is a great asset. Newer social science histories build on social science history's strengths and achievements, including its democratic inclusiveness, as they attempt to fulfill their promise and resolve limitations (see L. Tilly 1983; Floud 1984; see also L. Tilly 1989 for the debate in women's/feminist history; Baker 1999).

More a shift in conceptualization than in semantics, social science histories represent a major outcome (in progress) from SSHA's history. Social science histories raise major questions about that past and about the future. Toward a conclusion, I touch briefly on two connected clusters of issues: the project of interdisciplinarity, and the study of literacy. Taking "historical sociology" as an example, we note persisting theoretical and practical problems in linking disciplines and working interdisciplinarily. This concern of social science historians has no singular or easy answers. Although it is a more complicated matter than most early participants in the SSHA presumed, it continues to teach and provoke us, as it continues to add more than a few complications. Closely related is the rich example of the study of literacy considered as social science history.[46] Literacy studies represent one important field in which social science history makes wide-ranging contributions to social science, history, and matters of public debate and policy. Studies of literacy may also point toward some ways in which social science histories can promote special modes of understanding.

From the early days of social science history, the promise of a historical sociology attracted many social scientists and historians. It is prominent in SSHA's foundation and legacy. Within a continuing debate on the status of the "historical turn" in social science, the enterprise of historical sociology sparks a number of sharp criticisms (see McDonald 1996a,

1996b; Skocpol 1984; Skocpol et al. 1987; C. Tilly 1981; Hunt 1989; Bonnell and Hunt 1999; see also Ross 1991, 1995, 1998; Stone 1977, 1979). The story told is a tale of opportunities lost, the power of disciplines, the limits of interdisciplinarity, but also real advances. The lessons of historical sociology are ambiguous. They encourage us to think hard about shared or overlapping but also differing visions for social science histories in the next twenty-five years.

Reflecting on two decades' efforts, Abbott (1991, 201) observes that "one might have predicted that 'as sociology meets history' (C. Tilly 1981), there would arise a demand for synthesis, for a history-as-social-science that would combine the best of both disciplines. . . . But the synthesis has not arrived." Criticism points to several contributing factors. For Abbott, the quantitative history that took on the name "social science history" is one: it drew on a restricted range of social science (207). Craig Calhoun (1996, 327) elaborates: "Framing the project of historical sociology in methodological rather than substantive terms" weakened links to social theory and reduced "much historical sociology to conventional mainstream sociological research using data from the past. The thematic importance of historicity is too often lost."[47] In other words, a restricted conception of history paralleled that of social science.

Historians and sociologists "profoundly" misunderstood each other's disciplinary differences and agendas, the story continues. The central question—"whether the two disciplines are really about the same things or something different"— has not been pursued, suggests Abbott (1991, 211, 213). It is no mean question, even for the SSHA. In its absence, and in their practice, historians and social scientists make "some unique combination of choices among these dichotomies": generalizing and particularizing, quantitative and qualitative, radical and nonradical, political and social, macro and micro (ibid., 211). Abbott (ibid., 230) judges this "a terrible loss": "Conceptualization of social reality as processes of complex events is fundamental to the most effective theoretical traditions in both history and sociology. Only by following it can we address, much less solve, the problem of multiple temporal layers of change that lies at the heart of the history/sociology split" (see also Calhoun 1995, 1998; Sewell 1996).[48] Questions of theory and conceptualization compound, perhaps inseparably, those of method.

The "failure" of an ideal, theoretically robust, and synthetic interdiscipline of historical sociology exemplifies other encounters among the disciplines of social science history. It marks certain limitations and boundaries on interdisciplinary interrelations in which disciplines dialectically engage and transform each other. Instructively, it can direct us to major issues, sometimes unstated, in the linking of disciplines and what we might expect from such meetings. But it also restricts our ability to learn from disciplinary differences and their points in common, and thus increase our ability to probe and confront them. Perhaps there are limits to the radius of "historical" and "social science" turns. That question, and its implications for social science histories, calls out for attention at the SSHA.

"Failure" on that level does relatively little to impugn the ongoing enterprises that constitute the SSHA or obscure the achievements of more than three decades. Few social science historians have aspirations, or even considerations, on that dimension. The distinctions made by the critics of historical sociology identify social sciences histories that differ in ideals and agendas. Regardless, many—perhaps most—social science historians prefer to maintain their disciplinary identity and home base while participating actively in the SSHA. For better or worse, our employment and curricular structures rest on that foundation.

In his critique, Abbott (1991, 230) recognizes, perhaps ironically, the expanse of common ground before us: "Firm connections between history and sociology have tended to occur only within substantive areas or within general approaches like Marxism or feminism." The SSHA program comprises a roster of those "substantive areas." Reaching out, selectively, across history and the social sciences, those connections drive the SSHA and most of social science history today. They connect researchers across disciplinary, chronological, geographic, and conceptual bases. Broadly topical or thematic, they share aspects of conceptualization, theory and method, and understanding—and differences as well. They are embodied and achieve institutional expression in the networks, which are flexible, historical constructions. Today networks range from criminal justice, economics, and education to family/demography, migration, politics, race/ethnicity, states/societies, urban, and women/gender. There we find social science histories past and future.

Prominent among those "substantive areas" is the study of literacy, which has been an established interest of social science historians across disciplines and a presence at SSHA meetings from the early years. The history of literacy is also my longtime companion; it was the lure that attracted me to the new social science history almost thirty years ago and engaged me long after (see for example Graff 1979, 1987, 1993, 1995b). As it happens, literacy and history have much in common. Both are prone to perceptions of crisis and decline—precipitous declines that are sometimes claimed to threaten civilization as we know it. Both are susceptible to mythologization and are hard to define and measure. Social science histories of literacies challenge those charges, among other presumptions about literacy that have been influential in many academic disciplines, in public debate, and among policymakers (see Hirsch 1987; Gagnon and the Bradley Commission 1989; Stearns 1991, 1993; Graff 1979, 1987, 1989, 1993, 1995b, 1999b; Kaestle et al. 1991; Barton 1994; Barton and Hamilton 1998). The history of literacy is an instructive example of social science history with respect to its founding and the course of its development. It followed a path common to social science histories (see, in general for what follows, Graff 1987; Kaestle et al. 1991). On the one hand, pioneering social science historians of the 1960s and 1970s confronted a diffuse historical literature that made easy (if poorly documented) generalizations about the distribution of literacy across populations and also (even though vaguely) the great significance of literacy's presence, absence, or degree of diffusion. On the other hand, they confronted a social science literature, some of it with theoretical aspirations, generally derived from modernization approaches that placed literacy squarely among the requisites for progress by individuals and by groups. The historical writing rested on a thin base of mainly anecdotal evidence, with little concern about its accuracy or representativeness. The social science writing included modernization theories with stages and threshold levels, macrosocial correlations from aggregate data, and, occasionally, contemporary case studies. Writings in both areas treated literacy—whether conceptually or empirically—uncritically and as unproblematic. Literacy's key relationships, they assumed, were simple, linear, and direct, and its impact universally powerful. At the same time, most scholarly writing neglected the subject of literacy even when it was highly relevant.

Critical of earlier work, the new literacy studies that emerged in the 1970s and 1980s questioned the received wisdom that tied literacy directly to individual and societal development, from social mobility (+) and criminal acts (-) to revolutions in industry (+), fertility (-), and democracy (+). Skeptical about modernization models and with at least some of the conclusions taken from aggregative data, researchers who come from an impressive number of nations, disciplines, and specializations were wary about imprecise formulations, levels of generalization, and their evidential basis. Critical and revisionist in intellectual orientation, a generation of scholars sought to test old and newer ideas, hypotheses, and theories with reliable and relevant data.

Specifically, this meant identifying measures of literacy that, ideally, were direct, systematic, routinely generated, longitudinal, and comparable—quantitative indicators all—and building machine-readable databases to promote their use and enhance their accessibility to other researchers. In Sweden, this meant church registers; in France, marriage and military records; in Britain, marriage and census records; and in

Harvey J. Graff

North America, manuscript census records. The dream of a precisely comparative history remains illusive. Literacy studies have taught us to make comparisons more carefully, often restricting their range. As a recognizable field of literacy studies emerged, literacy's significance as an important variable for many subjects across the realms of social science histories was accepted. Its relevance expanded just as expectations of its universal powers were qualified and contextualized.[49]

Earlier expectations (and theories) that literacy's contribution to shaping or changing nations, and the men and women within them, was universal, unmediated, independent, and powerful have been quashed. Literacy—that is, literacy by itself—is now seldom conceptualized as independently transformative. To the contrary, we now anticipate and recognize its impact to be shaped by specific historical circumstances as context-dependent, complicated rather than simple, incomplete or uneven, interactive rather than determinative, and mediated by a host of other intervening factors of a personal, structural, or cultural historical nature rather than universal. In other words, literacy is a historical variable, and it is historically variable.

For example, literacy's students understand that the equation or synonymy of literacy acquisition with institutions that we call schools and with childhood is itself a fairly recent development. Other arrangements were once common. We recognize that the environment in which one learns to read or write has a major influence on the level of ability to use—and the likely use of—those skills. Social attributes (including ascribed characteristics like gender, race, ethnicity, and class) and historical contexts, which are shaped by time and place, mediate literacy's impacts, for example, on chances for social or geographic mobility. Literacy seems to have a more direct influence on longer distance migration. When established widely, that relationship will carry major implications for the historical study of both sending and receiving societies and for immigrants. Literacy's links with economic development are both direct and indirect, multiple, and contradictory. For example, its value to skilled artisans may differ radically from its import for unskilled workers. Literacy levels sometimes rise as an effect rather than a cause of industrialization. Industrialization may depress literacy levels through its negative impact on schooling chances for the young, while over a longer term its contribution may be more positive. Experiences of learning literacy include cognitive and noncognitive influences. This is not to suggest that literacy should be construed as any less important, but that its historical roles are complicated and historically variable. Today, it is difficult to generalize broadly about literacy as a historical factor, but that only makes it a more compelling subject.

Literacy studies have succeeded in establishing a new historical field where there was none. Statistical time series developed for many geographic areas and historical eras limit cavalier generalizations about literacy rates and their strong meanings, whether by demographers, economists, linguists, or literary historians. Three decades of scholarship have transformed how social science historians and many other students conceptualize literacy. Both contemporary and historical theories that embrace literacy are undergoing major revision because of this body of research and recent studies that point in similar directions. The view that literacy's importance and influences depend on specific social and historical contexts—which, in effect, give literacy its meanings: that literacy's impacts are mediated and restricted, that its effects are social and particular, that literacy must be understood as one among a number of communication media and technologies—replaces an unquestioned certainty that literacy's powers were universal, independent, and determinative.

Social science historians know how recently these ideas about literacy's transforming and developmental powers were central to theories that held sway in major areas of economics, demography, psychology, sociology, anthropology, history, and the humanities. The challenge to probe previous understandings with suitable historical data and test the "strong" theories of literacy attests to the contributions that social science history can make. The SSHA is one of the major arenas that foster this kind of critical and constructively revisionist research. It provides a place where ideas and data are exchanged—formally as written and less formally in oral communications in sessions and outside. (That's the kind of complicated communicative context that literacy's historians have learned to appreciate.) SSHA meetings promote interdisciplinary and international advances in criticism, collaboration, and new research that have had demonstrable effects on the theory and practice of literacy studies.

The emergence of literacy as an interdisciplinary field for contemporary students opens the way for a richer exchange between social science historians and other researchers for the mutual reshaping of inquiry past, present, and future that is part of the promise of social science history. Historical studies of literacy, finally, contribute to public discourse, debate, and policy "talk" internationally. The many crucial points of intersection include the demonstration that no "golden age" for literacy ever existed, that there are multiple paths to literacy for individuals and societies, that quantitative measures of literacy do not translate easily to qualitative assessments, that the environment in which literacy is learned affects the usefulness of the skills, that the connections between literacy and inequality are many, and that the constructs of literacy (its learning and its uses) are usually conceived far too narrowly.

Social science historians of literacy need to bring their criticisms and new conclusions to audiences throughout the academy and beyond. Along with other social science historians, they need to confront the limitations of two generations of study of primarily numerical records as they continue to build on that achievement. They need to probe the nature of literacy as a historical subject and variable. In part, they can do this by bridging the present gap between the history of literacy and new research on printing, publishing, and readership, on the one hand, and new perspectives in the humanities, anthropology, and psychology, on the other hand. Literacy studies join other social science histories in exploring new approaches to society and culture through narrative, feminist theories, literary theories, critical theory, and many other interdisciplinary connections across the human sciences in the early twenty-first century. For scholars wary of these interchanges, I emphasize that we undertake these encounters from our foundations as social science historians. That makes a difference.

Many Literacies and Historical Literacies

The identification and initial exploration of multiple or many literacies stand out among the most exciting recent discoveries about literacy. A recognition that alphabetic literacy—reading and writing as we know them—is one set of abilities and orientations (however valuable) among others, with which it interacts, is beginning to reshape thinking about cognition and communication.[50] Enormous implications follow from placing "traditional literacy" within learning and communicative contexts that may also include such "literacies" as numeracy, oral and aural abilities, spatial literacy or graphicacy (as geographers call it), visual abilities, cyber skills, and aesthetic sensibilities, among a great many other literacies touted. Many literacies appeal broadly to researchers and teachers today for reasons that begin with the intuitive and take seriously criticisms of schools that poorly teach a narrow range of literacy skills. They find support in new research about learning. Multiple literacies appeal to historians who wish to broaden the scope of new histories to include a wider realm of human abilities, modes of understanding, and means of communication. New attention to oral culture, nonverbal communications, visual expression, and numeracy mark this interest. Historians of science, for example, suggest that invention and discovery may depend more on visual than on alphabetic literacy. Notions of many literacies also carry implications for training social science historians. Social science history provides a rich laboratory and tool kit to study reading and writing among other literacies in challenging, innovative settings.

From social science histories and many literacies, it is not a large leap toward a new construct that I call historical literacies. The conceptions of both literacy and history that inform the historical literacies I propose bear little relationship to the ahistorical and underconceptualized historical literacy of memorized facts that is linked to E. D. Hirsch's notion of cultural literacy.[51] To the contrary, historical literacies derive from current thinking in both literacy studies and historical studies, and they have a special resonance with social science histories. Social science histories may have the power to promote special modes of inquiry and understanding that derive from and build on the wide-ranging competencies and sensibilities of many literacies and the unusual advantages of histories as ways of knowing and understanding in context. Historical literacies embrace the pluralism and scope that are inherent in integrated concepts of social science histories and multiple literacies. An encompassing set of analytic and synthetic skills and a wide-ranging approach to inquiry join specific modes of interpretation. Together they are rooted in the qualities that only historical thinking can provide. Thinking historically is a distinct mode of thought and path of understanding made possible by the disciplining powers of historical context: time, place, complex relationships, and consequences that arise from the possibilities of the historical moment. New conceptualizations and practices of literacies and histories may transform approaches to history by stressing multiple paths of access, understanding, and expression; multiple modes of inquiry, the fundamental importance of contexts of learning and practice; and the unique power of historical context as components of comprehension in historical terms. Historical imagination is another essential part of historical literacies. Together they promote historical understandings that can inform our apprehension of the present and the future, as well as the past: social science histories looking backward and looking forward.[52]

The Next Twenty-Five Years

In the Social Science History Association's first presidential address, Lee Benson (1978) forcefully stimulated certain "shocks of the new" when he enunciated his goal of "changing social science to change the world." To do that, he declared, SSHA must "restore the historical dimension to the scientific study of human behavior."[53] That was no small charge. Nor was it received uncritically: respondents agreed that Benson went too far.

Regardless of specific criticisms, Benson's spirit still resonates. Allan Bogue (1986, 157) reiterated that spirit when he stated that SSHA's "architects had a dream and . . . its influence will long be felt." In 2001 the influence continues to be felt. We honor it best as we endeavor to change history and the social sciences in order to understand the world better—that is, to understand the world historically. That is the goal of social science histories and historical literacies. The world may, or may not, change. Fittingly for the millennium, the promise of a historically dynamic social science history remains before us.

To the next twenty-five years!

NOTES

A shorter version of this essay was delivered as the presidential address to the twenty-fifth Annual Meeting of the Social Science History Association, Pittsburgh, 28 October 2000. The author thanks Daniel Gelo, Kolleen Guy, Michael B. Katz, James McDonald, and Daniel Scott Smith for their criticisms of an earlier version of the presentation; Charles Thurston and Michelle Herrera for assistance with library research; and Erik Austin for SSHA historical lore and advice.

1. How best to tell my tales is one of many important issues that I cannot discuss here. Parts of many stories intersect here, including my own. Each presentation begs questions of the modes of expression, from different forms of narrative (old or new style) to different forms of analysis, genre, emplotment, trope, and voice. Possible tropes, for example, include romance and comedy—to some they are a tragedy; to many others, a satire. Regardless, this story is both personal and collective, a story replete with ambiguities, indeed with contradictions. It is also a story with many lessons. See, in general, Cox and Stromquist 1998; Hexter 1971a, 1971b; LaCapra 1985; Megill 1985, 1995; Munslow 1997; Nelson et al. 1987; White 1966, 1978, 1987.

2. Questions persist over the status and achievements of social science history. Among a large, often ungainly literature, see Aydelotte 1971; Aydelotte et al. 1972; Benson 1972; Berkhofer 1969; Bogue 1973, 1983, 1986, 1987; Bogue and Clubb 1977a, 1977b; Fogel 1975, 1983; Kammen 1980; Kousser 1977, 1980, 1984, 1989; Landes and Tilly 1971; Lorwin and Price 1972; Reynolds 1998; Stearns 1980. See also Bender 1986; Handlin 1971, 1975, 1979; Hexter 1970, 1971a, 1971b; Higham 1989; Himmelfarb 1975, 1984, 1987; Monkkonen 1986; Munslow 1997; Novick 1988; Ross 1998; Schlesinger 1962; Scott 1988, 1991; Stone 1977, 1987;

Thelen 1987; Veysey 1979a, 1979b. M. J. Maynes gave some unpublished remarks on this topic at the SSHA meeting in Chicago, November, 1998.

3. Appleby blurs social history, quantitative history, and social science history into an amorphous social history, as do many others, including Eugene Genovese. She praises social history for raising "the consciousness of the entire discipline" about methods and data, and for adding so many ordinary people's lives to historical study. See also Charles Wetherell's (1999) incensed critique of Appleby.

4. Thanks to Dan Smith for pointing me to this comparison. The Historical Society has a very different agenda and ideals for the reform of the historical profession. See Fox-Genovese and Lasch-Quinn 1999.

5. There are many other examples, including the history of growing up, another of my interests; see Graff 1979, 1987, 1995a, 1995b.

6. Taylor refers to comments by Clifford Geertz: "Fifteen years in the life of a discipline is also a long time," Taylor (1992, xix) continued; "changes of the same magnitude have overtaken the history of urban cultures, which scarcely existed as a recognizable subspecies of history when I first began to write."

7. See, for example, the noted expressions of Schlesinger 1962; Handlin 1971, 1975, 1979; Hexter 1970, 1971a, 1971b; Hamerow 1987; Barzun 1972, 1974; and Himmelfarb 1975, 1984, 1987, among many others, more or less from a conservative side, and, avowedly from the left, Genovese and Fox-Genovese 1982 and Judt 1979.

8. I am not the only member of that class who became a professor or a historian. See Stone 1977, 1979, for an example of early enthusiasm followed by souring.

9. My first book, *The Literacy Myth: Literacy and Social Structure in the Nineteenth-Century City* (1979), was published in such a series: Charles Tilly's and Edward Shorter's *Studies in Social Discontinuity* series, from Academic Press.

10. I attended the Newberry Library Summer Institute in Quantitative, Demographic, and Family History in 1973. See Graff 1977, 1991, 1995b. In their presidential addresses, Bogue, Clubb, Flanigan, and Miller, among others, underscore the importance of the ICPSR in the construction of the SSHA and social science history more generally. See also Kousser 1977, 1980, 1984, 1989.

11. I refer to the conferences that launched the SSHA itself, as well as the annual Cliometrics meetings and the SUNY-Brockport conferences. Important for me was the "Little Community Conference" at Brandeis University in 1972, the site for my first professional paper. The invitation to participate came from graduate students who organized the conference and faculty who had read my first professional article in *Historical Methods* in 1971 on methods for studying literacy, based on my master's thesis.

12. For descriptions of an approach to social science history, see Graff 1991, 1995b: introduction; Katz 1975; Katz et al. 1982. To be sure, I am describing no utopia: I spent hundreds of hours coding quantitative data from microfilm onto

Harvey J. Graff

eighty-column IBM forms. In the University of Toronto history department, I was told that, until I had completed my comprehensive exams in no less than two to three years, I should plan to read at least one book a day in the library. On the organization of research in social science history, see also Hershberg 1981; C. Tilly 1981.

13. Dangers existed. In some "shops," supervisors' work advanced while students' was subordinated; top-down dictation could dominate over collaboration, imitation over creativity.

14. I became a U.S. and North American historian, with comparative bases in Western European and Canadian history. My interest in social theory found outlets. From my home base working with Katz, I learned a great deal from Toronto's strong and varied group of new historians: Natalie Zemon Davis, Edward Shorter, Jill Conway, and Ian Winchester. Charles Tilly recently had left Toronto for Michigan, but his influence remained.

15. From an initial examination of data from nineteenth-century Canadian manuscript censuses in the context of the new social history and social science history, literacy grew into my doctoral dissertation and a series of publications. This topic was timely in both the historical and the historicist perspectives.

16. For Canadian historiography, see, for example, the writings of Michael Bliss and Jack Granatstein. Critical responses were complicated in Canada, owing to questions about the importing of "foreign" methods from the United States and Europe.

17. The relationship of history in crisis to the phenomenon of "'new' histories" is ambiguous and contradictory but no less important for that. Histories of history reveal this tendency. Questions about politics and ideology arise— for example, questions about the relationships between "new left" historians, "new" histories, and social science histories—but I cannot take them up now. See Ross 1998; Higham 1989; Munslow 1997; Novick 1988; Olábarri 1995; Scott 1988, 1991; also Appleby et al. 1994; cf. Himmelfarb 1987; Handlin 1979; Schlesinger 1962; Hamerow 1987; AHR Forum 1989; Thelen 1987. My grasp of these issues was clarified by teaching in fall 1999, in anticipation of writing this address, a graduate proseminar that I titled "Histories Old and New." My thanks to the students.

18. Olábarri (1995) also discusses what these new histories have in common, and Ross (1998, 85) reminds us that these new histories belong to the history of the social sciences, as well as to history.

19. Ross (1998, 92) also states that "all three set out to remake American historiography on terms suggested by social theory; all have enriched historiography, but none has succeeded in its imperialistic ambition." C. Tilly (1981) credits the failure of "modernization" approaches in social science as a factor propelling historical social science. Stearns (1980) notes its importance for some historians.

20. Here I differ with Ross. I believe that this has been true to a greater extent than she allows. The relationship of each of these histories with quantitative social science history calls out for study.

21. Hobsbawm (1972a) refers to "social history" but is more concerned with what is called social science history. Stone (1977) writes about many of same topics under the rubric of "history and the social sciences." Benson originally proposed the title "Social Scientific History Association." Bogue (1986, 137) observed that "no one has yet offered a satisfactory descriptive label that can embrace the various brands of new history that became clearly visible during the 1960s; perhaps analytic or systematic revisionism, or eclectic empiricism fit best." The "new social history" has had a complicated history with social science history and the SSHA; see, for example, Bogue (1987, 340): "Everyone there [1974 Ann Arbor conference] was fully aware of the popularity of social history but believed that there were broad elements of similarity in the approaches found in all of the 'new' histories, sufficient to sustain cooperative activity." I am arguing against hard and fast distinctions between histories social scientific and histories new. I am not denying differences, some of them very significant. A more complete discussion of those relationships, while important, is not my task here. Too many discussions confuse by making and exaggerating distinctions. There are important issues in the (historical) sociology of knowledge here.

22. Reading "ruptures" is notoriously difficult. At the 1998 SSHA in Chicago, M. J. Maynes spoke movingly about some of the ways in which the profession has not changed with respect to "new histories and some of the human costs."

23. For Novick (1988), the wrecking ball swings from "a convergent culture" and "an autonomous profession" to "the collapse of comity," "every group its own historian," "the center does not hold," and "there was no king in Israel." On Novick's book, see Haskell 1990; Kloppenberg 1989; AHR Forum 1991. By the 1950s, the "presence of that increasingly visible minority [who thought of themselves as social scientists—among them SSHA's founders (William Aydelotte, Lee Benson, Allan Bogue, and Warren Miller)] prompted something of a disciplinary identity crisis," in Novick's (1988, 383) view. On the one hand, "Richard Hofstadter thought that 'at a very primitive level' many historians heard suggestions that their activity might be enriched by the social sciences as a reproach for 'shoddy work or intellectual superficiality'"; on the other hand, "for the many historians who had always thought of themselves as humanists, the suggestion that history should not just use social science but be a social science violated their deepest sense of their identity" (Novick 1988, 385; see also Hexter 1970, 1971b, 1972; Handlin 1979; Himmelfarb 1987; Barzun 1974; Genovese and Fox-Genovese 1982).

24. At the ICPSR, Warren Miller and Jerry Clubb provided a launching site for a new professional organization. See also Jensen 1969.

25. I recall my first meetings with many people, including Allan Sharlin, at

46

Harvey J. Graff

this event. Unlike Eric Monkkonen, I recall the museum reception in Greco-Roman ruins, not an Egyptian tomb. I don't recall it as a place "where we all felt crude and out of place" (Monkkonen 1994a, 162)! I was then a second-year assistant professor. I've attended all subsequent SSHA meetings. As I write, I am flooded by valued memories, which include sessions on several of my books and regular reunions with many friends and acquaintances.

26. Bogue (1987, 338) continued: "It is a commonplace to say that these gatherings were far more stimulating than those of the staid old matrons of the profession, the AHA [American Historical Association] and the OAH [Organization of American Historians]. That is still the case, I think." See also Bogue 1986, 1987, on aspirations, reactions, and others.

27. Monkkonen (1994a, 162) continued: "This was a period marked by small meetings—about one-third the size of this one [1993]—few members, and a sense of mutual exclusion from the professional mainstream coupled with a completely unjustified optimism." Ross (1998, 92) notes that the major new histories "set out to remake American historiography."

28. Nor was it "saved from extinction by an influx of young social historians who turned it into the vital organization." Their presence was anticipated and generally welcomed (Bogue 1987, 340).

29. As founding president, Benson worked to install networks. They were neither in the constitution nor part of planning. Although the number of networks has grown and some have ended, it was only recently discovered that SSHA has no formal provisions for changing networks! Susan Cotts Watkins focused on networks in her presidential address.

30. Ross (1998, 92) continued: for historians seeking science, the "model of science was most often the empirical, behaviorist, quantitative social science practiced in the United States." Without engaging in semantic quibbling, I think her use of "predominated" begs qualification. It casts a sense of homogeneity that may mislead. In some ways, it did—it was certainly a symbol for SSHA; in other ways, it did not. This issue bears further examination.

31. Ross offers no evidence. I am also unsure about her sense of the impact of critiques of quantification and positivism, although SSHA did change. Erik Austin, SSHA executive director, believes that 45 percent to 50 percent of current members are historians; the others are drawn from across a range of disciplines mainly in the social sciences (personal communication, January 2000); see also Bogue 1986, 1987; Higham 1989 [1965]; cf. Monkkonen 1986, 1994a, 1994b; Hareven 1996).

32. Daniel Scott Smith's noted report, "The Needs of a Mature Organization," after twelve years, in the 1989 presidential address, constitutes another sign.

33. On shorthand definitions and possible confusions, see Monkkonen 1994a.

34. A social science historian "begins where possible with an explicit statement of assumptions, concepts, and hypotheses [typically from the social sci-

ences], and he relies on evidence that is reproducible, verifiable, and potentially refutable" (Landes and Tilly 1971, 72).

35. "The systematic, standardized analysis of similar social processes or phenomena . . . in different settings in order to develop and test ideas of how those processes or phenomena work" (Landes and Tilly 1971, 73).

36. With respect to the new political history and the new economic and social histories, Bogue (1986, 137) emphasizes analysis over narrative, problems or themes over periods, process as well as event, ordinary voters over elites, and case study emphasis: "The combination of source materials differed. . . . [Which] in turn suggested the use of new methods and techniques more suited to the different source data." Aydelotte (1971) had relatively little to say specifically about quantitative methods in his book with that title. Compare with Higham 1989; Ross 1998; see also Fogel 1975; Fogel and Elton 1983; Hays 1980; Kousser 1980, 1984, 1989; McDonald 1996a; L. Tilly 1983; Sewell et al. 1992; Burke 1992; Rabb and Rotberg 1982; Gilbert and Graubard 1972; contrast with Handlin 1979; Schlesinger 1962; Barzun 1974; Himmelfarb 1987; AHR Forum 1989.

37. Conference programs offer the best guide, especially for the early years.

38. Monkkonen (1994b, 4) also writes: "The motives of jumping disciplines among historians differ somewhat from those in the other social sciences." See also Abbott 1991.

39. Similarly, single examples stand as the foundation for sweeping condemnations of the entire enterprise, especially Fogel and Engerman's (1974) *Time on the Cross* and Hershberg's (1981) *Philadelphia*. An especially excessive example is Windschuttle 1996. See also Evans 1997 and Himmelfarb's (1975, 1984, 1987) repetitions. These examples also illustrate the confusion of modernist new histories with the alleged effects of more recent linguistic, poststructural, or postmodern "turns."

40. From a less sympathetic vantage point, John Higham (1989, 251) also describes social science history's establishment: "Quantification gained general acceptance as a legitimate and sometimes essential instrument for historians, but its programmatic significance diminished. As its applications became more varied, more familiar, and even conventional in historical research, the mystique it had for enthusiastic practitioners in the 1960's began to fade."

41. Among the new currents are the following: "return to politics," "new institutionalism," policy studies, narrative and discourse, historical geography, world systems, macrohistorical dynamics, and theory and formal methods of diverse kinds.

42. This was also noted by Monkkonen in his presidential address, 1994a; Sewell 1992; Roth 1992; Baker 1999.

43. It is not coincidental that I established a working committee on the future of the SSHA during my year as president.

44. Sewell also addresses some of the problems. Neither traditional critics of social science history nor traditional supporters are pleased by this turn!

45. Both Sewell and Maynes comment on this, Maynes at some length in her presentation to the 1998 SSHA meeting in Chicago. See also Baker 1999. Sewell (1992, 487) also writes: "Until social science historians can show that specific text-reading strategies illuminate the meanings and dynamics of social movements and social processes, the positivistically inclined may feel justified in their skepticism. An analogy may be drawn to the early days of the encounter between social science and history. Throughout the 1950s, many historians borrowed concepts from social science theory; history texts of the period abound with role expectations, relative deprivation, and status inconsistency. But it was only in the 1960s and 1970s, when historians began to adopt the concrete research practices of social scientists, that the breakthrough to a new social science history occurred. Like the historical texts of the 1950s, these texts on narrative test out a new theoretical vocabulary and the issues that it implies. But I am convinced that we cannot realize the full potential of current interdisciplinary explorations along the borders of the social sciences and humanities without following literary theorists beyond their theoretical signposts into the concrete practices of their textual analysis." See also McDonald 1996a, 1996b; Scott 1988, 1991; Sewell et al. 1992.

46. The 2000 SSHA meeting included a roundtable on "Literacy as Social Science History: Its Past and Future." Chad Gaffield, David Mitch (who organized the session), Anders Nilsson, and David Vincent participated, and I chaired it.

47. Calhoun (1996, 328) continues: "But to reduce historical sociology to conventional sociology applied to past times is . . . to deprive it of its main significance."

48. Calhoun (ibid.) adds: "In order to realize its potential both within sociology and in relation to an interdisciplinary historical and theoretical discourse, however, historical sociology needs to address problems of the changing constitution of social actors, the shifting meanings of cultural categories, and the struggle over identities and ideologies. These need to be conceived as part and parcel of social relations, not separate topics of inquiry, and still less as the turf of other disciplines."

49. We have a much sharper conception, for example, of the roles of literacy in nation building, industrialization, urbanization, immigration, demographic transitions, shifts in demand and supply for schooling, the construction of modern differentiated social structures and their cultural concomitants including the emergence of class and mass culture, the spread of social institutions and their impact on lives, the maintenance of social order, and efforts to control disorder.

Disciplinary differences sometimes divide literacy's students; these include conceptual and theoretical interests, overarching questions, preferred methods, styles of analysis, and aspirations for research contributions. Economic historians, for example, are usually more interested in aggregate data, aggregative analysis, and relationships on a macro level so they may examine productivity, sector shifts, or labor force attributes. Social historians typically focus on individual-level records (reaggregated in the middle range) and micro-level analysis to examine immigration, mobility, work, education, or family, often by gender, class, race, and ethnicity. Demographic historians go both ways—for example, in tracking literacy's impact on fertility decline or migration. We learn from the common and the contrasting ground of disciplines.

50. Explicating this is the task for another occasion. In the meantime, see Graff 1993, 1999a, 1999b, and 1999c and works cited therein. Among those who influence my approach to literacy and learning are Daniel Calhoun, Howard Gardner, Barbara Rogoff, Jean Lave, Robert Sternberg, Michael Cole, Shirley Scribner, Shirley Brice Heath, David Barton, and their colleagues. There are dangers here, including the proliferation of too many literacies and the attendant trivialization of the concept.

51. Historical literacy is never defined by Gagnon and the Bradley Commission (1989). On Hirsch, see Graff 1989, 1995b, 1999a, 1999b; Stearns 1991, 1993.

52. For elaboration of at least some of the issues touched on here, see also Graff 1999a, 1999b; Calhoun 1995, 1996, 1998; C. Tilly 1981; Katz 1987, 1995; Hobsbawm 1972a, 1972b, 1981, 1993. My thinking about historical literacies is still preliminary. "Looking backward and looking forward" was the theme for the twenty-fifth anniversary meeting of the SSHA.

53. Benson (1978, 439–40) continued: "SSHA's particular advantage, I believe, is that it was consciously organized to restore the historical dimension to the scientific study of human behavior. Suppose we assume, as I do, that an ahistorical social science is a contradiction in terms, i.e., good social theory cannot be ahistorical. It then follows that SSHA can potentially play a significant role in the complex process of overcoming alienation in the American system of social science." For published replies, see Miller 1978; MacRae 1979; Kuklick 1979; see also Benson 1972.

REFERENCE LIST

Abbott, A. 1991. History and sociology: The lost synthesis. *Social Science History* 15: 201–38.
———. 1999. *Department and discipline: Chicago sociology at one hundred.* Chicago: University of Chicago Press.
AHR Forum. 1989. The old history and the new. With Theodore S. Hamerow, Gertrude Himmelfarb, Lawrence Levine, Joan Wallach Scott, and John E. Toews. *American Historical Review* 94: 654–98.
———. 1991. Peter Novick's *That noble dream:* The objectivity question and the future of the historical profession. With J. H. Hexter, Linda Gordon, David A. Hollinger, Allan Megill, Peter Novick, and Dorothy Ross. *American Historical Review* 96: 675–708.

Harvey J. Graff

Appleby, J. 1998. The power of history. Presidential address. *American Historical Review* 103: 1–14.

Appleby, J., L. Hunt, and M. Jacob. 1994. *Telling the truth about history.* New York: Norton.

Aydelotte, W. 1971. *Quantification in history.* Reading, Mass.: Addison-Wesley.

———. 1981. The search for ideas in historical investigation. Presidential address. *Social Science History* 5: 371–92.

Aydelotte, W., A. Bogue, and R. Fogel, eds. 1972. *The dimensions of quantitative research in history.* Princeton: Princeton University Press.

Baker, P., ed. 1999. Special issue: What is social science history? *Social Science History* 23: 475–591.

Barton, D. 1994. *Literacy: An introduction to the ecology of written language.* Oxford: Blackwell.

Barton, D., and M. Hamilton. 1998. *Local literacies: Reading and writing in one community.* London: Routledge.

Barzun, J. 1972. History: The muse and her doctors. *American Historical Review* 77: 36–64.

———. 1974. *Clio and the doctors: Psycho-history, quanto-history and history.* Chicago: University of Chicago Press.

Bender, T. 1986. Wholes and parts: The need for synthesis in American history. *Journal of American History* 73: 120–36.

Benson, L. 1972. *Toward the scientific study of history: Selected essays.* Philadelphia: Lippincott.

———. 1978. Changing social science to change the world. Presidential address. *Social Science History* 2: 427–41.

Berkhofer, R. Jr. 1969. *A behavioral approach to historical analysis.* New York: Free Press.

Bogue, A., ed. 1973. *Emerging theoretical models in social and political history.* Beverly Hills: Sage.

———. 1983. *Clio and the bitch goddess: Quantification in American political history.* Beverly Hills: Sage.

———. 1986. Systematic revisionism and a generation of ferment in American history. *Journal of Contemporary History* 21: 135–62.

———. 1987. Great expectations and secular depreciation: The first ten years of the Social Science History Association. *Social Science History* 11: 329–42.

Bogue, A., and J. Clubb. 1977a. History and the social sciences: Progress and prospects. *American Behavioral Scientist* 21: 165–312.

———. 1977b. History, quantification, and the social sciences. *American Behavioral Scientist* 21: 167–86.

Bonnell, V., and L. Hunt, eds. 1999. *Beyond the cultural turn: New directions in the study of society and culture.* Berkeley: University of California Press.

Bridenbaugh, C. 1963. The great mutation. *American Historical Review* 68: 315–31.

Burke, P., ed. 1992. *New perspectives on historical writing.* University Park: Penn State University Press.

Calhoun, C. 1995. *Critical social theory.* Oxford: Blackwell.

———. 1996. The rise and domestication of historical sociology. In *The historic turn in the human sciences*, edited by Terrence J. McDonald. Ann Arbor: University of Michigan Press.

———. 1998. Explanation in historical sociology: Narrative, general theory, and historically specific theory. *American Journal of Sociology* 104: 846–71.

Clausen, A. 1988. Social science history: Citation record, 1976–1985. Presidential address. *Social Science History* 12: 197–215.

Cohen, S. 1986. *Historical culture: On the recoding of an academic discipline.* Berkeley: University of California Press.

———. 1998. *Passive nihilism: Cultural historiography and the rhetorics of scholarship.* New York: St. Martins.

Cox, J., and S. Stromquist, eds. 1998. *Contesting the master narrative: Essays in social history.* Iowa City: University of Iowa Press.

Demos, J. 1970. *A little commonwealth: Family life in Plymouth Colony.* New York: Oxford University Press.

Eley, G. 1996. Is all the world a text? From social history to the history of society two decades later. In *The historic turn in the human sciences*, edited by Terrence J. McDonald. Ann Arbor: University of Michigan Press.

Evans, R. 1997. *In defense of history.* London: Granta.

Floud, R. 1984. Quantitative history and people's history: Two methods in conflict? *Social Science History* 8: 151–68.

Fogel, R. 1975. The limits of quantitative methods in history. *American Historical Review* 80: 329–50.

———. 1983. Foreword to *Clio and the bitch goddess: Quantification in American political history*, by Allan Bogue. Beverly Hills: Sage.

Fogel, R., and G. Elton. 1983. *Which road to the past? Two views of history.* New Haven, Conn.: Yale University Press.

Fogel, R., and S. Engerman. 1974. *Time on the cross.* Boston: Little, Brown.

Fox-Genovese, E., and E. Lasch-Quinn, eds. 1999. *Reconstructing history: The emergence of a new historical society.* New York: Routledge.

Gagnon, P., and the Bradley Commission on History in the Schools, eds. 1989. *Historical literacy: The case for history in American education.* New York: Macmillan.

Genovese, E. 1999. A new departure. In *Reconstructing history: The emergence of a new historical society*, edited by Elizabeth Fox-Genovese and Elisabeth Lasch-Quinn. New York: Routledge.

Genovese, E., and E. Fox-Genovese. 1982. The political crisis of social history: Class struggle as subject and object. In *Fruits of merchant capital.* New York: Oxford University Press.

Gilbert, F., and S. Graubard, eds. 1972. *Historical studies today.* New York: Norton.

Graff, H. 1977. "The new math": Quantification, the "new" history, and the history of education. *Urban Education* 11: 403–40.

———. 1979. *The literacy myth: Literacy and social structure in the nineteenth-century city.* New York: Academic Press.

———. 1987. *The legacies of literacy: Continuities and contradictions in western society and culture.* Bloomington: Indiana University Press.

———. 1989. Critical literacy versus cultural literacy: Reading signs of the times. Review of *Cultural Literacy,* by E. D. Hirsch. *Interchange* 20: 46–52.

———. 1991. Towards 2000: Poverty and progress in the history of education. *Historical Studies in Education* 3: 191–210.

———. 1993. Literacy, myths, and legacies: Lessons from the past—thoughts for the future. *Interchange* 24: 271–86.

———. 1995a. *Conflicting paths: Growing up in America.* Cambridge, Mass.: Harvard University Press.

———. 1995b. *The labyrinths of literacy: Reflections on literacy past and present.* Rev. ed. Pittsburgh: University of Pittsburgh Press.

———. 1999a. Interdisciplinary explorations in the history of children, adolescents, and youth—for the past, present, and future. *Journal of American History* 85: 1538–47.

———. 1999b. Teaching and historical understanding: Disciplining historical imagination with historical context. In *The social worlds of higher education: Handbook for teaching in a new century,* edited by Bernice A. Pescosolido and Ronald Aminzade. Thousand Oaks, Calif.: Pine Forge Press.

———. 1999c. Teaching [and] historical understanding: Disciplining historical imagination with historical context. *Interchange* 30: 143–69.

———. 2001. The shock of the "'new' (histories)": Social science histories and historical literacies. Presidential address. *Social Science History* 25: 483–534.

Greven, P. Jr. 1970. *Four generations: Population, land, and family in colonial Andover, Massachusetts.* Ithaca, N.Y.: Cornell University Press.

Hamerow, T. 1987. The crisis in history. In *Reflections on history.* Madison: University of Wisconsin Press.

Handlin, O. 1971. History: A discipline in crisis. *American Scholar* 40: 446–64.

———. 1975. The capacity of quantitative history. *Perspectives in American History* 9: 7–28.

———. 1979. *Truth in history.* Cambridge, Mass.: Harvard University Press.

Hareven, T. 1996. What difference does it make? Presidential address. *Social Science History* 20: 317–44.

Haskell, T. 1990. Objectivity is not neutrality: Rhetoric vs. practice in Peter Novick's *That noble dream. History and Theory* 29: 129–57.

Hays, S. 1980. *American political history as social analysis.* Knoxville: University of Tennessee Press.

Hershberg, T., ed. 1981. *Philadelphia: Work, space, family, and group experience in the nineteenth century.* New York: Oxford University Press.

Hexter, J. 1971a. *Doing history.* Bloomington: Indiana University Press.

———. 1971b. *The history primer.* New York: Basic Books.

Hexter, J., and William O. Aydelotte. 1971. Letters. In *Quantification in history,* edited by William O. Aydelotte. Reading, Mass.: Addison-Wesley.

Higham, J. 1989. *History: Professional scholarship in America.* Baltimore: Johns Hopkins University Press.

Himmelfarb, G. 1975. The "new" history. *Commentary* 59: 72–78.

———. 1984. Denigrating the rule of reason: The "new history" goes bottom-up. *Harpers* (April).

———. 1987. *The new history and the old.* Cambridge, Mass.: Harvard University Press.

Hirsch, E. D. Jr. 1987. *Cultural literacy: What every American needs to know.* Boston: Houghton Mifflin.

Hobsbawm, E. 1972a. From social history to the history of society. In *Historical studies today,* edited by Felix Gilbert and Stephen R. Graubard. New York: Norton.

———. 1972b. The social function of the past: Some questions. *Past and Present* 55: 3–17.

———. 1981. Looking forward: History and the future. *New Left Review* 125: 3–20.

———. 1993. The new threat to history. *New York Review* (16 December): 62–64.

Hunt, L., ed. 1989. *The new cultural history.* Berkeley: University of California Press.

Jensen, R. 1969. History and the political scientist. In *Politics and the social sciences,* edited by Seymour Martin Lipset. New York: Oxford University Press.

Judt, T. 1979. A clown in regal purple: Social history and the historians. *History Workshop* 7: 66–94.

Kaestle, C., H. Damon-Moore, L. C. Stedman, K. Tinsley, and W. Vance Trollinger, Jr. 1991. *Literacy in the United States: Readers and reading since 1880.* New Haven, Conn.: Yale University Press.

Kammen, M., ed. 1980. *The past before us: Contemporary historical writing in the United States.* Ithaca, N.Y.: Cornell University Press.

Katz, M. 1968. *The irony of early school reform: Educational innovation in mid-nineteenth-century Massachusetts.* Cambridge, Mass.: Harvard University Press.

———. 1969. Social structure in Hamilton, Ontario. In *Nineteenth-century cities: Essays in the new urban history,* edited by Stephan Thernstrom and Richard Sennett. New Haven, Conn.: Yale University Press.

———. 1975. *The people of Hamilton, Canada West: Family and class in a mid-nineteenth-century city.* Cambridge, Mass.: Harvard University Press.

———. 1987. *Reconstructing American education.* Cambridge, Mass.: Harvard University Press.

———. 1995. *Improving poor people: The welfare state, the "underclass," and urban schools as history.* Princeton: Princeton University Press.

Katz, M., M. Doucet, and M. Stern. 1982. *The social organization of early industrial capitalism.* Cambridge, Mass.: Harvard University Press.

Kloppenberg, J. 1989. Objectivity and historicism: A century of American historical writing. Review article. *American Historical Review* 94: 1011–30.

Kousser, J. 1977. The agenda for "social science history." *Social Science History* 1: 382–91.

———. 1980. Quantitative social-scientific history. In *The past before us: Contemporary historical writing in the United States,* edited by Michael Kammen. Ithaca, N.Y.: Cornell University Press.

———. 1984. The revivalism of narrative: A response to recent criticisms of quantitative history. *Social Science History* 8: 133–49.

————. 1989. The state of social science history in the late 1980s. *Historical Methods* 22: 13–20.

Kuhn, T. 1962. *The structure of scientific revolutions*. Chicago: University of Chicago Press.

Kuklick, B. 1979. Benson and Miller in perspective. *Social Science History* 3: 242–44.

LaCapra, D. 1985. *History and criticism*. Ithaca, N.Y.: Cornell University Press.

Landes, D., and C. Tilly, eds. 1971. *History as social science: The behavioral and social sciences survey—history panel*. Englewood Cliffs, N.J.: Prentice Hall.

Laslett, P. 1965. *The world we have lost*. London: Methuen.

Lockridge, K. 1970. *A New England town, the first hundred years: Dedham, Massachusetts, 1636–1736*. New York: Norton.

Lorwin, V., and J. Price, eds. 1972. *The dimensions of the past: Materials, problems, and opportunities for quantitative work in history*. New Haven, Conn.: Yale University Press.

MacRae, D. Jr. 1979. Changing social science to serve human welfare. *Social Science History* 3: 227–441.

Maynes, M. J. 1992. Autobiography and class formation in nineteenth-century Europe: Methodological considerations. *Social Science History* 16: 517–37.

————. 1995. *Taking the hard road: The life course in French and German workers' autobiographies in the era of industrialization*. Chapel Hill: University of North Carolina Press.

McDonald, T., ed. 1996a. *The historic turn in the human sciences*. Ann Arbor: University of Michigan Press.

McDonald, T. 1996b. What we talk about when we talk about history: The conversations of history and sociology. In *The historic turn*, edited by Terrence McDonald. Ann Arbor: University of Michigan Press.

Megill, A. 1985. *Prophets of extremity: Nietzsche, Heidegger, Foucault, Derrida*. Berkeley: University of California Press.

————. 1995. "Grand narrative" and the discipline of history. In *A new philosophy of history*, edited by Frank Ankersmit and Hans Kellner. Chicago: University of Chicago Press.

Miller, W. 1978. Some reflections on "Changing Social Science to Change the World." *Social Science History* 2: 442–48.

Monkkonen, E. 1986. The dangers of synthesis. *American Historical Review* 91: 1146–57.

————. 1994a. Lessons of social science history. Presidential address. *Social Science History* 18: 161–68.

————, ed. 1994b. *Engaging the past: The uses of history across the social sciences*. Durham, N. C.: Duke University Press.

Moore, B. Jr. 1966. *Social origins of dictatorship and democracy: Lord and peasant in the making of the modern world*. Boston: Beacon Press.

Munslow, A. 1997. *Deconstructing history*. London: Routledge.

Nelson, J., A. Megill, and D. McCloskey, eds. 1987. *The rhetoric of the human sciences*. Madison: University of Wisconsin Press.

Novick, P. 1988. *That noble dream: The "objectivity question" and the American historical profession*. Cambridge: Cambridge University Press.

Olábarri, I. 1995. "New" new history: A longue durée structure. *History and Theory* 34: 1–29.

Pescosolido, B., and R. Aminzade, eds. 1999. *The social worlds of higher education: Handbook for teaching in a new century.* Thousand Oaks, Calif.: Pine Forge Press.

Rabb, T. 1982. Toward the future: Coherence, synthesis, and quality in history. In *The new history: The 1980s and beyond. Studies in interdisciplinary history,* edited by Theodore K. Rabb and Robert I. Rotberg. Princeton: Princeton University Press.

Rabb, T., and R. Rotberg, eds. 1982. *The new history: The 1980s and beyond. Studies in interdisciplinary history.* Princeton: Princeton University Press.

Reynolds, J. 1998. Do historians count anymore? The status of quantitative methods in history. *Historical Methods* 31: 141–48.

Ross, D. 1989. Historical consciousness in nineteenth-century America. *American Historical Review* 89: 909–28.

———. 1991. *The origins of American social science.* Cambridge: Cambridge University Press.

———. 1995. Grand narrative in American historical writing: From romance to uncertainty. *American Historical Review* 100: 651–77.

———. 1998. The new and newer histories: Social theory and historiography in an American key. In *Imagined histories: American historians interpret the past,* edited by Anthony Mohlo and Gordon S. Wood. Princeton: Princeton University Press.

Roth, R. 1992. Is history a process? Nonlinearity, revitalization theory, and the central metaphor of social science history. *Social Science History* 16: 197–243.

Schlesinger, A. Jr. 1962. The humanist looks at empirical social research. *American Sociological Review* 27: 768–71.

Scott, J. 1988. *Gender and the politics of history.* New York: Columbia University Press.

———. 1991. The evidence of experience. *Critical Inquiry* 17: 773–97.

Sewell, W. Jr. 1992. Introduction: Narratives and social identities. *Social Science History* 16: 479–88.

———. 1996 Three temporalities: Toward an eventful sociology. In *The historic turn in the human sciences,* edited by Terrence McDonald. Ann Arbor: University of Michigan Press.

Sewell, W. Jr., G. Steinmetz, and M. J. Maynes. 1992. Special section: Narrative analysis in social science. *Social Science History* 16: 479–537.

Skocpol, T., ed. 1984. *Vision and method in historical sociology.* Cambridge: Cambridge University Press.

Skocpol, T., O. Zunz, L. Cornell, and W. Roy. 1987. Historical sociology and social history: Comment and debate. *Social Science History* 11: 17–62.

Stearns, P. 1980. Toward a wider vision: Trends in social history. In *The past before us: Contemporary historical writing in the United States,* edited by Michael Kammen. Ithaca, N.Y.: Cornell University Press.

———. 1991. The challenge of "historical literacy." *Perspectives: American Historical Association Newsletter* 29 (April): 21–23.

Harvey J. Graff

———. 1993. *Meaning over memory: Recasting the teaching of culture and history.* Chapel Hill: University of North Carolina Press.

Steinmetz, G., ed. 1999. *State/culture: State-formation after the cultural turn.* Ithaca, N.Y.: Cornell University Press.

Stone, L. 1965. *The crisis of the aristocracy, 1558–1641.* Oxford: Oxford University Press.

———. 1977. History and the social sciences in the twentieth century. In *The future of history,* edited by Charles F. Detzell. Nashville, Tenn.: Vanderbilt University Press.

———. 1979. The revival of narrative: Reflections on a new old history. *Past and Present* 85: 3–24.

———. 1987. *The past and the present revisited.* London: Routledge.

Taylor, W. 1992. *In pursuit of Gotham: Culture and commerce in New York.* New York: Oxford University Press.

Thelen, D., ed. 1987. A round table: Synthesis in American history. With Nell Irwin Painter, Richard Wightman Fox, Roy Rosenzweig, and Thomas Bender. *Journal of American History* 76: 107–30.

Thernstrom, S. 1964. *Poverty and progress: Social mobility in a nineteenth-century city.* Cambridge, Mass.: Harvard University Press.

Thompson, E. P. 1963. *The making of the English working class.* London: Victor Gollancz.

Tilly, C. 1964. *The Vendée.* Cambridge, Mass.: Harvard University Press.

———. 1981. *As sociology meets history.* New York: Academic Press.

———. 1984. *Big structures, large processes, huge comparisons.* New York: Russell Sage.

Tilly, L. 1983. People's history and social science history. Presidential address. *Social Science History* 7: 457–74.

———. 1989. Gender, women's history, and social history. With comments by Gay L. Gullickson and Judith M. Bennett. *Social Science History* 13: 439–82.

Veysey, L. 1979a. Intellectual history and the new social history. In *New directions in American intellectual history,* edited by John Higham and Paul Conkin. Baltimore: Johns Hopkins University Press.

———. 1979b. The "new" social history in the context of American historical writing. *Reviews in American History* 7: 1–12.

Wetherell, C. 1999. Theory, method, and social reproduction in social science history. *Social Science History* 23: 491–99.

White, H. 1966. The burden of history. *History and Theory* 5: 111–34.

———. 1978. *Tropics of discourse: Essays in cultural criticism.* Baltimore: Johns Hopkins University Press.

———. 1987. *The content of the form.* Baltimore: Johns Hopkins University Press.

Windschuttle, K. 1996. *The killing of history: How literary critics and social theorists are murdering our past.* New York: Free Press.

TWENTY-FIVE YEARS LATER

SSHA IN THE EYES OF

ITS FOUNDING SPIRITS

Presidential Plenary Session, 26 October 2000, 6:30 P.M.

Harvey J. Graff

Welcome to this evening's plenary session, one of the events with which we are celebrating the twenty-fifth anniversary of the Social Science History Association. A range of special activities promotes and highlights the theme. Special presidential and thematic sessions focus both appreciatively and critically on the past and future of social science history. This session features founders' and past presidents' reflections on social science history. Other sessions focus on teaching social science history, the philosophy of social science history, and Pittsburgh as a site for social science history.

Among the many ways in which we mark this important anniversary, the two evening plenaries are very special. They stand out. Although the aims of the two differ, together they overlap in terms of their respective contributions to our celebration. Tonight we present a founders' session, which we are calling: Twenty-Five Years Later, SSHA in the Eyes of Some of its Founding Spirits. Tomorrow: Looking Backward and Looking Forward, Social Science History at 2000.

I have asked participants of tonight's event to respond informally, briefly, and personally to two questions: First, in your view, what is the most important legacy of SSHA's founding and quarter century of development? What do you think that new younger members should know about the association's history and founding?

Secondly, what salient issues of the period of the founding of SSHA persist today? How do they challenge us?

I realized when I sat down last week to write out introductions of the panelists, to do justice to them would eat up entirely too much of the session. If there are people at this meeting who require little formal introduction, it is those here.

Allan Bogue, William Flanigan, Daniel Scott Smith, Barbara Hanawalt

Let me tell you who is with us. Allan Bogue from the University of Wisconsin, the second president from 1977–1978; William Flanigan from the University of Minnesota, the president 1980 to 1981; Daniel Scott Smith, president from 1987 to 1988, from the University of Illinois at Chicago; and Barbara Hanawalt from Ohio State University, president 1989 and 1990. Two former presidents who had planned to join us were unable to do so. I convey the regrets of Louise Tilly and Robert Fogel.

Allan Bogue

It is a real pleasure to be able to attend the twenty-fifth anniversary meeting of the Social Science History Association. I do greatly regret the fact that a larger number of those of us who sat around the table at Ann Arbor on the day that Michigan's Secretary of State approved our request for incorporation are not present. Alas, Bill Aydelotte and Warren Miller have died. Lee Benson and Ted Rabb are retired from teaching but maintain varying degrees of involvement in scholarly concerns. Jerry Clubb, also retired, is not on this panel, but he will appear on one tomorrow. Of our first two journal editors, Bob Swierenga continues his pathbreaking research on Dutch immigration, and Jim Graham lives adjacent to Jerry Clubb in retirement overlooking the Strait of San Juan De Fuca, the two no doubt doing the definitive count of the number of ships passing through. And I am sorry also that Bob Fogel was forced to cancel his participation. Most people think of Bob in terms of *Time on the Cross*, or the counterfactual analysis of the importance of railroads, or investigation of the height and nutrition of past generations, but his chairmanship of the History Advisory Committee of the Mathematical Social Science Board and its sponsorship of the Princeton University Press series, *Quantitative Studies in History* were very important in shaping the social science history of the 1960s and 1970s.

In organizing this panel, Harvey Graff suggested that we should think both about the significance of our past history and venture some thoughts about the future as well. Given the word "science" in our organization's name one wonders if there were any social laws involved in our founding or evident in our early history. I have thought, a bit fancifully, about this and decided that the latter was certainly true. At least three social laws were in play, though others may add to the list or dispute my choices. First, "Harvard is not always right," or conversely, "Harvard is sometimes wrong." My evidence follows: In December 1970 the American Historical Association met in Boston, and Bob Rotberg and Ted Rabb hosted a luncheon for the editorial boards that they had selected for the *Journal of Interdisciplinary History,* their new journal, which was then off to a promising start, its first issue dated autumn 1970. After the meal the editors led a discussion of plans for the future of the *JIH,* and Bob Rotberg suggested that the initial enthusiasm that it had generated perhaps indicated that it would be appropriate to found an association to foster the development of interdisciplinary history. Obviously Rotberg and Rabb understood that the annual meeting of such an association might well feature scholarly papers that would be appropriate for publication in the *Journal of Interdisciplinary History.* At this point enter Harvard. Stuart Hughes and Bernard Bailyn rose in their places and scoffed at the idea. There were, they believed, too many associations already whose activities and meetings drew conscientious scholars away from their desks. The Harvard gentlemen thoroughly trashed Rotberg's suggestion, and discussion moved on to other matters.

As well as being a member of one of the *JIH* editorial boards, I was at that time chairman of the AHA's Quantitative Data Committee, a group that had been organized in 1963–64, particularly at the instigation of Lee Benson, and which was charged with identifying quantitative data appropriate for the use of historians, fostering their preservation in machine-readable form, and advertising its usefulness. Warren Miller, then developing the Inter-University Consortium for Political (and later Social) Research at Ann Arbor, saw Benson's efforts as a means of developing a historical data dimension in the ICPSR archive that he had initially organized to maintain and distribute the data from the presidential panel-polling activity that Angus Campbell had begun at the University of Michigan at the end of the 1940s. With Miller's support Benson prepared a grant proposal on behalf of the AHA, and the proceeds allowed the Quantitative Data Committee to conduct a series of conferences to identify useful bodies of quantitative historical information, and papers given at two of the conferences appeared ultimately as the book *The Dimensions of the Past: Materials, Problems, and Opportunities for Quantitative Work in History,* edited by Val R. Lorwin and Jacob M. Price. Meanwhile, Benson and the committee had been recruiting state representatives to assist in the task of exhuming state electoral returns, and—with the assistance of ICPSR and the Social Science Research Council—the committee sponsored a summer methods conference on the use of quantitative data in electoral and legislative research. After I succeeded Benson as chairman of the AHA committee in the late 1960s, we continued to advance the earlier agenda, most notably with the use of a National Endowment for the Humanities grant to collect early national electoral returns.

At the same meeting in which the Harvardians rebuffed Bob Rydberg, Paul Ward, the executive secretary of the AHA, informed me that its council had concluded that historians were now agreed that quantitative data were good things and that the committee was no longer needed. The committee was given three years in which to wind up its business.

Within the next several weeks I talked on the telephone to Jerry Clubb, then director of the ICPSR Archives and a very active member of the AHA Quantitative Data Committee, and we agreed that we ought to create a new vehicle—an association—to support the activities that the AHA proposed to abandon. We also agreed that Clubb would seek support from Warren Miller and I would try to sign up Lee Benson. Both men liked the idea, although Benson initially offered only the use of his name. Soon however, he became completely committed and would be particularly enthusiastic in supporting the idea of establishing the network structure that became an important part of the association. I drafted a questionnaire explaining the situation and asking for support, and we sent it out to everyone who we believed might be interested. The responses were encouraging, and we moved on from there to that day in Ann Arbor when the incorporation document was issued.

But here enters social law number 2 in play: "Things seldom go as planned." Our constitution proclaimed as the association's major objective "improvement of the quality of historical explanation in every manner possible, but particularly by encouraging the selective use and adaptation in historical teaching and research of relevant theories and methods from related disciplines, particularly the social sciences." This was to be done, we promised, by developing a high-quality publication program, by organizing regional and national conferences "to foster research areas in which work is particularly experimental or pathbreaking in nature as well as those that have already attracted considerable numbers of adherents," encouraging introduction of the new histories into the curriculum, sponsoring summer institutes and other venues where historians might learn relevant skills, fostering the retrieval, archiving, and processing of relevant bodies of data, educating funding agencies on special needs of history-oriented researchers, working for maximum freedom of access to data of particular interest to social science historians, developing grant proposals to provide funds for association projects along these lines, and taking any other appropriate action that association members believed necessary to achieve such objectives.

If SSHA had done all of these things, it would have really been a quite differently unique organization than it ultimately became. For a host of reasons the organization retreated from or never took up many of the challenges posed in its constitutional statement of objectives, becoming in its institutional objectives similar to many other disciplinary learned societies—focused mainly on the production of an annual conference meeting and maintenance of a scholarly journal. But the end result has not been a disappointment by any means. The annual meeting has provided a unique mixing bowl for not only historians but members of other disciplines, who ground their work in change through time—and the journal has provided an excellent setting for their scholarly productions. Although not unique to SSHA, the network structure has resulted in much fruitful cross-disciplinary interaction within the memberships as well as developing many excellent panels for the association's annual meeting.

I am less certain about the application of the third social law, although not in its ultimate truth. In reviewing developments in political research during his career, Warren Miller affirmed that "the events that constitute life . . . form a series of intersecting probability distributions." He then went on to note that "some of the crucial events in the history of the development of political behavior research were so improbable that they probably really didn't occur at all" (Miller 1989, 147).

If one adds the history of the AHA Quantitative Data to the history of SSHA the improbabilities are also somewhat overwhelming. Consider the following: Stull Holt from the University of Washington was acting executive secretary of the AHA when Lee Benson pressed for formation of the Quantitative Data Committee and was invaluable in obtaining the consent of the Council for organizing it. But this was the same Stull Holt who published a book of poetry entitled *An American Faculty,* a kind of Spoon River treatment of the faculty of an American University—perhaps the University of Washington—and one of the poems ran:

> The historian alone has the effrontery to claim
> That it is his task to synthesize all knowledge
> And to tell the complete story of the entire man.
> That is why we must reject those who say
> That only by quantification can facts be established.
> (WKSLHW 1974, 110)

Briefly, and in more serious vein, allow me to consider the Social Science History Association's accomplishments and the challenge that it faces for the future. During the last twenty-five years the members of this association have written a great deal of very good history, however you define it. This association has facilitated the process by providing a forum at its annual meetings where innovative people can interact across the scholarly disciplines.

The members of the association can also be proud that the original intent of creating an association that would be particularly supportive of younger scholars has been maintained. The feature of offering a large number of panels at our meetings was specifically planned to give younger scholars an opportunity to present papers whose titles could then appear in their CVs. I do not believe that the journal of any well-established association has been more open to assistant professors and doctoral candidates than we have.

Furthermore, I believe the networks have also helped to make membership in this association a richer experience than one finds in other history associations.

I conclude with a short reaction to those critics who have written this association off as a mere vestige of a passing phase of historiographic development—they are wrong—abysmally wrong as this meeting's registration and program shows. The Social Science History Association may change its appearance and to some degree its function, but its mission of walking the disciplinary frontiers and promoting interaction across them will remain the mission upon which the development of a richer and informative history depends.

William Flanigan

If you want an illustration of the difference between a show horse and a workhorse, Al did all of this and much more at the founding of this association. My name appeared on a letter that was sent out announcing that the organization existed. And I do not believe I did anything else to contribute to the founding of the organization. I was a political scientist, and along with the sociologists, the economists, and the geographers that were involved in the founding, we were really peripheral.

The work, the inspiration, all the drive for the organization came from Al and Jerry and others, all of whom were historians. Also, the founders were an unusually political group of historians. It seems to me, the founding was another Warren Miller improbable event. He was a political scientist with really no business treading into political history. Political historians were certainly welcome in the presence of political behaviorists, but political behaviorists, whose status in their profession was shaky enough, thought it was risky to be seen with historians. It was an odd set of individuals and interests that came together at the founding.

It was data driven, and that inspiration came, I think, from several of the individuals Al mentioned, but also from the new institution of the

Inter-University Consortium for Political Research, and the effort of that organization to expand its base beyond a few political scientists in a few universities, and political history, along with the census, were the two obvious avenues of expansion for that organization.

There was a second drive, and it seems to me Al did not put this as forcefully as it impresses me (thinking back to that period) and that is: there was a real grievance felt by the historians, by the historians who were pushing for this. Certain types of scholars, particularly by junior scholars in the area of political history, were not being given the opportunities they deserved at meetings and in the publications that then existed in the history profession. They certainly would have had a difficult time breaking into the political science journals, the sociology journals, so that there was a need for opportunity in the history profession. These motives, it seems to me, drove the founding.

The presence of political scientists, sociologists, economists, and geographers was really necessary for the credibility of this social science and social history approach, but we were not necessary to actually get any work done or accomplish anything in the early years. And it is a good thing that we were not called on to do much.

But we were also in a different position, whether we were fairly young or more advanced, because we were in professions where we were welcomed at the meetings and welcomed in the journals, and we were under a certain amount of expectation to perform in those areas. So for the most part, the people involved from outside of history were not looking for this as a new opportunity, except with respect to research.

And as I think back on this organization, what strikes me from the beginning, and it still impresses me today, is the extent to which participation in this organization is driven by research interests. I was struck by this when I stood in line for breakfast at the very first meeting. The people on both sides of me were talking about their research.

I had been to enough professional meetings at that time to know that was very unusual. You ran down your department, you talked about the job market, you did a number of things while standing in line, but to talk about your research was really striking. And there never has been a job market at this organization. There is not really a reunion atmosphere around this meeting. The only thing that brings people here is research. And it makes it—at least for a political scientist—a remarkably attractive organization for that very reason.

It also had another very strange effect right from the beginning, and that was that there were an awful lot of unemployed researchers around, and that does not characterize other meetings. I met more people here without jobs than at all the other presentational meetings I have attended.

64

Allan Bogue, William Flanigan, Daniel Scott Smith, Barbara Hanawalt

I do not think that is a great thing about the organization, but I believe it represents the degree to which this organization has been seen as an opportunity. I do not know whether all those various individuals ultimately found that it is a successful way to get into academia, but the research basis of the organization was reflected in those people and those attitudes.

It is my recollection, and I should have asked Al if this is true, that the first meeting of this organization was a so-called regional meeting at Madison, Wisconsin. This did not displace the annual meetings, which were still to begin. It was a somewhat spontaneous activity, it seemed from the outside. Now, of course, we all know that Al and a bunch of people probably worked day and night for months to make it happen spontaneously, but it was not a national meeting, and this organization had never had a meeting. But a letter went out to people who had expressed an interest or probably more than likely were on the consortium mailing list at one time or another. An incredibly large crowd turned up in Madison for this. It was a pep rally for the organization as much as anything, and it was a remarkable showing of the kind of enthusiasm that was going to exist right from the beginning in this organization.

I have said almost nothing about the questions that we were directed to answer, because I thought immediately when those questions appeared on my e-mail that the great accomplishment of this organization—and what the people active in it now should know and be proud of—is the people who were around at the founding are almost totally irrelevant to the organization. It has moved beyond that, it is strong, and it is full of active scholars. It is so different from twenty-five years ago, for the individuals, the topics of the panel. I can not imagine a better sign for an organization than to have changed that way. I think you are all to be congratulated. Thank you.

Daniel Scott Smith

Well, I was actually present at the founding, but I am not one of the founders. Indeed, I have been present at every annual meeting of the SSHA. But I can accurately be considered as a historian of the second generation in the organization.

I will take the liberty to draw in two ways on my other main academic identity as an early American historian. First, I want to talk about the idea of declension, a familiar theme to students of New England Puritanism. That is, there was a Golden Age of the Founders, and since then it is all been downhill. In following this theme, I impose my interpretation of the Original Intent of the Constitution of the founders. In short, what they intended about the social science history "City Upon a Hill" is what I say they intended.

The theme is: How did the Social Science History Association become the social sciences histories association? That is, how do you account for the fact that fragmentation describes the declension (or evolution) of the SSHA since its founding? I want to talk about four areas very briefly: theory, data, the intended audience, and the relationship of the SSHA to the structures of academia.

Theory: When the founders wrote and talked about theory, my sense, at least, was that those who were coming from history departments were converts to a new religion of social science. As converts, they saw theory as some kind of magic that tied (or would tie) things together. Now, what happened, of course—and I think this is where the roles of quantification and statistics come in—was that the favored theories tended to be analytical rather than synthetic. Social scientists in the middle of the twentieth century divided phenomena into parts and then tried to account for them. That was the dominant mode of explanation in the beginning and through the 1980s; some of us still find these exercises quite useful. Second-generation types, however, tended to be fond of aphorisms such as "theories are to be used but not believed."

Data: Certainly the founders believed that more (and more systematic) evidence, preferably quantitative, was needed to support the more rigorous analysis that was required for social science history. The creation of the Inter-University Consortium for Political (now including Social) Research (ICPSR) at Ann Arbor exemplifies this development in social science. The project in the 1960s to encode county- and state-level published census data and electoral results exemplifies this goal in the field of United States history. This orientation toward large data sets and quantification continues in segments of the organization. Certainly this is the case of the demographers, with whom I am most closely affiliated. Nor has this empirical project died at the grand scale as is illustrated by the Integrated Public Use Samples of Census Data (IPUMS) that are being created at the University of Minnesota. And these data archives are useful, important, and for some now indispensable in their research endeavors.

However, theory for historians as done by scholars located in history departments, or rather what is thought to be the cutting edge, has changed dramatically. I would characterize it as postempirical, if not nonempirical, and theoretical in a sense never dreamt of by the founding generation. Anecdotes are in, systematic documentation is out.

Audience: In this area, the declension has been nearly total. I think the founders had in mind two audiences that we do not address any

Allan Bogue, William Flanigan, Daniel Scott Smith, Barbara Hanawalt

more. The first audience is that of public policy makers and shapers of public opinion. Lee Benson in particular was identified with this aspiration. This utopian aspiration was certainly not realized, and it is rarely attempted any more. Certainly it plays no part in the activities organized under the aegis of the SSHA. The second audience is that of the general educated public. And here again, I think Bill has accurately defined the SSHA as a research-driven organization. We come to the SSHA meetings to hear discussions of research and to talk with others in our specialized fields.

Academia: Here is the heart of the story of declension. I think the original goal was what might be called interdisciplinarity, that is, a merger and an intermingling of people from different disciplines either collaborating, or ideally one person having more than one perspective. That did not happen.

What did happen and where the organization is now is multidisciplinarity. It is organized around different topics or subject areas. As was said earlier, this has become a meeting of meetings. If you are seriously interested in historical demography or the history of the family, the SSHA convention is *the* meeting to attend in the United States. It is my sense that there are six or seven or eight other such meetings going on when the SSHA meets. The SSHA thus is a conglomeration of people from different disciplines interested in particular subject matters.

Finally, why did this happen? Why the declension from the original intent or vision of the founding generation? The main agent of declension was the tyranny of disciplinarity. What really drives academia in terms of rewards, in terms of jobs, in terms of defining who are the most relevant peers still takes place within specific disciplines—history, economics, political science, and so forth. As long as this remains true, the original goals of the founders never will be reached and never can be reached. So sinners we shall be in the foreseeable future if not forever: the Disciplines made us do it. In the meantime, the SSHA is a valuable, vital institution for serious scholars, and we all should be thankful for that. Thank you.

Barbara Hanawalt

Bernard Cohen, an anthropologist, has attended our meetings once in a while. He wrote a very good essay in *Comparative Studies in Society and History* in 1980, in which he outlined anthropology and history as a state of play. And he concludes this by poking fun at historians, but also by speaking about how disciplines become established.

And it is probably relevant to what has been said here. That is, often the discipline starts with a big book, or in, I think, social science history, it would be several and in various fields. This is followed by workshops, and the workshops being successful, it moves on to an association, and the association being successful, it founds a journal. And then if it is really a successful association and movement, it will then persuade departments around the country that they really need to hire somebody in this field.

Now, certainly this does describe the Social Science History Association, for pretty soon after the founding it became absolutely necessary that every serious department in the country—with the exception of Harvard and the Ivy League—did feel the need to have a quantitative historian on their faculty. These people provided wonderful training to graduate students, and they got them very involved in the Social Science History Association. The perpetuation of training and membership has worked out nicely for the association.

But as Dan said, the urgency seems to have worn off in this field. This is not a category you see advertised in association job lists. But I agree with Dan that this is more of a movement with the times rather than a setback. And when I look at the sessions over the past years, I think about how many different theoretical approaches there are now in the program.

At one time, the people who were doing cultural history felt very much on the fringe, and they would have one or two sessions at meetings. I also think back to Dan when he was president saying that his concern was: How can we move the association forward to be more inclusive? Would we be in danger of simply ending up with the same people talking to the same people every year? And fortunately, that has not happened, and the association has been able to move with the times and has been very inclusive.

I agree with what a number of the speakers have already said: that there was a hostility to quantitative history. Probably nobody knows that better than I, who was doing quantitative history of the Middle Ages. And if you think political scientists were a problem or American historians were a problem, medievalists simply could not take it. It was to them something like raping a legal record, if that is physically possible. But their reaction was emotional in this regard.

Indeed, in 1975–1976, I was the associate editor of the *American Historical Review.* Bob Quirk was the editor, and he told me flatly that the *AHR*, under his editorship, would never publish a quantitative history article. There really was that hostility that you were talking about, and it was very explicitly stated at times.

Allan Bogue, William Flanigan, Daniel Scott Smith, Barbara Hanawalt

For me in particular, but for many people going to the SSHA meant that there was an appreciative audience, an audience that was willing to include somebody as far out of field as I am. But another thing I found, again being very far out of field, was that a surprising number of people, when I arrived at the meetings, had read what I had written. And this was certainly more than any of my historian colleagues had done. But it was a delight to feel that inclusion.

Moving on to inclusion, I want to say it is also an association, having started in the early 1970s when women were still fighting for positions in associations, and not very successfully in the standard associations, that was very inclusive. I served in my first position in the Social Science History Association on the ad hoc committee on Women. I think the last meeting perhaps that occurred at this committee—and certainly the last meeting of the ad hoc committee that I attended—degenerated into a discussion among three of the women on whose husband was the best quantitative historian. I won't reveal any names. The committee disbanded because at this point so many of us had served on the program committee, on the council, and Louise Tilly had been nominated for president. The association simply evolved to be inclusive of women.

May I also say as further evidence of inclusiveness and to the delight of the association members, the association has evolved to be inclusive of many foreign visitors. They take the trouble and the expense to come every year. This too has added a wonderful dimension to the association. Thank you.

REFERENCE LIST

Miller, W. 1989. Research life as a collection of intersecting probability distributions. In *Crossroads of Social Science: The ICPR 25th Anniversary Volume,* edited by Heinz Eulau. New York: Agathon Press.
WKSLHW. 1974. *An American faculty.* New York: Vantage Press.

LOOKING BACKWARD AND

LOOKING FORWARD

Social Science History at 2000,

Critical Perspectives

Presidential Plenary Session, 27 October 2000, 6:30 P.M.

Harvey J. Graff

Tonight, we simultaneously look backward and look forward, looking at social science history at 2000. I have asked tonight's participants to reflect on two questions or issues in framing their remarks. They will each speak for five or ten minutes, and then we'll have time to talk together.

I asked them to respond, at least in part, to these questions: First, in your view, what are the most important lessons or accomplishments of the SSHA's first twenty-five years?

In your view, secondly, what are the most compelling problems or questions that arise from that history, and that members and the association itself need to address?

It is a special pleasure for me to introduce the panelists and sit among them. First, Andrew Abbott—and I am proceeding alphabetically—from Sociology at the University of Chicago; Ira Katznelson, History and Political Science, Columbia University; M. J. Maynes, History, University of Minnesota; and William Sewell, Political Science and History, University of Chicago. (Michael Katz, History, University of Pennsylvania; also participated in the session.)

Andrew Abbott

In charging us to reflect about the important lessons of SSHA's past and the important problems in its future, Harvey Graff left us a very open charge. With respect to the past, I think we are all likely to be in agreement. As for the future, different kinds of interests are likely to make us see different kinds of problems.

Like most of my colleagues, I think the important lesson from the past is that it is possible for an organization like SSHA to survive. SSHA does not transact jobs. It is not a major book sales or acquisitions venue. It brings together a bizarrely diverse crowd of people: diverse in terms of discipline, substantive interests, and methodological commitments. Many of the customary foundations for solidarity are thus absent. Under those conditions, SSHA's survival shows that intellectual common interest and mutual respect can, all by themselves, hold together an association that we all find extraordinarily exciting. And even though the intellectual topology of SSHA is very complex, the association does not break down into local factions, as it could easily do, but rather maintains a dizzying variety of interconnections between very unlikely colleagues.

So, survival is the first and most important lesson of the past. It is possible to have an "academic" association that stays alive intellectually, something many of us doubt from our experience with our disciplinary associations. My second lesson from the past captures another facet of this survival. SSHA has changed with the changing patterns of scholarship. It began with a strong project of quantitative historical inquiry and has grown away from that, although not without some pains and difficulties. It has kept its eye on all the exciting and committed scholarship about the past. That has meant a turn toward culture in the relatively recent past. But culture will pass, too, and if we remain true to the spirit of the association, we will leave culture and gender behind when they lose their excitement as did cliometrics before them. There will be something else in the future.

As for the future problems of the association, they will in one sense be the same as those of the past: How do we keep an exciting association going? How do we keep creeping professionalism from turning it into a homogenized venue for career making? How do we keep damp fingers raised to feel out the new intellectual winds? Fighting routinization and factionalism will be the same problems in the future as they were in the past. I have great hopes for the association's success with them.

What I would rather talk about here is one particular intellectual challenge we will face. That challenge is the rise of computational methods. By computational methods I do not mean new kinds of statistics. I mean the use of computers to do new kinds of things: storing and searching huge qualitative databases or arraying for analysis immense quantitative historical datasets in which not only the values of variables, but also the meanings of the categories change over time.

The latter of these tasks is the more obvious. It will not be very long—probably within the professional lifetime of our younger members—before every single U.S. Census is complete online: not Steve Ruggles's wonderful microsamples but the entire collection of raw data. It is already possible to have such data for the entire electronic history of the stock market. Given state social service systems, it is also possible to generate complete, linked datasets that include every person who has any form of contact with the state, be it through welfare, schooling, criminal justice, unemployment, or property taxation. We will shortly be able to generate complete historical data on trajectories through such systems for the entire period of electronic record keeping—now going on forty years in many of these systems. Databases on things like genealogy and past consumer markets are already enormous.

In short, we are going to be in possession of "historical data"—in the sense of data with serious over-time extension—that is not sample data but rather population level data. In many of these systems, that data will have been measured in real time, continuously. We have no idea what to do with such data. All of our standard analytic routines are designed to use small samples to produce big inferences to larger populations. We have no idea what to do with "everything on the entire population." Nor do we have any real idea how to deal with over-time drift in the definitions of data categories or in the shape and extent of units of analysis. Things like gender are sound enough, but who would want to think that a high school education has anything like the same causal meaning in 1890 as in 1990? Or that the occupation of accountant in 1880 is the same, in terms of what it determines about an incumbent, as in 1980? Or that AT&T in 1950 is AT&T in 1985 or in 2001? We now already have historical datasets in which such category drift is inescapable, and the problem is going to get rapidly worse as the period of electronic record keeping gets longer and longer.

Nor is qualitative historical research going to be untouched. Computerized searching of text databases will see enormous advances in the near term. A word processor that scans your grammar is an obvious ancestor of a database search system that will easily identify the authors of anonymous documents, that will seriate in an afternoon textual variants that used to take a lifetime to order, that will even undertake much larger tasks of classification and textual analysis. Suppose you are interested in understanding Locke's views about property and freedom. A program that can retrieve and classify every time these words occur within three sentences of each other might be very useful, and of course such programs already exist. So do the required online full-texts of an extraordinary amount of Western culture. We are surprisingly close to push-button scholarship.

Andrew Abbott, Ira Katznelson, Mary Jo Maynes, William H. Sewell, Jr.

My intent is not to sound like one of those wired idiots who runs around yelling "we will bury you," like Khrushchev at the UN. I do not think new computational forms are going to replace human scholars. But they are going to become absolutely central modes of research, and if we do not seize them and put them to our own good use, somebody else is going to start redefining what social science history is. And that is a problem because those people are very unlikely to have any historical sense. In fact, like many people, they probably do not believe that history in any genuine sense—an incommensurability between past and present—really exists. Such people are not going to worry about category drift. They are not going to have a sense of the historical indeterminacy of units of analysis like countries, cities, states, and regions. We cannot let their reifications shape what social science history becomes as a discipline.

Ira Katznelson

I cherish this Association for its heterogeneity, capacity for surprise, commitment to the best positive and normative values in modern scholarship, and, perhaps above all, for its demonstrated capacity to change and to grow. Here, many of us who otherwise would not intersect meet, debate, challenge, and learn. Not bound by the rules and conventions of single disciplines or by the fashions and job markets of any, the Social Science History Association produces a special realm of intellectual freedom.

The quarter century of the SSHA spans most of my adult scholarly life. I recall attending one of the first meetings. My initial impression (just thirty, I was still impressionable!) was that this is one of the oddest organizations I ever had encountered. Every panel's membership included historians and social scientists. The historians were mostly quantitatively oriented, self-consciously analytic, and systematic in method and research design. Seeking to overcome what they saw as the limits of traditional narratives, they badly wanted to make social science, as they saw it, constitutive of their scholarship. Yet the political scientists and sociologists who attended were the humanists in their disciplines, very much open to various critical impulses, including those that called into question the very nature of social science and history as causal enterprises. Indeed, many of these qualitative social scientists were fleeing from what they viewed as the tyranny of numbers and the straightjacket of positivist methodologies. The results of these encounters were predictable. Each group talked past the other. The dominant mode of conversation was mutual incomprehension.

Looking Backward and Looking Forward: Social Science History at 2000

The most important accomplishment of the association in the past quarter century has been the erasure of this stylized form of noninteraction. It no longer exists. At each meeting, a plethora of ways of working is represented. Indeed, the very distinction of quantitative and qualitative hardly captures what most of us who attend actually do. Many of us cross these boundaries every day. More interesting, these words hardly capture the rich and various ways we conduct our scholarly inquiries.

What the Association has achieved is the creation of an uncommonly tolerant environment where substantive work about big and deep problems of wide import is valued alongside methodological self-reflection. The basic assumption undergirding our panels is that the participants, in all their disciplinary and methodological diversity, are likely to have important things to say about fundamental issues. Understanding and translation rule the day; that is, understanding work quite different from one's own in its particular terms and translating methods and findings into languages and formats that make them useable inside diverse research programs.

The SSHA thus gives pluralism a good name. At its best, this spirit comes close to the kind of social science Albert Hirschman advocates in his wonderful essay on "Rival Interpretations of Market Society" (1982). Noting that key works on this central institution of modernity offer deeply contradictory theories, hypotheses, and ways of working, Hirschman insists we should refuse to choose, at least *a priori* (of course, he has his own preferences). Instead, we should craft social science marked by an oscillation of perspectives in which each perspective or "school" maintains its integrity and passion for truth on the understanding that each might be "true" for some aspects of "reality" or in some historical circumstances. This is a counsel for both intellectual depth and scholarly modesty. Oscillation and an embrace of complexity replace a war of each against all as well as efforts to meld diverse perspectives into single grand designs.

What is remarkable, among other traits, about Hirschman as a model for the association is that his economics always is constituted by his self-conscious engagement with large themes in political theory. In this regard, the SSHA might be considered wanting. Very few colleagues place political theory in gear with their historical or social scientific scholarship. This is a pity because some of the deepest and most vexing questions we inquire after have emerged out of the great lineage of political thought, including contemporary political theory. To my taste, almost every one of these issues about fairness, justice, and a decent politics and society at once is institutional and empirical as well as theoretical and normative. The more to regret, then, that the boundary dividing political theorists from empiricists is crossed much less often than more frequent and also valuable border-crossing ventures with social theory.

A few years ago, I had the signal privilege to be president of this association. I called my presidential address, "Du Bois's Century." I chose this subject and this title for two reasons. In his own writing, W. E. B. Du Bois combined a commitment to deep particularity with a confidence in the deep universality of humankind in a manner that puts adversaries in recent "culture wars" to shame. Further, I wanted to recall this association to failures in which we share, failures signified by the manner in which the author of this country's first great community study, *The Philadelphia Negro* (1898), was denied a decent place within mainstream higher education. At the start of the twenty-first century, we still are not an inclusive body of scholars. Whether the new century will, in a full sense, become Du Bois's century, remains one of our great unknowns.

Mary Jo Maynes

I will restrict myself to two points in response to Harvey's questions about the lessons and accomplishments of the SSHA's first twenty-five years, and the challenges for our future. First, we need to define "social science" at least as broadly as the social sciences do (in terms of theoretical frameworks, methods, questions, and sources). Second, we need to push ourselves toward a more global orientation.

On the first point, at the core of the social science history of the first generation, there were many problematics that built on the claims of the social sciences to be like the natural sciences: demographic models, microeconomics, and resource mobilization. Several of our larger networks—so crucial to the ongoing work of and recruitment into the organization—were built around these approaches. But since the beginning, there have been other, quite different, intellectual tendencies represented. Other problematics of long interest to members had roots in critical epistemologies such as class analysis or early forays into materialist feminist analysis. More recent cross-disciplinary projects gravitate toward new concerns. We see, for example, new attention to problems of the self-positioning of the researcher, critical commentary on the structures and frameworks of historical investigation, interest in systematic ways to approach the analysis of textual evidence, or concern with intersubjectivity. Some of these interests pick up on interpretive and hermeneutic traditions that bring the social sciences and history more into conversation with what have been core concerns for the humanities. But these problems are also well within longstanding traditions of social-scientific inquiry defined more inclusively.

So we find shifting problematics that all are arguably within the realm of intersection of history and the social sciences. I can only quickly exemplify: in historical sociology, one notes a conceptual drift from the terms of class analysis to habitus; in political science, a shift of emphasis from analysis of election results to new institutionalism; in geography, interest in the spatial dimensions of memory alongside the economics of location; in economic history, attention to the social-historical construction of the global consumer as well as to the measurement of growth. None of these shifts are absolute; studies based on the older paradigms still claim attention. My point here is that shifts of this sort are simultaneously undermining and revitalizing social science history as it was imagined two decades ago. I would argue for both the continuing significance of the older approaches and the validity of the new ones. It would behoove us, for the sake of institutional and intellectual vitality, to learn to live with epistemological schizophrenia, and to learn and to teach to be conversant in a range of problematics rather than being fundamentalists.

On the second point—thinking globally—in my field, or at least in my experience, one enormous change since the SSHA was first organized has been the increasing interest in comparative and global approaches. Some areas of or approaches to social science history lend themselves better than others to comparison for reasons of data incomparability or divergent historiographies. Moreover, some parts of the globe have been easier than others to incorporate into our program.

Here too I can only briefly exemplify. Examples such as race theory, which now informs work in sociology and geography as well as history and cultural studies, also necessarily raises questions about frontiers and boundaries and positionality with respect to global hierarchies. Historians of migration have long needed to think globally. Demographic history offers another arena where global frameworks have always been operative (although originally with insufficient alertness to the connections between global power hierarchies and the institutions that structured demographic research). We are now seeing demographic and family history enter a new phase of comparative inquiry. One of the most exciting developments of the Minnesota Population Center (formerly known as the Census Project), with its long and solid connections to the SSHA's annual program, has expanded to collect and study not only U.S. census data but also census data from Latin America, Europe, and Africa.

Moreover, scholars from some parts of the world beyond the United

States have been represented at our meetings—especially Europeans—while we are not as strong in recruiting scholars from "the South." I did look at this year's program with this particular question in mind, and it struck me that some of the sort of effort I am suggesting is already well reflected there. For example, one of the presidential sessions specifically invited "Southern" historians and social scientists to reflect on the projects of historical social science. I attended another wonderful session, which was a book session on James Lee and Feng Wang's *One Quarter of Humanity*—a book on Chinese historical demography. This session was very, very exciting. It brought together historical demographers working in Asia with others whose research is based in Europe. As Tamara Hareven noted there, this kind of new work on Chinese historical demography is making Europeanists think differently about Europe. This is just one example, but it makes the point that forays across geographic boundaries, or formulations that call upon global perspectives, not only broaden our comparative horizons but make us think differently about our work, wherever it is based.

So my second plea, then, would be to keep up this effort and push it harder. I would particularly urge us to build on our impressive success at bringing European scholars into our organization to find ways for the SSHA to recruit scholars from beyond North America and Europe. This is not a challenge just for the SSHA, but it is a challenge that I would particularly like this organization to take on.

William H. Sewell, Jr.

I have not come to the Social Science History meetings every one of its twenty-five years, but have attended pretty frequently ever since the 1970s. I am a great fan of the SSHA because these are, as far as I am concerned, consistently the most stimulating meetings anywhere in the social sciences. Year in, year out, as the content of what actually goes on in the meetings changes, there remains a palpable sense of intellectual excitement. I want to think about why that is the case, why the excitement has persisted through all these years.

I think its persistence depends on three distinctive features of the SSHA. The first is that this is not only an interdisciplinary space, but in a very real sense a nondisciplinary space. I often tell my graduate students that they do not call them disciplines for nothing. The disciplines discipline: they set standards, award degrees, have official journals, decide who gets jobs, who gets awards, et cetera, et cetera. What is special about the SSHA meetings is that the stakes at play in our discussions are only intellectual. There is no job market. There is no disciplinary pecking order, and above all, there is no power to shape university institutions. I think it is a huge advantage that we are so weak. Our weakness is our strength.

The second distinctive feature, which the other panelists have noted, is the association's flexibility. My sense is that in the beginning there was a wished-for disciplinary project in the SSHA. This was to be where history and positivistic social science would come together, do an end run around the American Historical Association, and maybe create a new discipline or quasi discipline of historical science at the intersection between positivist social science and positivist history. For various reasons, that never happened.

Instead, there has been an extraordinary flexibility. The SSHA meetings seem to register faithfully the changing pulse of interdisciplinary social science in general, which means that by now there is probably almost as much activity at the boundaries between history and the humanities, or social science and the humanities, as between history and the social sciences on the positivist end. Keywords like "identity" and "historical memory" appear as often in titles of papers or sessions as keywords like "occupational structure" or "demographic transition."

The third distinctive feature of the SSHA is its real intellectual diversity. While it is true that the meetings register the changing pulse of interdisciplinary social science, the association as a whole does not chase after academic fashion. Rather, its motto is "Live and let live." Hence, for example, the more positivist style of quantitative social history that was the founding impulse for the SSHA continues to thrive. This remains the premier place for exchange among scholars doing that style of work, and those of us who, for one reason or another, have become renegades from quantitative history can go to their sessions and get our batteries recharged about it. There is a coexistence of genuinely different but mutually tolerant epistemologies in these meetings, and I think that is a tremendous strength.

How, as historical social scientists, do we explain the SSHA's special features: its non-disciplinarity, flexibility, and diversity? Paradoxically, one major reason for the special character of the SSHA is that it is a weak organization. It is run on a shoestring. It does not have a permanent staff. It does not run a job market. The president—as I am sure past presidents would testify—has very limited and very brief powers. I looked through the program, and as far as I could count, the president got to pick ten of 116 sections. Maybe he got to nudge for a few more. Even that limited power lasts just one year. Then somebody with a different agenda will

Andrew Abbott, Ira Katznelson, Mary Jo Maynes, William H. Sewell, Jr.

come in and do something completely different. The power of the president is both small and evanescent.

So if the president has no power, and there is a laughable budget and no permanent staff, what makes the SSHA tick? I would argue that the organizational continuity and the power have resided in the networks, not in the association, per se. The networks are intellectually autonomous and are not difficult to form or to disband. They put together the program, and they do it according to their independent intellectual agendas, which reflect the wishes of their members. This is an acephalous, decentralized, rhizomatic organization. It is anarchistic, and it works. I am not sure how and why this peculiar network-based form of organization came into being, but I think it is the secret of our success.

I do not want to make prognostications about the future. I think the only thing that history definitively tells us is that we cannot predict the future. I think we should continue doing what we have been doing, and that is to stay disorganized and stay powerless. I therefore disagree with Michael Katz's idea that we should get involved with the AHA and tell history departments how to run their graduate programs. I do not think we as an association should get more deeply involved in the affairs of any of our "home" disciplines. We should remain powerless to create anything except this extraordinary forum for intellectual debate. More by luck than by design, we have hit upon a remarkably flexible and effective anarchistic organizational pattern. So my advice for the future is: "Vive l'anarchie!"

REFERENCE LIST

Hirschman, A. 1982. Rival interpretations of market society: Civilizing, destructive, or feeble? *Journal of Economic Literature* 20 (December): 1463–84.

Part Two

TEACHING SOCIAL SCIENCE
HISTORY

The discussion of teaching social science history centered on a fundamental issue. Instead of the often-mentioned questions of how to train more graduate students as social science historians or to combat postmodern perspectives in student training, anthropologist Daniel Segal took on the thorny question of how we can work with students in those most widespread, basic, and potentially atavistic of history courses, Western Civilization and its developing offspring, World Civilization. Although our own research and scholarship may be very self-aware, Segal contends that Western Civilization—a cosmopolitan project in the 1920s, which has become a neoconservative project in the present age—represents the Achilles heel of history because it sees non-Westerners as the Other, outside of time, and predating civilization. It is, in other words, ahistorical in its uncritical focus on Civilization, as anthropology is not. Segal challenges history teachers to expose the assumptions of the "civilization" textbooks and to teach our students to do the same. Thus Segal complements the perspective of the session "Southern Perspectives on Historical Social Science" by challenging the conceptual apparatus of common approaches to history.

WORLDING HISTORY

DANIEL A. SEGAL

The West is not in the West. It is a project not a place.
Edouard Glissant, Caribbean Discourse

For as long as history has been a discipline, which is to say a century or so, history has been tied to a subset of humanity, one commonly identified in geographic terms. As a discipline, history has focused primarily on Europe or, more broadly, on the West, construed as an extension of Europe—as "Europe plus," one might say. Concomitantly, history has paid relatively little attention to the rest of the world. This essay examines both this circumscribed gaze on humanity by disciplinary history and the difficulties of overcoming it—that is, the difficulties of *worlding history.* I argue that history's provincialism—what I would term its "Western problem"—cannot be overcome by means of an empiricist strategy of simply adding the history of other places and peoples to history as we know and teach it. The reason for this is that exclusion from history is something more than simply neglecting Others. Rather, exclusion from history is organized along a gradient scale of social evolution defined, at its apical point, by the European/Western Self. It is not, in short, that Others are simply overlooked, but more precisely that they are placed *before* history or, at the very least, at various points or stages before history's leading edge. Adding accounts of the past of other places and other peoples does not itself remove, or even speak to, this organizing principle; quite to the contrary, additional histories are all too easily captured by and placed into this social evolutionary scheme. Worlding history thus requires not just histories of more and more places but a deployment of theory. It is in this sense that I advocate a dialogue between history and particular strands of the social sciences, most notably anthropological critiques of social evolutionary models and anthropological relativizing and defamiliarization.[1]

It is worth noting that historical writing and research, even as practiced in Europe and the West, has not always exhibited the specific pattern of geographic provincialism with which we are familiar. This pattern itself is a historical phenomenon. Back in the nineteenth century—to lean on an arbitrary division of time—historical scholarship in Europe

Daniel A. Segal

and North America foregrounded national units much more than any supranational unit, whether Europe or the West. In this context, history contributed a great deal to the project of substantiating the existence of specific national units, be they units crafted along the lines of previously existing monarchal realms (as with France) or units with novel borders (as with Germany).[2] Much, though certainly not all, of this nationalist and nation-making historical scholarship was produced by scholars who focused primarily, if not exclusively, on the national unit with which they shared an "identity" (e.g., French historians who wrote about France, U.S. historians who wrote about the United States, and so on).[3] So too, those historians who did focus their work on nations other than "their own" generally exhibited high levels of identification with, if not chauvinism about, their chosen national subject.

If one looks in the aggregate at the various national units that were the foci of various historians' gazes, one finds that together they comprise the supranational unit of Europe/the West, for very little of this nationalist historical practice focused on places outside of, or other to, Europe/ –the West. One could then say that this earlier practice of history prefigured, or prepared the way for, the discipline's subsequent linkage to the larger European and Western civilizational units. Yet it is important to see that this linkage with a larger areal and civilizational unit was incompletely realized before the early twentieth century.

The differences in the geographies of historical practice in the nineteenth and early twentieth centuries are subtle but nontrivial. To begin with, let us recall that in the nineteenth century, the larger civilizational unit that contained the aggregate of nation-states we now deem "Western" was most commonly identified *not* as "Western" but as "Christian." Moreover, as much as the national units within Christian civilization were themselves treated as historical objects, this was largely not the case for "Christian civilization" itself. Rather, what substantiated Christian civilization as a totality was less historical representation than appeals to the revealed "Truth of the Gospel." By contrast, during the first decades of the twentieth century, historians increasingly took European/–Western civilization as a subject of historical study and used this larger civilizational unit, in a variety of ways, to enframe more narrowly focused studies of national units. Thus, the movement upward in scale of the historian's gaze—from nation-state to a larger civilizational unit—took place as an aspect of a refashioning of that civilizational Self, from "Christian" to "Western."

This new linkage of history with "the West" was at the same time an aspect of history's refashioning as an academic discipline, for in its day this shift was understood as involving a departure from nationalist historical work that was chauvinistic and romantic, in favor of work that was cosmopolitan and disinterested, even scientific. Indeed, it would not be too much to say that part of what imbued "the West" as a historical subject with (seemingly) universal status was that "the West" was a unit above and beyond the often divisive nationalisms that had been championed by the earlier (and protodisciplinary) instantiation of historical practice.

In the United States, the new cosmopolitanism of disciplinary history was accelerated, if not pioneered, by the New Historians, and under their influence it came to be manifest in the discipline's signature course offering for undergraduates—"Western Civ," which emerged in the 1920s and became an established pedagogic genre in the 1930s. More generally, the new cosmopolitanism of disciplinary history was manifest in the gradual emergence of a model stipulating that departments of history, in order to be accorded a certain level of professional status, had to have sufficient coverage of the entire "Western tradition" and not just their own national(ized) history. In this way, in both scholarship and the curriculum of higher education, national histories, as much as they continued to be produced, were placed in a new context and, concomitantly, were no longer quite what they had been in an earlier moment: whatever was true of the work of an individual historian, history *as a discipline* now placed national histories in a larger, more cosmopolitan, framework. Indeed, even when no mention of a larger civilizational unit occurred in a historical work, this new, more cosmopolitan, stance or voice could itself indicate and provide a new contextualization of national histories.

In recent decades, however, the larger Western framing provided by disciplinary history has ceased to be seen as robustly cosmopolitan. In the wake of the dismantling of European empires and of the diversification of student bodies at U.S. colleges and universities, history's privileging of the West now appears as provincial, much as overtly nationalist histories appeared chauvinistic and romantic (i.e., unscientific) in the early twentieth century, as history coalesced as a discipline. Moreover, in this new context, the political valence of Western Civ has shifted dramatically: it has become a neoconservative cause. So too, the cosmopolitan impulse that had previously produced Western Civ now animates concerted efforts to world history—that is, to shift the unmarked locale of history upward once more, from the West to the world. This can be seen in at least two sites or projects. One of these projects aims to extend further the geographic coverage of history departments, a move that is heavily dependent on both the way positions are defined upon retirements of senior faculty and the distribution of areal expertise among new Ph.D.s. The second project aims to formulate a survey of World

Daniel A. Segal

History that would take the place in the curriculum once held by Western Civ—that is, as both a widely accepted element of general education and as the standard introductory course to the study of history. It is this second project that I will focus on here.

My comments on this project reflect a doubled or twofold perspective. In recent years, the primary focus of my scholarly work has been the history of undergraduate level Western Civ survey courses, from their initial emergence in the 1920s up through the present moment.[4] Yet along with pursuing this research on the history of Western Civ, I have also been developing and teaching a survey of modern world history, one designed and represented as a more worldly, less provincial, alternative to Western Civ. In short, I myself have participated in the pedagogic project of worlding history. My coeval positioning as a scholar and practitioner has made me keenly aware of what I term "gotcha-hermeneutics." What I mean to invoke by this confessedly improbable term is the extent to which much contemporary cultural criticism proceeds by catching practitioners (museum curators, filmmakers, and so on) in unwitting articulations of ideologies of domination without ever indicating fully just what would count as a satisfactory reform of their practice. As valuable as much of this work of cultural critique is (and I have participated in it myself), what is worrisome to me is that it risks suggesting that it is only critics and theorists who can do antihegemonic work. My goal, by contrast, is to look for ways to bring criticism and theory into practice—and specifically into pedagogic practice.

When we review attempts to world history in recent decades, we find that the most common strategy for carrying out this project has been to add histories of other places and other peoples: given the West, add the rest. This is in no case more visible than in the way many publishers in the 1990s produced world history textbooks for undergraduate level survey courses. Taking an already published Western Civ textbook for which they held the copyright, these publishers produced a cognate work for the world history market by hiring new authors to write chapters on other parts of the world, and then inserted those chapters into the existing text. On its own, without any further refinement, such an additive approach is an empiricist strategy. It seeks to world history by filling in geographic gaps with additional material about other places. While no one can doubt that worlding does indeed require greater attention to other parts of the world, this additive strategy quickly gives rise to a compelling reason not to take worlding too far or too seriously. The objection is that given limits of time, one can add only so much; teaching history—and in particular, teaching a survey course—would be impossible if one kept adding more and more of the world.

To develop a more focused and effective approach to worlding history requires that we recognize that history's provincialism is something more than the neglect of the rest of the world. As a means of illustrating how better to understand the provincialism of history—and specifically, of history as taught to our undergraduates—I want to turn to two figures from a recent Western Civ textbook, *The Challenge of the West: Peoples and Cultures from the Stone Age to the Global Age.* Published in 1995, this textbook was authored by a team of prestigious historians led by Lynn Hunt.

Before focusing on the two images I have selected however, it is worth pausing to reflect on the very title of this textbook. For my purposes, what is striking is that in the title itself, we find not one but two voices.[5] As any faculty member considering using this book would know, in an earlier moment, the words preceding "the West" in the title of a work of this genre would have been something like "The Rise of . . . " or "The Heritage of . . . " For faculty then—and for some students as well—the phrase, "The Challenge of the West," reads exactly as if a traditional or older voice has been replaced or corrected by a revisionist voice. Yet the result is not a happy one, for if the reader moves past the title to the work itself, s/he finds no clear explanation of what is meant by the phrase "the challenge of the West," nor any evidence that this phrase reflects the text's contents. Rather, if one reads the text itself, one finds a largely conventional narrative of the history of Western Civ modified, most notably, by attention to gender. One thus might hypothesize that the title has more to do with positioning and marketing this textbook—as one that avoids either celebrating or demonizing the West—than encapsulating it.

Turning to the two images I have selected from this text, the first is a photograph of a !Kung San woman living in the Kalahari (see figure 1). Though it is reproduced here in black and white, in *Challenge of the West* it appears in color. The photograph was taken sometime in the 1970s, and the photographer is the anthropologist Margery Shostak, author of *Nisa: The Life and Words of a !Kung Woman* (1983), a work that has been widely used in introductory level courses in both anthropology and women's studies.[6] In *Challenge of the West,* this photograph appears very close to the beginning of the work; it is printed on the third page of the prologue, which is itself titled "Before Civilization." To be even more specific, it appears in a section of the prologue given the subtitle, "The Paleolithic Period," a phrase that appears, as a running head, immediately above the photograph. Moreover, the legend beneath the photograph tells us that "this woman . . . exemplifies the only way human beings could support themselves before the invention of agriculture." Elsewhere on the same page, the text reports that "the !Kung San" are among the "few small groups of people" who "still live" in the manner

Daniel A. Segal

Photograph of a !Kung woman used in Challenge of the West as a figure in the text's prologue, "Before Civilization." The photograph was taken by anthropologist Marjorie Shostak in the 1970s. Asked about the presence of this woman's image in a discussion of the time "before civilization," Lynn Hunt responded: "Is it preferable to simply not represent them at all?" (e-mail to author, 5 November 1997).

of "prehistoric groups" (1995, xxxix). In short, at the very beginning of a text that serves as an overall history of Western civilization, we have a full-color photograph of a dark-skinned, African woman, more or less coeval with ourselves, deployed as an illustration of human life in "the Paleolithic period" of "prehistory"—and of human life "before civilization."

The second photograph, also produced in color in the textbook, is of a man and a woman—each recognizably "Middle Eastern"—working in a field of grain (see figure 2). This photograph was also taken by a prominent anthropologist—namely Lila Abu-Lughod, author of *Veiled Sentiments: Honor and Poetry in a Bedouin Society* (1986); though not taught as widely as *Nisa*, this too is a work that has gained considerable usage in undergraduate courses. The photograph is from Abu-Lughod's ethnographic research with Awlad Ali Bedouins, though the textbook conflates the photographed subjects—quite discordantly, as they would see it—with Egyptians. In *Challenge of the West*, this photograph appears in chapter one, a chapter concerned with the general topic of "First Civilizations" and placed, in the narrative, immediately after the prologue, "Before Civilization." As laid out on the page, Abu-Lughod's photograph is paired with a reproduction of a painting from ancient Egypt, in which we also find people working with grain (see figure 3). The didactic point of the pairing is made explicit in the legends that accompany these images. The first legend tells us that "techniques of harvesting and winnowing grain . . . have changed little in many parts of contemporary Egypt." The second adds, "Some people"—an inchoate referential phrase the photograph serves to illustrate—"still use the method of winnowing grain that ancient Egyptians used, throwing it into the air by hand" (Hunt et al. 1995, 12). So here we find brown-skinned persons of "the Near East," persons alive (like us) in the time of color photography, figured as the equivalents of an earlier time and earlier civilization—one of the very "first," we are told. Moreover, just as the photograph of these persons is situated in a chapter that follows an account of "prehistory," itself graced by a photograph of a black African woman, it in turn is followed by a much more extensive and historical narration of the West. The sequencing of colors, places, times, and civilizational stages is anything but nuanced.

It is worth noting that both of these photographs moved from the sites where they were taken (the Kalahari and the Egyptian western desert) to their locations in this textbook (in sections on "before civilization" and "first civilizations," respectively) without the knowledge of either Shostak or Abu-Lughod, and vice versa, without the authors of *The Challenge of the West* knowing very much about the persons in the photographs

Daniel A. Segal

Photograph of an Awlad 'Ali Bedouin man and woman winnowing barley and used in *Challenge of the West* as a figure in chapter one, concerned with "First Civilizations." The photograph was taken by anthropologist Lila Abu-Lughod, most likely in 1987 (e-mail from L. Abu-Lughod to the author, 20 January 1999).

The Harvest in Egypt
This Egyptian painting depicts agriculture along the fertile banks of the Nile River. Techniques of harvesting and winnowing grain (separating the edible core from the inedible chaff) have changed little in many parts of contemporary Egypt.

Preparing Grain in the Traditional Way
Some people today still use the method of winnowing grain that ancient Egyptians used: throwing it into the air by hand so the breeze can blow the light chaff away from the heavier core.

Juxtaposition, as printed in *Challenge of the West*, of Lila Abu-Lughod's photograph of Awlad 'Ali Bedouins (see figure 2) and an ancient Egyptian scroll. Asked about this placement and use of her photograph, Abu-Lughod responded: "It drives me crazy when people make links to ancient Egyptians and talk about five thousand years ago. In particular, these Bedouin, who grow barley [and who] have been living in this area for hundreds of years, came originally from Libya and trace their descent to Arab tribes who swept through North Africa from the Peninsula in the eleventh century. They have no ties to ancient Egyptians and only recently came into Egypt. As you will know from *Veiled Sentiments*, they feel themselves to be quite distinct from the people of the Nile Valley and have a distinctive history. So the link to ancient Egypt is absurd. The second problem is that the man in the background is not using his hands but a pitchfork to hurl the grain into the air" (e-mail from L. Abu-Lughod to the author, 20 January 1999).

or their immediate cultural-social contexts. There are a number of reasons why the circulation of these images did not also involve a circulation of greater biographical and/or ethnographic knowledge about the persons represented in them. To begin with, historians generally do not, as part of their professional practice, read ethnographic texts. In addition, much of the work selecting and obtaining illustrative material for textbooks is handled not by academic authors but by a photography editor or researcher in the employ of the publisher. For persons in such positions, what is of import is not the cultural-social context outside of the photographic frame, but the visual content of an image and access to legal rights to reproduce it. In this regard, let us note that in U.S. and international law, these legal rights are only rarely attached to the subjects of photography, as distinct from the person who operates the camera ("the photographer"). Moreover, in the case of both photographs, the chain of connections between the authors of *Challenge of the West* and the photographed subjects was even more extended and indirect, for both Shostak and Abu-Lughod had deposited their photographs (and the legal rights to reproduce them) with a specialized photographic agency, Anthro-Photo File, an institution whose role in the circulation of ethnographic images has been undeservedly neglected by historians of anthropology.[7] Given this constellation of factors, it is not surprising that the exchange that mediated the movement of these images into *Challenge of the West* and their consequent recontextualization therein, was not a rich cross-cultural (or even cross-disciplinary) dialogue, but a monetary and legal transaction—specifically, a royalty payment.

What these images illustrate, moreover, is that the Western-centrism of Western Civ is not a matter of simply neglecting non-Western Others, but of inserting them into a preexisting social evolutionary emplotment of human existence: it is this emplotment that is, quite precisely, the new context that has been provided for these images. Moreover, this same pattern of emplotment—with no more than minor variations—can be found throughout the history of the teaching of Western Civ, going back to the publication of the very first Western Civ textbook in 1926. Others have always been present between the covers of Western Civ texts, but always located as precursors to the West.[8]

So too, and of more immediate importance to my discussion of worlding, we can find very much this same emplotment of human diversity in the way publishers over the last decade have retrofitted Western Civ texts as World History texts. What publishers have added to the former to make the latter is revealed by noting the areal expertise of the authors hired to write the supplement that is added to the older, Western texts. To give one example, the cover of *Civilization in the West* lists three authors, all historians of Europe; the cover of the "World History" sibling of this work, *Societies and Cultures in World History,* lists one additional author, a professor of East Asian history.[9] Similarly, if one compares *Western Civilization* with its sibling work, *World History,* the additional author is also a professor of East Asian history.[10] As these examples suggest, the primary ingredient that "worlds" history in these textbooks is the area formerly known as "the Orient"—which is to say the non-European Other that, for some two centuries, has most been accorded the status of a "civilization," albeit an "ancient" and "stagnant" one. Thus, even when this worlding of history brings in a fair amount of historical information about China and Japan, it inscribes anew the division of humanity into civilization and "peoples without history."[11]

It follows from these observations that to "world" history in a robust manner requires not just a supplement—not just adding Others—but a pursuit of the more complex project of contesting received linkages of peoples with times and developmental statuses. This requires dismantling both the practice of encasing human difference in sequenced stages of time and, what is fundamental to this entrenched practice, the very division of human time into prehistory and history. Only by dismantling this binary can we begin to locate all of humanity in history—rather than placing some of humanity before "history" and before "civilization."

A corollary of these points is worth noting as well. As is evident from the example of these two photographs, the social evolutionary matrix I have identified is an interdisciplinary one, for it involves not history as an isolate but history set in relation to anthropology. It thus follows that we cannot contest this matrix unless we are open to reconfiguring the relationship between history and anthropology, and concomitantly, open to reconfiguring the two disciplines themselves. How could it be otherwise, we might ask, given the extent to which the intellectual division of labor between history and anthropology has been based upon a decomposition of humanity into peoples with and without history respectively?

But what then is to be done? How can we, as teachers, contest the social evolutionary matrix that links black Africa to prehistory, the Middle East to the beginnings of civilization, and the West to history? To do this effectively requires that we recognize that when a college-level textbook, such as *Challenge of the West*, places human variation into a social evolutionary matrix, it is unlikely that the textbook is introducing students to ideas unknown to them. Rather, when a textbook does this, it is trafficking in a way of thinking with which students are almost certainly conversant long before they arrive at college. Thus, to contest this scheme, one must do more than abandon it: one must make it visible and open to inquiry.

As an initial illustration of what this would involve, consider merely the use of the term "civilization." Both in responses to my own work on these issues and in other contexts, I have heard textbook authors and some faculty who teach these texts assert that in using the concept of "civilization"—as in the phrase "Before Civilization"—the textbooks are not, in fact, subscribing to any scheme of social evolution or ranking of social forms. The argument that is deployed to support this claim is that "civilization" is somehow used in the textbooks in a purely technical sense— that is, to refer to social groups of a certain scale or those possessed of a certain technology—and that no grander theory or understanding is intended or articulated. Such a defense of the term strikes me as naïve, if not disingenuous. Who can believe that even if a textbook stipulates some such technical definition of "civilization," that doing so is sufficient to exorcise the cluster of evaluative and social evolutionary meanings that today saturate this word? How can conventionalized meanings that are so powerfully enforced in so many other contexts be removed simply by definitional fiat in a textbook? Surely it would be better not to pretend that the word does not mean what it most certainly does mean for most students and, instead, offer our students the tools needed to reflect on the term and its complex history.

In this regard, it is worth noting that though they all make use of the civilization concept, in the ways illustrated by *Challenge of the West*, not a single existing Western Civ or World History textbook provides a sustained discussion of uses and critiques of this concept. What must be added to our textbooks—if we are serious about worlding history, as distinct from being satisfied with the presence of Others behind history— is not just history about more places but the sort of argument Steven Feierman provides. The civilization concept, says Feierman, involves "a complex of elements" that are said to cohere "political and economic hierarchy, towns, commerce and intercommunication, writing, the plough, high densities of population and historical dynamism" (1993, 177). When we look carefully at African histories, however, we find numerous cases in which "the interrelations do not hold" (177), and thus we have no basis for continuing to treat these elements as indices of some distinct stage or form of human sociality. As Feierman concludes: "The elements have no explanatory significance if treated as a check list" (178). Moreover, if we stubbornly insist on using the civilization "complex" when looking at African history, we will disregard and overlook other, quite different, linkages of social institutions. To give just one example, drawing on research by John Janzen, Feierman discusses how trade in the Kongo in the seventeenth century—involving, on an annual basis, ivory from as many as four thousand elephants and as much as forty tons of copper—was supported not by anything recognizable as a "state" per se, but by a dispersed "healing association" or "drum of affliction" (178). The overall point then is that the "civilization" concept serves us poorly in Africa—which is itself sufficient to conclude that it is ill-suited to the project of worlding history.

There is a more general lesson here as well. The example of "civilization" shows us that we cannot move forward with the project of worlding history unless we bring theory—by which I mean a self-conscious and critical examination of our own conceptual schemes—into our pedagogy and textbooks. But doing this is no simple matter. Textbooks—as any of us who have read or taught them know—are written in a stead-fastly monologic and authoritative voice. They offer a series of declarative sentences about their chosen subject matter, presenting these claims—in Clifford Geertz's apt phrase—as a "view from nowhere" (2000, 137). By contrast, critical reflection requires a multiplicity of voices: to examine a concept such as "civilization" requires both that we ventriloquate, with as much integrity as possible, voice(s) that endorse and use this concept, and that we respond with other, critical, voices and perspectives. So too, critical reflection about such a concept requires that we self-consciously look at language and habits of representation, and that we suspend our easy comfort with making declarations about the world "out there," as if it were possible to know that world without the mediation of language, broadly construed. In sum, critical reflection—or if one wishes, "theory"—is always both dialogic and metalingusitic.

As this suggests, for our textbooks to provide students entrée to critical reflection about a concept such as "civilization" would involve a fundamental change, not just in the geographic coverage of textbooks but in their prose. And we should not expect that this would be welcomed, or even permitted, without a struggle. The writing that would result would be "complex"; it would be "demanding." It would require that students read not just words and sentences, but that they track voices as they read and that they reflect on the constitutive powers of language and the conventional character of representations. But it is just such writing, at least as much as any matter of content, that is policed and disciplined by the editors employed by textbook publishers, as expressed in their demands that textbook prose be "accessible" and transparent. My point is certainly not to advocate or excuse bad writing or murkiness. Nonetheless, if we are serious about worlding history, we must be prepared to write and speak against the grain of common sense, for it is in common sense, as much as in our textbooks, that Others are located not in history but in its wake.

Discussion Following Daniel Segal's "Worlding History"

Questioner: When you interviewed Lynn Hunt, did you raise the issues that you pointed out here, concerning the photographs? And how did she respond?

Daniel Segal: A crucial thing about interviewing Lynn Hunt—speaking as an anthropologist—is that to a great extent Lynn Hunt and I live in same social world. We read a lot of the same stuff; we are exposed to many of the same ideas; we attend some of the same conferences. The result of this, methodologically, is that it is almost impossible for me to formulate a question for her about her textbook that does not quickly conjure up, for her, pretty much the same line of argument that I myself am developing in asking the question. When I say to her, "I would like to ask you some questions about the photograph of the !Kung woman in the opening section of the text," she is not listening to the question in the context of working with a production or photography editor at a publishing house; instead, she is interacting with a colleague, one whom she recognizes as having certain theoretical interests and concerns. As a result, she was in many ways able to anticipate and even produce my questions. So when I asked her about that photograph, she knew quickly what I was getting at. In short, I cannot get her to speak about the image without a great deal of self-consciousness and awareness of the point of my question.

Questioner: Did she ask you how you would have done it differently?

Segal: Well, one of her responses was, "Is it preferable to simply not represent them at all?" In other words, would you rather we leave the !Kung and other Africans out entirely? To which my response was this: I do not believe that I should be forced to choose between leaving Africans out of history and placing them in prehistory. The other option is to write the persons in the photographs into the textbook's narrative of the late twentieth century—which is when those persons are or were living.

Ron Aminzade (Sociology, University of Minnesota and Chair of the Presidential Session on Teaching Social Science History): Thinking of Dan's paper, I want to ask: should we even be using textbooks? Given the structure of the publishing industry and the pressures from editors, should we just abandon the textbooks? I would like to hear Dan's thoughts on this.

Segal: In my own world history course, I use only primary documents as readings, and then in addition to the lectures, I meet weekly with students in groups of no more than twelve. This is very labor intensive. My own institution—Pitzer College—has supported this by giving me extra teaching credit for it. But that is what has made it possible, which leads me to the general answer to your question: ideally, perhaps, get rid of the textbooks. But as a practical matter, for colleagues who work at, say, the California state colleges, or even currently as education is organized at our big public research university, with the size of introductory level classes, my approach is not a practical suggestion.

I think it is important to keep in mind the material conditions under which lots of colleagues work, conditions that do not allow that and do not support the kind of privileged teaching that I am able to give at a small private liberal arts college. So my answer is that textbooks are going to be with us for some time. I think they can be made a lot better, and I think it is worth making them a lot better.

Questioner: It seems to me that the problem that you are addressing is not so much about textbooks as it is about a prevalent developmental model of world history. Do you have some strategies to address that?

Segal: If I understand your question, I think the point you are making is a very important one. The ideas I am discussing are both profoundly disturbing and profoundly distributed. They are in all sorts of places. You can do a reading of a set of Disney movies and find some of these same ideas, I think. You can do a reading of all sorts of things and find them. But as a strategic point, I would say that while these ideas are circulated by all sorts of producers of images, all sorts of producers of commemoration, schooling plays a particular role in that it accredits ideas. Schooling is not the sole or even the primary source of social evolutionary ideas, but when social evolutionary ideas appear in the undergraduate curriculum, that says to students, "This is a way of thinking that is proper for an educated person; this is a legitimate way of thinking." So in relationship to these ideas, there is an accreditation function of schooling. Moreover, that accreditation function is, like schooling itself, pyramidal. It is ranked, so that when students are introduced to ideas in high school, that accredits those ideas, but then there is a higher level of accreditation when those ideas are repeated in tertiary education. Given this, it seems to me a strategic intervention to focus on textbooks and undergraduate courses.

Let me make a second point as well. I could write about how Disney flicks contain all sorts of powerful racist and social evolutionary images. But the Walt Disney Corporation is much less likely to care about or be influenced by what I write than are my colleagues who write textbooks, or even the editors at publishing houses. We author these textbooks; we review them; we teach them. It is plausible then that we can change them. True, there are all sorts of institutional barriers to making them different, but I think our chance of changing them is significantly better than our chance of changing the next Disney flick or the next Eminem rap song.

Questioner: I want to come back to the question about the interview with Lynn Hunt. How is it that somebody who is so smart could have used that photo in that way? And why was she unwilling to take on the challenge of doing it differently herself?

Segal: The reason I used the illustration from Lynn Hunt's textbook is not that I want to pick on Lynn Hunt, nor is that I can not find quite similar problems in other textbooks. Rather, it is to make the point that

Daniel A. Segal

even when a textbook author is a strong intellect and possessed of much status in the profession, the author really does not write her or his textbook; rather she or he writes into a codified genre: textbook authors fill in the chapters in an existing outline, an existing formula. If I showed this in the case of someone of much less stature, it would prove much less. It would be easy to imagine: "Well, that person can be told what to do by the publisher." Using Lynn Hunt's textbook as my example shows the distribution of the author function, by means of a set of conventions and institutional relationships, beyond the biographical author or authors.

NOTES

1. For a discussion of the distinctive character of anthropological relativizing and defamiliarization, see Segal 1999.
2. On the relationship of U.S. nationalism to the more frequently studied European cases, see Segal 1994.
3. On the cultural specificity of notions of identity, see Handler 1994. For an account of nation-states that registers their contingency, see Segal 1988, Handler and Segal 1996.
4. For a fuller account of this research, see Segal 2000.
5. My discussion of voicing in this passage and later in this article draws on the work of Bakhtin, notably Bakhtin 1981, 1984.
6. I was unable to obtain much specific information about this photograph or the woman depicted in it. Marjorie Shostak died before I began to investigate the image. I have spoken about the image with her husband, anthropologist Melvin Konner, who also worked with the !Kung, but he did not recognize the woman in the photo or know of the specific circumstances in which the photo was taken.
7. For information about Anthro-Photo, I am grateful for discussions with Lila Abu-Lughod, as well as with Nancy De Vore, who runs Anthro-Photo.
8. For documentation of this point, see Segal 2000.
9. Compare Kishlansky, Geary, and O'Brien, *Civilization in the West*, 2d ed., with Kishlansky, Geary, O'Brien, and Wong, *Societies and Cultures in World History*. In the fuller list of credits given inside this textbook, five additional scholars are identified as having contributed smaller supplements to the text. Of these five, one contributed still more material on China, two contributed material on the Middle East, another contributed material on Africa, and the last contributed material on Latin America. The lesser billing given to these five authors indicates accurately the lesser attention given to the additional parts of the world for which they had responsibility. Moreover, the patterns of coverage and exclusion are complex. One needs to consider, for example, the absence of any contributors with expertise about Oceania or Native Americans, as well as the selection of topics within, say, African or Latin American history.

10. Compare Spielvogel, *Western Civilization,* with Duiker and Spielvogel, *World History.*

11. This paragraph is drawn from Segal 2000, 797–98; the phrase, "peoples without history," is drawn from Eric Wolf's (1982) own ironic use of the phrase.

REFERENCE LIST

Abu-Lughod, L. 1986. *Veiled sentiments: Honor and poetry in a Bedouin society.* Berkeley: University of California Press.
Bakhtin, M. 1981. *The dialogic imagination: Four essays.* Translated by Caryl Emerson and Michael Holquist and edited by Michael Holquist. Austin: University of Texas Press.
———. 1984. *Problems of Dostoevsky's poetics.* Translated and edited by Caryl Emerson. Minneapolis: University of Minnesota Press.
Duiker, W., and J. Spielvogel. 1994. *World history.* Minneapolis: West. Pub. Co.
Feierman, S. 1993. African histories and the dissolution of world history. In *Africa and the disciplines,* edited by Robert H. Bates, V. Y. Mudimbe, and Jean O'Barr. Chicago: University of Chicago Press.
Geertz, C. 2000. *Available light: Anthropological reflections on philosophical topics.* Princeton: Princeton University Press.
Handler, R. 1994. Is "identity" a useful cross-cultural concept? In *Commemorations: The politics of national identity,* edited by John R. Gillis. Princeton: Princeton University Press.
Handler, R., and D. Segal. 1996. Nationalism. In *The encyclopedia of cultural anthropology,* edited by David Levinson and Melvin Amber. New York: Henry Holt and Company.
Hunt, L., T. Martin, B. Rosensqein, R. P. Hsia, and B. G. Smith. 1995. *The challenge of the West: Peoples and cultures from the Stone Age to the Global Age.* Lexington, Mass.: D.C. Heath.
Kishlansky, M., P. Geary, and P. O'Brien. 1991. *Civilization in the West,* 2d ed. New York: Harper Collins.
Kishlansky, M., P. Geary, P. O'Brien, and B. Wong. 1995. *Societies and cultures in world history.* New York: HarperCollins.
Segal, D. A. 1988. Nationalism, comparatively speaking. *Journal of Historical Sociology* 1 (3): 300–321.
———. 1994. Living ancestors: Nationalism and the past in post-colonial Trinidad and Tobago. In *Remapping memory: The politics of timeSpace,* edited by Jonathan Boyarin. Minneapolis: University of Minnesota Press.
———. 1999. Ethnographic classics, ethnographic examples: Some thoughts on the new cultural studies and an old queer science. In *Kulturstudien heute (The Contemporary Study of Culture),* edited by I. Korneck, et al. Wien: Turia und Kant.
———. 2000. "Western civ" and the staging of history in American higher education. *American Historical Review* 105 (3): 770–805.

Daniel A. Segal

Shostak, M. 1981. *Nisa: The life and words of a !Kung woman.* Cambridge: Harvard University Press.
Spielvogel, J. 1994. *Western civilization,* 2d ed. Minneapolis: West. Pub. Co.
Wolf, E. 1982. *Europe and the people without history.* Berkeley: University of California Press.

Part Three

SOCIAL SCIENCE HISTORY

PAST AND PRESENT

Many presentations reflected on the Social Science History Association and its work. We include four of them here to provide historical and scholarly context for both graduate students and experienced scholars. The first two papers draw on Richard Steckel's analysis of meeting programs since 1976. Steckel focuses on the meetings themselves, providing a history of the organization as it has grown from a regional to a national, then international conference, with evolving areas of concentration. This overview provides a brief framework for the works that follow. The next paper, by James Z. Lee, thoughtfully evaluates the history of one of the most significant of SSHA networks, Historical Demography and Family History. This is not a triumphant narrative; rather Lee emphasizes the challenges to historical demography and family history to be more historical and more communicative, for example. Lee points to the exemplary EurAsian project. Together, these two papers open a window on the long-term developments and options for social science history and prepare the reader for the sections to come that are devoted to substantive issues.

Following, Michael Brown takes on the contested and complex study of race. Stepping out of social science practice to assess the history of understanding racial inequality, Brown writes about the dismissal of race by scientists and its establishment as a social construct, noting that the problematic of race has been transformed by the work of the past two decades, including the studies of whiteness. Brown insists on a new understanding of segregation and race domination, following the dismantling of biological models of race and prejudice. By so doing, Brown offers a history of the study of race, not only by social scientists but also by scholars of culture like Toni Morrison. This is social science history and more, as befits an assessment of this complex topic.

The final contribution to this section is a reflective roundtable on the history of literacy. Here the opening historiographical comments on literacy and social science history could well be applied to the study of race, historical demography, and other phenomena. Thirty years ago, literacy (like the reduction of fertility rates, for example) was perceived as a signal of progress by a social science literature steeped in modernization theory. Like the fertility transition, literacy has come to be understood as more complex and context-dependent than the scholars of the 1960s understood it to be. This discussion of literacy is a fitting capstone to this section, then, insofar as it offers an analysis of one substantive area of inquiry for social science historians in particular depth. Harvey J. Graff introduces the themes of the history of literacy as explored in the SSHA, then Chad Gaffield tracks the way that the study of literacy has been complicated by its scholars and demonstrates its connections to other areas of inquiry; David Mitch pushes at the necessity for a continuing critical edge to the study of literacy and assesses future directions; Anders Nilsson assesses the concepts and measures surrounding literacy as human capital, for example, and measurable by signature. Finally, David Vincent focuses on the post as a great indicator of literate exchange and poses the basic questions that must be addressed by a continuing history of literacy. Like James Lee, the authors here suggest that scholars in their network engage with the metanarratives of other networks in order to continue to extend scholarship into new and fruitful areas.

THE EVOLUTION OF THE SOCIAL

SCIENCE HISTORY ASSOCIATION

MEETINGS, 1976–1999

RICHARD H. STECKEL

When founded in the mid-1970s, the Social Science History Association (SSHA) was a small organization with a modest interdisciplinary scope and roots geographically centered in the Midwest and the Northeast. Over the following quarter century it grew to embrace vast national and international audiences engaged in increasingly diverse interdisciplinary research topics. Its success even spawned a similar organization in Europe.

This paper uses methods of inquiry familiar to social science historians in seeking to understand this remarkable transformation. The source materials are the annual meeting program books, which list the names of chairs, paper titles, paper givers, and discussants. To give broad chronological coverage while keeping the project manageable, I selected the years of 1976, 1980, 1985, 1990, 1995, and 1999 for study. All program information given in the books was recorded on Excel spreadsheets, from which various statistical patterns were extracted on participation, origins of participants, and the subjects of discussion as represented by networks. As someone who participated in nearly all of the meetings since the late 1970s and who has been involved in many committees of the organization, I add personal insights into this extraordinary growth.

Growth

Table 1 shows that the meetings were relatively small and growth was slow in the 1970s. Participants on the program numbered 275 at the first meeting, held in Philadelphia in 1976.[1] The number

Richard H. Steckel

Table 1: Number of Participants on the Program by Year

Year	Number	Location
1976	275	Philadelphia
1980	289	Rochester
1985	466	Chicago
1990	533	Minneapolis
1995	769	Chicago
1999	985	Ft. Worth

Source: SSHA program books.

grew by only fourteen at the Rochester meetings of 1980, but thereafter the pace accelerated. From 1980 to 1999 the number of participants more than tripled, growing at annual average rate of 6.5 percent. The Chicago meetings of 1985 attracted 466 participants, and another 67 were added for the Minneapolis meetings of 1990. A leap to 769 participants occurred at the 1995 meetings at Chicago, and Ft. Worth embraced nearly a thousand in 1999. Needless to say, the meetings are not only alive and well but also vibrant with activity.

Associations with a traditional disciplinary focus that predominate within SSHA do not match this record of growth over the same period. Table 2 shows that all of the major primary associations for SSHA members were much larger but grew more slowly since the late 1970s. Annual growth rates ranged from 1.9 percent (American Sociological Association) to 2.6 percent (American Anthropological Association) but even the latter was just over one quarter of the rate in the Social Science History Association. If the disciplinary memberships are a general indicator of an upper limit to size, an enormous potential for growth remains within SSHA.

Origins

There are many ways to discuss origins, including geographic regions, institutions, and departments. Table 3 presents the regional origins of the participants, of which almost 90 percent at the first meeting originated in the Northeast or the Midwest, with nearly two-thirds coming from the former region. A majority came from the Northeast at the next meeting, but significant gains were made from the West (9.69 percent) and the Southeast (7.61 percent). The Northeast continued to fall, and by the mid- and late 1990s their share stabilized at about 23 percent.

Table 2: Growth of Registration at Annual Professional Meetings

Group	Average meeting registration		Annual growth rate (percent)
	1977–1979	1998–2000	
American Historical Association	2,640	4,158	2.2
American Sociological Association	3,259	4,813	1.9
American Anthropological Association	2,908[a]	4,849	2.6
American Economic Association	4,673	7,928	2.5
American Political Science Association	2,561	5,883	4.0
Social Science History Association	282[b]	985[c]	6.0

[a] 1978–1980.
[b] Participants determined from program books, average of 1976 and 1980.
[c] Participants determined from the program book for 1999 only.
Sources: Telephone conversations, e-mails, or faxes from group headquarters, March–April 2002.

Table 3: Geographic Origins of Participants on the Program

	Number	Northeast (percent)	Central (percent)	Western (percent)	Southeast (percent)	Foreign (percent)	N. A.[a] (percent)
All	3317	31.05	31.96	11.15	11.37	13.69	0.78
1976	277	62.45	25.27	5.05	4.33	2.89	0.00
1980	289	52.60	25.95	9.69	7.61	3.46	0.69
1985	466	30.69	39.70	9.23	12.02	7.30	1.07
1990	533	29.08	40.90	9.19	11.26	8.82	0.75
1995	769	23.02	33.16	13.13	10.79	18.99	0.91
1999	983	23.40	26.14	13.73	14.65	21.26	0.81

[a] Not available.
Source: SSHA program books.

The most dramatic change in origins was the rise of participants from abroad, many of whom were attracted by topics in family history or historical demography. The share was under 5 percent up to 1980 and just under 9 percent in 1990, but exceeded 21 percent in 1999. Foreign participants are now the third largest group, approaching the rates of those from the Northeast (23.4 percent) and the Central states (26.14 percent). The appeal of interdisciplinary history is now international, and Europeans recently formed an organization with goals and operating procedures parallel to those of SSHA.

No single university or organization has dominated the meetings, but there have been some consistent players. Universities located in large cities where meetings have been located have some advantage, because

Richard H. Steckel

Table 4: Number of Institutions Having Eight People or More on the Program

Year	Number
1976	4
1980	6
1985	9
1990	8
1995	18
1999	24

Source: SSHA program books.

scholars are more likely to come if they live nearby. Consistent with the predominance of the Northeast and the Central states, it is not surprising to find Pennsylvania and Harvard—major schools of the Northeast—and the Big Ten schools, particularly Michigan, Minnesota, and Wisconsin, plus the University of Chicago, as the most important suppliers of participants. Only one school (Michigan) appears among the top ten in all six years studied, but Pennsylvania and Chicago appear five times, and Harvard and Minnesota appear four times.

Pennsylvania holds the record for the largest share of participants (20.73 percent), but it occurred under the special circumstances of the first meeting, which was held at Penn in 1976. Thereafter only one school had more than a 10 percent share: Minnesota, 12.2 percent when the meetings were held in Minneapolis. With these exceptions, all schools have had less than a 5 percent share.

The growing institutional diversity of the meetings can be identified by the tendency for the share of the "other" schools to rise over time. This share was 53.09 percent in 1976 but had risen to 79.70 percent in 1999. At the same time the number of institutions represented among the participants climbed from 109 to 362.

Data in Table 4 show that critical masses of interest in social science history have emerged at numerous institutions. Only four schools had as many as eight participants at the first meeting in 1976, and nine years later the figure was nine. The most substantial growth occurred in the 1990s, however, when eighteen schools (1995) and twenty-four (1999) sent eight or more participants.

Departments and Research

Scholars situated in history departments have always been the most numerous participants. According to Table 5, their num-

The Evolution of the Social Science History Association Meetings, 1976–1999

Table 5: Percent of Total Participants on the Program by Department
and Number of Departments

1976	1980	1985	1990	1995	1999
History (43.64)	History (50.17)	History (44.42)	History (47.84)	History (42.13)	History (39.90)
Pol. Sci. (12.36)	Pol. Sci (11.76)	Sociology (11.59)	Sociology (12.38)	Sociology (15.60)	Sociology (13.30)
Sociology (10.55)	Economics (11.07)	Economics (9.44)	Economics (9.38)	Economics (9.62)	Economics (7.72)
Economics (9.09)	Sociology (10.38)	N. A. (6.44)	Pol. Sci. (3.75)	N. A. (4.29)	Pol. Sci. (5.28)
N. A. (5.82)	African Studies (1.73)	Pol. Sci. (5.15)	N. A. (3.38)	Pol. Sci. (4.29)	Geography (2.84)
Anthropology (2.91)	Am. Studies (1.38)	Anthropology (4.51)	Anthropology (2.81)	Geography (2.21)	Anthropology (1.93)
Philosophy (1.82)	Criminal Justice (1.38)	Education (1.93)	Geography (2.25)	Anthropology 91.43)	Economic Hist. (1.83)
3 Depts. Tied (1.09)	Social Sciences (1.04)	Hum. Soc. Sci. (1.93)	Education (1.88)	American Stud. (1.17)	Government (1.52)
Other (12.73)	Other (11.07)	Other (14.59)	Other (16.32)	Other (19.25)	Other (25.69)
No. Depts. (35)	No. Depts. (32)	No. Depts. (48)	No. Depts. (53)	No. Depts. (91)	No. Depts. (134)

Source: SSHA program books.

bers reached a slight majority (50.17 percent) in 1980, and only recently fell below 40 percent (39.90 percent in 1999) for the first time. Sociologists have usually been second in participation (four out of six years) with rates of 11.59 to 15.6 percent. Also important have been political scientists (twice the second most numerous, both in the early years) and economists (five times third and once fourth). Geography, Anthropology, and American Studies frequently appear among the top eight department represented on the programs.

"Other" departments have risen in importance over the past quarter century. Amounting to 12.73 percent at the first meeting, this group reached 25.69 percent in 1999. Parallel with this growth was an increase in the number of departments represented from 35 to 134. Much of this growth occurred in the 1990s, when the share from abroad also rose dramatically. A connection between these two phenomena has yet to be established, but one might exist if overseas scholars were less likely to fit into categories of traditional departments at American universities.

Richard H. Steckel

Networks

Members of the SSHA will no doubt be interested in the evolution of areas of research represented at the meetings. Inevitably, this is difficult to measure with precision simply because so many panels are interdisciplinary. In fact, it has been a rule of thumb that panels include members from at least two different departments, and often three or four are represented at a single session. Thus, it is not surprising that the topics of the papers on the panels often are difficult to categorize. No single classification scheme is likely to be approximately accurate unless it is extraordinarily detailed. But if this is done, it is once again difficult to comprehend the meaning of large shifts. Inherently one is caught between the tensions of a desire for accuracy, which requires detailed classification, and a desire to generalize, which requires some broad categories.

That said, I plunge into this challenging problem by discussing growth and evolution of networks depicted in Tables 6 through 11. While there has been some growth in the number of networks over time (for example, from sixteen in 1976 to seventeen in 1999), their evolution is the more interesting feature of change. The dynamics reveal a pattern of ebb and flow that overlays an element of consistency. Throughout its history, four strands of research have always been found within the organization: Family/Demography, Politics, Labor, and Methodology. Four durable new networks joined by 1980: Economic History, Criminal Justice/Legal, Urban, and Education. But several research groups faded away or were subsumed under other networks, including Social Structure/ Social Mobility, Social Theory/Social Policy, and Large-Scale Societal Change, which combined to account for nearly 30 percent of the participants at the first meeting in 1976. Four additional networks joined by 1985 (Women, Migration, Rural, and Historical Geography), but Bureaucracy and Elites as well as Social Organizations/Ethnicity were lost (the latter reemerged by 1990 as Race/Ethnicity). Family History and Demography combined by 1985. Additional new appearances were religion (by 1990), Culture, and States/Societies (by 1995), and Macrohistorical Dynamics (by 1999), but the tables make clear that the predominant research groups of the organization were established by 1990.

Another way to studying change is by identifying the number of participants on the program who were on panels connected with or sponsored by an active network. Even this approach is made difficult by the fact that some program books do not list the networks sponsoring the panels, especially in the early years. I acknowledge the procedure is

The Evolution of the Social Science History Association Meetings, 1976–1999

Table 6: Percent of Program Participants by Network Affiliation of Session, 1976

Network	Number	Frequency (percent)
Total	275	100.01
Social Structure and Social Mobility	38	13.82
Historical Demography and Economic Development	38	13.82
Electoral Behavior and Political Parties	35	12.73
Methodology	29	10.55
Social Theory and Social Policy	24	8.73
Family History and Historical Demography	18	6.55
Workers and Industrialization	15	5.45
Large-Scale Societal Change	15	5.45
History and Epistemology of the Sciences of Man	11	4.00
Elites and Societal Processes	11	4.00
Legislative Behavior	10	3.64
Historical Comparative Bureaucracy	9	3.27
Ethnohistory	8	2.91
Ideas and Behavior	5	1.82
Community Processes	5	1.82
Religion and Society	4	1.45

Source: SSHA program book.

quite inexact as a measure of research focus, and so any conclusions drawn from the data in Tables 6 through 11 should be made with caution. At the first meeting in 1976, papers could be grouped into sixteen networks or areas of research, shown in Table 6. The largest numbers of participants were found in Social Structure and Social Mobility, Historical Demography, Politics, and Methodology. These four areas alone accounted for 50.9 percent of the total.

At the 1980 meetings in Rochester, the number of networks shrank to eleven, with Economic History being the biggest contributor (16.26 percent), Labor second (14.19 percent), and Politics (12.8 percent) and Justice (12.11 percent) close together for third and fourth. Unfortunately, I do not have the network affiliations for the sessions in 1985 (but these might be inferred in future work).

The Family/Demography network emerged with the largest participation in 1990, accounting for 104 of 533 participants, or 19.51 percent of the total. Also important were Education (11.63 percent), Labor (11.44 percent), and Justice (11.26 percent). Economics, which had been the largest group in 1980, placed sixth.

A trend toward cosponsorship of sessions was apparent in 1995, a movement that intensified in 1999. Family/Demography once again

Richard H. Steckel

Table 7: Percent of Program Participants by Network Affiliation of Session, 1980

Network	Number	Frequency (percent)
Total	289	99.99
Economic History*	47	16.26
Labor	41	14.19
Electoral, Party and Legislative	37	12.80
Criminal Justice and Legal*	35	12.11
Family History	33	11.42
Theory, Methods and Teaching	23	7.96
Urban*	19	6.57
Demography	19	6.57
Social Organizations, Ethnicity	17	5.88
Bureaucracy and Elites	12	4.15
Education*	6	2.08

* New network from 1976.
Source: SSHA program book.

Table 8: Percent of Program Participants by Network Affiliation of Session, 1985

Network	Number	Frequency (percent)
Total	81	100.01
Family History/ Historical Demography	15	18.52
Women's History*	10	12.35
Legislative, Electoral and Public Policy	9	11.11
Economic History	8	9.88
Other	8	9.88
Methodology	7	8.64
Urban History	6	7.41
Workers and Industrialization (Labor)	5	6.17
Rural History*	4	4.94
Education and Society	3	3.70
Crime and Deviance	2	2.47
Historical Geography*	2	2.47
Migration*	2	2.47
Historical Geography	2	2.47

* New network from 1980.
Source: SSHA program book in which the network was inferred from session titles and paper topics.

Table 9: Percent of Program Participants by Network Affiliation of Session, 1990

Network	Number	Frequency (percent)
Total	533	100.01
Family/Demography	104	19.51
Education	62	11.63
Labor	61	11.44
Criminal Justice/Legal	60	11.26
Race/Ethnicity*	44	8.26
Economics	39	7.32
Methods/Theory	39	7.32
Politics	39	7.32
Urban	38	7.13
Migration/Immigration	17	3.19
Women	14	2.63
Religion*	8	1.50
Rural	5	0.94
Not Available	3	0.56

* New network from 1985.
Source: SSHA program book.

placed first in 1995, with 14.3 percent of the total, followed by Economics (12.09 percent), and Politics (9.1 percent). The trend toward cosponsorship reduced the concentration of single network sponsorship, as 68 participants (8.8 percent) fell into the joint category.

Last year the largest number of participants was jointly sponsored (21.93 percent), many by more than two networks. Once again, Family/Demography was the largest provider of participants, with 12.79 percent of the total. Migration/Immigration occupied the second slot with 9.54 percent, and Economics was third with 7.72 percent of the total.

Possible Ingredients of Success

It may be impossible to establish why SSHA has been relatively successful, but I think several factors were involved. One is a larger movement of growing success and acceptance for interdisciplinary work. Although this work can occur within traditional departments, these administrative units can be impediments by using their control over hiring, promotion, salaries, teaching loads, and course subject matter. Accentuating these tendencies is growth of the literature

Richard H. Steckel

Table 10: Percent of Program Participants by Network Affiliation of Session, 1995

Network	Number	Frequency (percent)
Total	769	99.97
Family/Demography	110	14.30
Economics	93	12.09
Politics	70	9.10
States/Societies*	61	7.93
Criminal Justice/Legal	43	5.59
Labor	42	5.46
Theory/Methods	42	5.46
Race/Ethnicity	41	5.33
Migration/Immigration	33	4.29
Historical Geography	32	4.16
Presidential Network*	32	4.16
Rural	29	3.77
Religion	22	2.86
Urban	22	2.86
Theory/Methods and Gender (cosponsored)	21	2.73
Gender	20	2.60
Politics and Urban (cosponsored)	14	1.82
States/Societies and Gender (cosponsored)	14	1.82
Culture*	9	1.17
Gender and Criminal Justice/Legal (cosponsored)	5	0.65
Gender and States/Societies (cosponsored)	5	0.65
Race/Ethnicity and Theory/Methods (cosponsored)	5	0.65
Culture and Politics (cosponsored)	4	0.52

* New network from 1990.
Source: SSHA program book.

within traditional fields, which has been so great that it often crowds out or otherwise leaves little room for intellectual speculation in interdisciplinary activities. Just keeping abreast of new developments within one's field is challenging, adding to the centripetal forces operating within departments. I suspect that the greatest flowering of interdisciplinary work over the past quarter century has occurred within a variety of interdisciplinary research centers established within academia. These centers or institutes often target particular research problems using expertise housed in numerous traditional departments. With budget authority granted by central administrations, they hire or subsidize the hiring of people to undertake research on topics for which collaboration is quite beneficial to progress.

The Evolution of the Social Science History Association Meetings, 1976–1999

Table 11: Percent of Program Participants by Network Affiliation of Session, 1999

Network	Number	Frequency (percent)
Total	985	100.05
Family/Demography	126	12.79
Migration/Immigration	94	9.54
Economics	76	7.72
Historical Geography	60	6.09
Criminal Justice/Legal	52	5.28
Women/Gender	46	4.67
Politics	41	4.16
Urban	38	3.86
Methods/Theory	37	3.76
States/Society	36	3.65
Education	34	3.45
Rural	33	3.35
States/Society	27	2.74
Race/Ethnicity	15	1.52
Economics, Family/Demography, Historical Geography	14	1.42
Labor	14	1.42
Family/Demography, Rural	12	1.22
Migration/Immigration, Race/Ethnicity	12	1.22
Religion	12	1.22
Labor, Women/Gender	11	1.12
Macrohistorical Dynamics, Methods/Theory	11	1.12
Macrohistorical Dynamics, States/Society	11	1.12
Migration/Immigration, States/Society	11	1.12
Macrohistorical Dynamics*	10	1.02
Politics, Women/Gender	10	1.02
Culture, Methods/Theory	9	0.91
Not Available	8	0.81
Economics, Migration/Immigration	7	0.71
Family/Demography, Rural	7	0.71
Migration/Immigration, Women/Gender	7	0.71
Criminal Justice/Legal, Education, Race/Ethnicity	6	0.61
Culture, Family/Demography	6	0.61
Historical Geography, Rural	6	0.61
Labor, Race/Ethnicity	6	0.61
Labor, Rural	6	0.61
Migration/Immigration	6	0.61
Culture	5	0.51
Economics, Methods/Theory, Politics, Rural	5	0.51
Economics, States/Society	5	0.51
Education, Race/Ethnicity	5	0.51

112

Richard H. Steckel

Table 5.11 (*continued*)

Network	Number	Frequency (percent)
Education, Women/Gender	5	0.51
Family/Demography, Women/Gender	5	0.51
Family/Demography, Migration/Immigration	5	0.51
Migration/Immigration, Religion	5	0.51
Migration/Immigration, Rural	5	0.51
Poster Session	5	0.51
Religion, States/Society	5	0.51
Urban, Women/Gender	5	0.51
Religion, Urban	4	0.41
States/Society, Women/Gender	4	0.41

* New network from 1995.
Source: SSHA program book.

Most regular participants would probably agree that stimulating meetings are a very attractive feature of the SSHA. Numerous people with whom I have discussed the subject tell me that they would like to attend as many as several sessions offered at many time slots. Combined with this rich menu of choices is an air of informality, helpfulness, and approachability of participants. It is easy to meet people at the meetings to discuss ideas or plan sessions.

The networks have been quite effective in generating sessions that are attractive to so many people. As the section on networks makes clear, it has been relatively straightforward to create new networks that represent the latest thinking in various areas of social science history, which in turn attracts participants. Within this framework it has been easy to involve junior faculty and graduate students on the program, leading to growth. These newcomers like what they see, and many are willing to come back. Indeed, in light of their success I think the most interesting question to ask about the networks is why they have not been more widely imitated by traditional disciplinary associations.

SSHA is not the primary association or affiliation for virtually all participants. Despite this obstacle, the association has consistently been able to renew its strong leadership. Year after year, the major positions—whether the presidency, executive committee, the program committee, or others—have attracted a capable and committed group of leaders who have been willing to devote their time and talents to the purposes of social science history. It is clear that a large and growing number of social scientists believe in the future of social science history.

Conclusions

In the past quarter century, the Social Science History Association meetings have grown from modest affairs (under three hundred participants), which drew people mainly from the Northeast or the Midwest, into a major national and international conference with nearly one thousand involved in the program. This success recently spawned an imitation in Europe, which bodes well for the future of an interdisciplinary approach to the study of the past. Critical masses of scholars interested in this approach can now be found at more than two dozen institutions.

Scholars from history departments have always been the largest group represented on the programs, with sociology, political science, and economics also being major players. A substantial trend toward greater diversity in the intellectual homes of participants occurred in the 1990s.

The organization was initially founded with an emphasis on a diverse set of questions embracing nearly all fields in the social sciences. While this diversity has grown over the years, demographic and interrelated questions of migration and family structure have been the most widely represented on recent programs. I have heard several participants say that the meetings have become the best available for historical demography, which interrelates with many disciplines. In no way, however, do these questions dominate the meetings. At their most numerous in 1990, Family/Demography accounted for less than one-fifth of all participants. Critical masses of scholars gather to hear research on many topics from a variety of fields such as Immigration/Migration, Politics, Economic History, Justice, Geography, Labor, and Religion. Clearly, no single field of research "owns" the meetings, and I doubt that anyone involved would want to see that happen. While the professional associations of our home disciplines are still vibrant and well attended, it is gratifying to me that so many scholars now seek inspiration at SSHA.

NOTES

1. Participants include the chair, paper givers listed on the program (whether or not present at the meetings), and the discussants. Chairs who also served as discussants are counted as participating twice, and individuals who served on more than one panel are similarly counted more than once. Members of roundtables are included as participants.

HISTORICAL DEMOGRAPHY

AND FAMILY HISTORY

JAMES Z. LEE, WITH THE HELP OF

RICHARD STECKEL

Paradox

While the emergence of population and family history long preceded the establishment in 1976 of the Social Science History Association (SSHA), the heyday of historical demography and family history coincided with the association's early history. This is equally apparent in family history as in historical demography, which will be the main disciplinary focus of our talk today.[1] The Princeton Project published their major research monographs on the European fertility decline in the 1970s and their more widely cited summary volumes in 1986 and 1990.[2] The Cambridge Group for the History of Population and Social Structure published their most well-known demographic volume in English population history in 1981, although there was also a subsequent volume in 1997 as well.[3] Finally, the Institut National d'Etudes Demographiques (INED) summarized three decades of family reconstitution in several summary series on the population history of France in the 1980s.[4]

The paradox, however, is that while the golden age of population and family history is well past, the Historical Demography and Family History (HDFH) network has never been as active or as popular in the SSHA as we are today. This year, our network will present more papers, have more panel participants, and continue to take up a progressively larger proportion of the available panel venues than we ever have before. Figure 1 is a summary of the SSHA conference programs from 1976, 1980, 1985, 1990, 1995, and 2000.[5] The number of panels have sextupled from five to thirty.[6] Moreover, in spite of a 50 percent increase in the number of networks from eleven to seventeen,[7] the proportion of HDFH panels at the SSHA as a whole has doubled from 10 to 20 percent.[8] Including this roundtable, there are almost 170 HDFH network

114

Population and Family History at the Social Science History Association

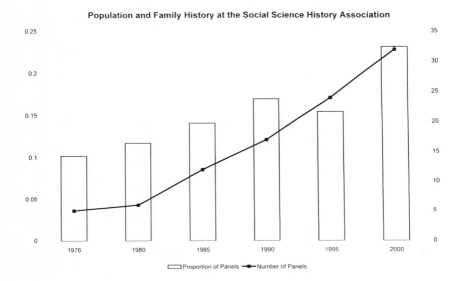

panel participants in Pittsburgh, almost thrice the numbers of any other SSHA network.[9]

Renaissance

The current popularity of historical demography and family history, however, is a product of very different circumstances from the world order of the golden age. While that "old" world order was characterized by central planning in a distinctly tri-polar universe of great powers and great scholars energized by revolutionary ideologies or the academic agendas of the "new" history, the "new" world order in HDFH, like the real world around us, is a period of aging powers, old ideologies, tired academic agendas, international proliferation, and fluid coalitions.[10] As a result, while previous participation in the HDFH networks was almost solely American, our current panel participation is extremely international. Figures 2 and 3 summarize the national origins of panel participants to the historical demography and family history network from 1976 to 2000 at five-year intervals. The number of participants has increased from 33 to 168, excluding cosponsored panels. The proportion of non-U.S. participants has also risen from 3 to 63 percent. Today, in contrast with 1976 when there was only one non-U.S. HDFH

James Z. Lee and Richard Steckel

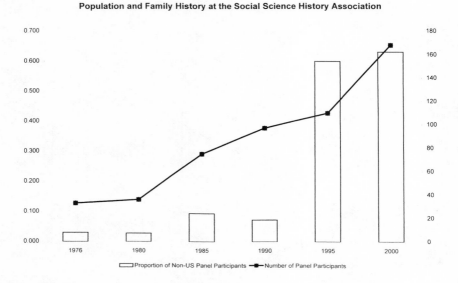

Population and Family History at the Social Science History Association

Proportion of Non-US Panel Participants ▪ Number of Panel Participants

panel participant,[11] there are now over one hundred non-U.S. participants from nineteen countries of origin.

The surge in non-U.S. participation is partly a product of the increasing professional standardization of the academe in certain European and
Asian countries, which is in turn part of the larger movement beyond the
academe toward internationalization and an international English language community.[12] It is partly a product of the decline of the old world
order; partly a product of the genuine appeal of the interdisciplinary,
nonhierarchical, network nature of the SSHA; and it is partly a product
of an informal network of personal and professional relations where a
few individuals, such as Tamara Hareven, have tirelessly recruited and
encouraged international participation,[13] and where such international
participants as Tommy Bengtsson, Anders Brandstrom, Antoinette
Fauve-Chamoux, Beatrice Moring, Frans Van Poppel, Michel Oris, David
Reher, Roger Schofield, Solvi Sogner, Jan Sudin, Gunnar Thorvaldsen,
Richard Wall, and others have discovered an academic venue so reward-
ing that they return almost every year—sometimes even at their own expense.[14] Individual contributions here matter greatly to our network's
popularity. And many whom I have not mentioned deserve special
recognition in this regard for the continued success of our network.

Increased standardization in our profession has encouraged many
international scholars to publish their research in the major internationally refereed academic journals, most of which publish in English and

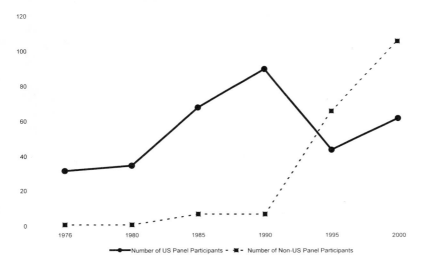

Population and Family History at the Social Science History Association

many of which recruit at the SSHA.[15] Moreover, in addition to such international funding agencies as the European Science Foundation, a number of national funding agencies and universities attach increasing importance to international collaboration, international reputation, and international standards. Such emphasis and support, of course, vary dramatically from country to country and are partially responsible for the distribution of international participation. Table 1 identifies the national origins of the non-U.S. participants during the six annual meetings under observation. Most come from the Scandinavian countries, the United Kingdom, the Netherlands, followed by Japan, France, Canada, Italy, and Benelux. While the absence of other foreign nationals is understandable, including the absence of virtually any Germanic scholar, almost any Hispanic scholar, and any scholars from many other countries, the low participation from France, especially from INED, as well as the increasing presence of the Japanese, is striking. Clearly, those scholars and countries participating in the new world order will lead it. Those who do not will not have this opportunity.

Challenges

At the same time, the current world order poses a major challenge to historical demographers and family historians in the

James Z. Lee and Richard Steckel

Table 1. Population and Family History Panel Participants at the Social Science History Association, Place of Origin of Non-U.S. Participants from Six Annual Meetings

Nationality	1976, 1980, 1985	1990, 1995, 2000
Austria	0	5
Benelux	1	7
Canada	2	10
France	0	13
Germany	0	4
Italy	0	10
Japan	0	15
Mexico	0	4
Netherlands	0	20
Scandinavia	0	58
Spain	1	4
United Kingdom	4	30
Others	0	6

United States. While our field may be growing, our numbers are shrinking as a proportion of the field. This is especially true for those of us whose primary affiliation is in history. American historians used to account for almost two-thirds of all network panel participants, but now account for little more than a third.[16] We are inexorably aging, and with few exceptions we have been unable to reproduce ourselves and train and hire our future replacements.[17]

If we are not careful, this means that the new world of social science history will be a world where Americans and historians will be increasingly marginal. We have already surrendered huge programmatic historical initiatives to the social scientists. And we can detect an increasing European presence even in our editorial and publication capacity with the increasing prominence of European publishers and European editors and editorial board members.[18] If we are not careful, the European Social Science History Conference (ESSHC), established in 1996, may eventually supplant the SSHA as the major international venue for social science history. They have already surpassed us in terms of number of papers, panels, and participants. Compared with thirty HDFH panels at the 2000 SSHA, the 2000 ESSHC family/demography network organized fifty-two panels, thirty-one network sessions and twenty-one related sessions, while the ESSHC ethnicity/migration network organized sixty-two sessions, including forty network sessions and twenty-two related sessions, a total of more than one hundred panels.[19]

Moreover, while population and family history continues to be active in some American population studies centers, historical demography as a whole is far less popular in the American academe than it was a quarter century ago. In this sense, at least, historical demography is doing less well than other fields in social science history. Economic history, in addition to their network meetings at the SSHA, has been able to establish two economic history associations and holds annual meetings in the United States as well as quadrennial meetings elsewhere. Political history has become so central to political science that the American Political Science Association (APSA) regularly allocates political historians as many as one-tenth of the panels at their annual meeting. By contrast, historical demography has been able to organize no more than two panels at the upcoming annual meeting of the Population Association of America (PAA), only two panels at the quadrennial meeting of the International Union for the Scientific Study of Population (IUSSP), and at most one occasional panel at the American Sociological Association or the American History Association.[20] Is it then surprising that young American social scientists are increasingly less interested in population history just as young American historians are increasingly less interested in historical demography. We cannot blame our relative unpopularity entirely on postmodernism and cultural studies. At least in our immediate disciplinary associations, the PAA and IUSSP, we need to reclaim the foreground ourselves.

Solutions

If American historical demography is to remain vibrant, we need to reinvigorate our field. We need to think of new directions of scholarly investigation to recruit more graduate students and to attract and train other historians so that they can contribute to our scholarly research. I can suggest several solutions that build on the comparative advantages of our current situation where we might consider promoting research. While some of these suggestions are hardly new, the likelihood of their success is better than ever before.[21]

First, as Steven Ruggles has advocated in another venue, we need to take advantage of our position at the beginning of the twenty-first century and extend our research agenda to embrace the twentieth century, in its entirety.[22] We should respond, in other words, to "the historical turn in the social sciences," with a new contemporary turn in history.[23] This means not only discussing the "historical background" of current phenomena, it means collecting contemporary as well as historical data and doing the analysis of such phenomena ourselves. This will allow historical demography and family history to recapture some of the

James Z. Lee and Richard Steckel

relevance that fueled much of the initial interest in the "new" social history. It will also allow us to regain some of the funding sources we have largely abandoned to the social sciences.

Second, we should take advantage of the increasingly international proliferation of historical demography and family history to expand our investigation of comparative population and family history. Just as we need to increase our *temporal* reach, so we also need to broaden our *spatial* areas of interest, not just in Western history but beyond as well. The debate over the comparative standards of living, for example, have recently invigorated interest in comparative economic history. The demographic aspects of this debate are still very much up for grabs. What work has been done has been largely by economic historians.[24] With few exceptions, the demographic historians have been surprisingly silent—surprisingly since our community of scholars is far more international and our demographic data far easier to compare historically than the community of economic historians and historical economic data.

As a result, in spite of the rapid proliferation of individual and aggregate level population data for much of the world during the last three hundred years, we have yet to use these data to redefine our spatial understanding of world population history. The only population history atlas to appear in the last twenty-five years is out of print, out of date, and was written by a geographer rather than a demographer (McEvedy 1978). While there are ongoing projects to replace this atlas at the international level,[25] there are no formal projects as yet to do this for the United States, in spite of the flood of American censal data available from IPUMS. We have yet to use IPUMS to redefine our spatial understanding of American history. And yet as Tommy Bengtsson, an historical demographer from Sweden, has suggested, such data allow us to construct a new social demographic atlas of the United States to replace the censal geography of South Atlantic, East-South Central, West-South Central, New England, Mid-Atlantic, East-North Central, West-North Central, Mountain, and Pacific West with a new demographic geography as well as a new demographic history.

Strategies

Regardless of which projects we pursue, it is important that we aggressively follow two strategies in seeking solutions. First, to produce the spatial and temporal dimensions of our new demographic history, we have to match our increased empirical knowledge from new data with similar increases in social science methods and scientific advances in visual presentation. Otherwise the new perspectives and increased resolution these cross-sectional and longitudinal data provide will be wasted. We need, in other words, to increase our level of social scientific expertise to compete with our social scientific colleagues in demography, economics, geography, and sociology. At the moment, our ability to absorb new quantitative techniques is singularly slow. As a result, the gap in our analytical tools compared to the social sciences is increasing rapidly. While event history time-series techniques have been common in demography for over two decades, they have only begun to be used recently by population historians and are still far from common. Moreover, in spite of the wealth of community and household level data in many of these new individual level data sets, we have yet to capture these dimensions through multilevel modeling. And yet without such techniques, as well as such ambitions, we run the risk of becoming an increasingly marginal academic field, of eventually degenerating from analysts to archivists, fit only to provide the historical grist to be ground by other millers with the finer social science mills at their disposal.

Second, we need to take advantage of our ability as historians to communicate our results from these analyses to a general audience. History, unlike the other social sciences, has always claimed an ability to write for a larger audience of "educated" readers rather than just "professional" readers. But while many of our colleagues in family history have written successful books according to such standards, the same cannot be said for most historical demography. In spite of the popular interest in death, marriage, and sex, it is hard to identify any book in historical demography as compelling as *Centuries of Childhood, Family Time and Industrial Time,* or *The Family, Sex, and Marriage in England* (Aries 1962; Hareven 1982; Stone 1977). In spite of the popularity of the Malthusian narrative, it is also hard to find any book in historical demography that has the relevance or importance of *The Population Bomb* or, for that matter, of *How Many People Can the Earth Support* (Erlich 1968; Cohen 1995).

Examples

One conspicuous example, which attempts to move in several such directions spatial comparison and social science methodology, is the EurAsian Project in Population and Family History (EAP). Inspired by Professor Akira Hayami, a population historian of Japan, the EAP is a collaborative project of over twenty other historical demographers from several countries dedicated to study the effects of economic conditions and social organization on population behavior in different

James Z. Lee and Richard Steckel

social settings. Since 1995 they have engaged in a comparative and collaborative study in the demographic and family history of selected largely preindustrial, largely rural populations from eastern Belgium, northeastern China, northern Italy, northeastern Japan, and southern Sweden using similar types of data, similar methods of analysis, and similar sets of calculations. This has required the conception of a formal analytic framework to understand population responses to exogenous stress as well as the construction of a number of specific detailed and dynamic models of demographic behavior, and a variety of large, longitudinal data sets of specific historical communities that currently span two continents, three centuries, five countries, and over twenty populations with 0.5 million household-level observations and 2.5 million individual-level observations.[26]

They can consequently take a unique formal dynamic approach and study historical change at the individual, household, kin group, and community level, and situate them in terms of their relations to each other and to economic conditions.[27] Focusing specifically on demographic events such as birth, death, marriage, and migration, which are less susceptible to cultural construction and data distortion, they use event history time-series techniques to make formal comparisons that place each individual within a multiplicity of overlapping changing contexts at different levels of aggregation and in different kinds of settings.[28] They study how such economic conditions as occupation, food prices, and wages, and such social conditions as household and kin composition and relationships affect a person's ability to marry, to have children, to migrate, to survive. They use, in other words, demographic models to make comparisons between individuals, households, kin groups, and communities that span centuries, countries, even continents. These results, many of which have been presented here at the SSHA, may or may not be "typical" of their respective national populations and periods, but they offer an alternative demographic vantage from which to generalize about human behavior not at the national level, but controlling for specific cultural, economic, and historical contexts from the individual level on up.

The EAP will communicate our findings in a series of four summary scholarly monographs on mortality, fertility, nuptiality, and migration, the first of which is almost ready to go to press (Bengtsson, Campbell, and Lee). This will take several years to complete. What remains, as Michael Haines has suggested in a recent discussion, is the even more difficult task of how to disseminate our research results to a wider audience. At the moment, their publications are designed for the scholarly literature. They need to make them accessible to the trade literature as well.

So far, they have not done so. To write such a synthesis, they still need to understand how their work expands our understanding of the only metanarrative common to historical demography, the Malthusian narrative. This was the successful strategy of the most influential book in recent times in historical demography, *The Population History of England* by E. A. Wrigley and R. S. Schofield. It is also the strategy of James Lee's recent book, coauthored with Wang Feng, *One Quarter of Humanity: Malthusian Mythology and Chinese Realities.*

Wang and Lee wrote *One Quarter of Humanity* as an elaboration on the Malthusian narrative. We also wrote it as an exercise in broad historical and sociological synthesis for the "educated" reader as well as the professional reader. Although our book is a work of scholarship with one hundred pages of scholarly apparatus, appendices, notes, and references, it is also short, with only 146 pages in the main text, including thirty maps and figures and fourteen tables. In contrast with Wrigley and Schofield's 1981 book, we do not perform any actual demographic calculations in our book. Instead, we summarize the results of calculations that we have published elsewhere, situating them in their broad historical and spatial context and discussing their implications for our understanding of comparative sociology. Given our spatial sensibilities, we construct a stylized model of a Chinese demographic system and contrast this model with the European demographic system identified by Flinn (1981) as well as an ideal Malthusian model. Finally, given our temporal strategy, we show the relevance of the previous Chinese demographic system to our understanding of Chinese population behavior today and suggest that the Chinese demographic system provides a nuanced alternative to the overly simplified Malthusian fears of some for future world population trends.

While such exercises have a long way to go before we can rise to the level of family history, they offer some new embellishments to the Malthusian narrative that we at the EAP, and historical demographers in general, need to explore in more detail. For historical demography to flourish, we will need even more such embellishments in the future, exploring the links between short-term economic change and population change, between long-term population growth and economic growth, between demographic history and ecological, economic, geographic, and social history.

At the same time, we should strive to explore the HDFH dimensions of the metanarratives of the other networks at the SSHA. The demographic and family dimensions of criminality and law, of culture, economics, education, geography, labor, macrohistory, methods, politics, race and ethnicity, religion, states, cities, and gender are readily

James Z. Lee and Richard Steckel

apparent. Let us explore them, and in so doing also build new bridges to other fields in social science history and to other networks in the Social Science History Association.

NOTES

1. The situation is similar, however, for family history. While the initial pioneering work of such European founders as Aries (1962, 1971) and Laslett and Wall (Laslett 1971, Laslett and Wall 1972) preceded the establishment of the SSHA, many of their subsequent books coincided with the early history of the association (Aries 1977; Duby 1978, 1981, 1983, 1994; Laslett 1977; Wall, Robin, and Laslett 1983; Laslett and Kertzer 1995), as did the equally important contributions of such American scholars as Hareven (1978a, 1978b, 1982), Hareven and Langenbach (1978), Ruggles (1987), Stone (1977, 1990, 1993, 1995), and others.

2. Livi-Bacci (1971), Knodel (1974), Van de Walle (1974), Lesthaeghe (1977), Livi-Bacci (1977), Anderson et al (1979), Coale and Watkins (1986), and Watkins (1990).

3. Wrigley and Schofield (1981), Wrigley, Davies, Oeppen, and Schofield (1997). See, however, the critique by Ruggles (1999).

4. The most well-known are the five summary volumes produced by Dupâquier in 1988. But see also such series as the *Dictionnaire d'histoire administrative et démographique* published by the Centre National de la recherche scientifique under the direction of Jean-Pierre Bardet.

5. Richard Steckel provided digital files of the 1976, 1980, 1985, 1990, and 1995 annual programs, while Erik Austen provided some important notes for the 1980 program, and David Hacker some important assistance with the analysis of the 2000 annual program.

6. These counts required some hand identification and calculation since the early programs do not explicitly identify the networks, and since historical demography and family history originally were separate, and historical demography was paired with economic history.

7. Two other networks—migration and immigration, and rural—overlap considerably with historical demography and family history.

8. The count of panels from the 2000 annual meeting includes cosponsored panels.

9. This count of panel participants from the 2000 annual meeting does not include cosponsored panels.

10. The most important of these new coalitions may well be the recent cooperative arrangements of the demographic history associations of France, Italy, and Spain: la Société de la Démographie Historique, la Societa de Demographia Storica, and l'Associacion de Demographia Historica, who have organized several joint seminars and workshops during the last few years.

11. The lone international participant was Professor Neal Sovani from the

Gokle Institute in Poona, India, who served as a discussant on a panel in historical demography and economic history with Robert Fogel, Nathan Keyfitz, Irving Kravis, David Landes, and Roger Revelle.

12. Thus whereas earlier scholars in population and family history learned French and oriented themselves around the "stages" offered at INED and Ecole des Hautes Etudes en Sciences Sociales, younger European scholars today tend to be indigenously trained and oriented toward the English academe. Consequently, when the European historical demographic community organized a summer school in historical demography in Florence in 1997, one of the unexpected difficulties was that while the professors, who were largely from France, Italy, and Spain, were all able to teach in French, many of the students who were not from France were more comfortable in English than French (Michel Oris personal communication).

13. Frans Van Poppel, for example, relates in a personal communication that "I had first attended a Population Association of America meeting in the United States in 1982, but Susan Watkins, with whom I had been in touch, encouraged me several times to come to the Social Science History Association. She said this was just the place for someone working at the intersection of demography, history, and social science. At that time there were only a few other Dutch in attendance at the SSHA, most of whom did not attend the demography and family history panels. I was struck, however, by the completely different way in which discussions took place at the SSHA. There was plenty of time for presentation and for discussion by everyone and not only by a discussant."

14. The issue of such expenses is important. Whereas most participants from North America, northern Europe, and Japan are able to raise at least travel funds from their universities or extra-university grants, many participants from elsewhere in Europe, such as France, have had to pay their travel funds out of pocket (Fauve-Chamoux personal communication).

15. With the exception of the *Annales de demographie historique* (1965–), which publishes in English as well as French, the other major journals in population and family history—the *Journal of Family History* (1976–), *The History of the Family, an International Quarterly* (1996–), *Continuity and Change* (1986–), *Social Science History* (1976–), *Historical Methods* (1978–), *Population Studies* (1950–), as well as *Journal of Interdisciplinary History* (1970–), *Population and Development Review* (1975–), *European Journal of Population Studies* (1985–), and *Journal of Economic History* (1941–)—all publish almost exclusively in English. In addition, *History of the Family, Change and Continuity, Social Science History,* and *Historical Methods* recruit actively at the SSHA.

16. This is based on the institutional affiliation of the U.S.-based HDFH panel participants in 1976 and 2000.

17. The most notable exception is Steven Ruggles at the Integrated Public Use Microdata Series project (IPUMS) at the University of Minnesota, who has already produced several very successful Ph.D.s in social science history and has many more current graduate students. Other exceptions are Myron Gutman at the University of Texas and Douglas Anderton at the University of Massachusetts.

18. Six of the top ten journals of our field—*Annales de demographie historique,*

James Z. Lee and Richard Steckel

Journal of Family History, History of the Family: An International Quarterly, Continuity and Change, European Journal of Population Studies, and *Population Studies*—are published and or edited abroad.

19. I would like to thank Karin Hofmeester of the ESSHC for providing copies of the 1996, 1998, and 2000 ESSHC final programs.

20. According to a personal communication from Douglas Anderton, both of the PAA panels have a "heavy orientation to the United States," with little room for the internationalization of the SSHA.

21. Several of these suggestions, in fact, parallel previous efforts launched by the Social Science Research Council Mathematical Board for the Social Sciences under the overall direction of Charles Tilly and Richard Easterlin.

22. Ruggles oral comment at the Conference on Household and Family in Past Time Revisited, Mallorca, September 1999.

23. Terrence J. McDonald and his colleagues largely from the University of Michigan discuss these issues in a book of the same name (McDonald 1996).

24. See, for example, the demographic analyses by Wong (1997) and Pomeranz (2000).

25. The Historical Demography Committee of the IUSSP organized a meeting on the population history of the last millennium to meet in 2001, which will eventually yield an atlas of world population history for the last one thousand years, focusing in particular on the last three hundred years.

26. Such data are uncommon since they require laborious, longitudinal reconstruction of populations from historical census-type registers with continuous or almost continuous registration; and since we further require populations with large numbers of individuals and long sweeps of time that include the entire community, provide information on individual occupation, household structure, and individual or household status, and have parallel serial information on either grain prices or farm wages. The EAP mortality analysis, which was completed several years ago, uses a smaller data set of 1.5 million individual observations.

27. The word "dynamic" is used to express the influence of one variable on another over time; for example, how bad harvests influence births and deaths during the following years. Generally dynamic analysis in historical demography has been applied to aggregated data of births, marriages, and deaths to analyze short-term effects of economic variations or long-term relationships between population and living standards. This has been done with a variety of models and methods. See Bengtsson and Saito (2000) for an overview. Historical studies at the micro level are usually static, often because they have to collapse long time periods in order to produce enough events to support statistical analysis.

28. These techniques, which have been used only in a very limited number of studies, combine time series and life event analysis to resolve problems created by censoring and truncation, and provide time-varying determinants at individual, family, household, and community level.

REFERENCE LIST

Anderson et al. 1979. *Human fertility in Russia since the nineteenth century.* Princeton: Princeton University Press.

Aries, P. 1965 (1962). *L'enfant et la vie familiale sous l'Ancien Régime (Centuries of childhood: A social history of family life),* translated by Robert Baldick. New York: Vintage Books.

———. 1971. *Histoire des populations françaises et de leurs attitudes devant la vie depuis le XVIIIe siècle.* Paris: Éditions du Seuil.

———. 1977. *L'homme devant la mort. Philippe Ariès.* Paris: Éditions du Seuil.

Ariès, P., and G. Duby, ed. 1985–1987. *Histoire de la vie privée.* Paris: Seuil.

Bardet, J.-P., ed. 1981–1996. *Dictionnaire d'histoire administrative et démographique.* Paris: Centre National de la recherche scientifique.

Bengtsson, T., C. Campbell, and J. Z. Lee, et. al. 2004. *Life under pressure: Mortality and living standards in Europe and Asia, 1700–1900.* Cambridge: MIT Press.

Bengtsson, T., and O. Saito, eds. 2000. *Population and the economy: From hunger to modern economic growth.* Oxford: Oxford University Press.

Burguière, A., ed. 1996. *Histoire de la famille (A History of the family),* translated by Sarah Hanbury-Tenison, Rosemary Morris, and Andrew Wilson. Cambridge, Mass.: Harvard University Press.

Burguière, A., et al. 1980. *Family and sexuality in French history,* edited by Robert Wheaton and Tamara K. Hareven. Philadelphia: University of Pennsylvania Press.

Coale, A. J., and S. Watkins, ed. 1986. *The decline of fertility in Europe.* Princeton: Princeton University Press.

Cohen, J. 1995. *How many people can the earth support.* New York: Norton.

Duby, G. 1978. *Medieval marriage: Two models from twelfth-century France,* translated by Elborg Forster. Baltimore: Johns Hopkins University Press.

———. 1983 (1981). *Chevalier, la femme et le prêtre (The knight, the lady, and the priest: The making of modern marriage in medieval France),* translated by Barbara Bray. New York: Pantheon Books.

———. 1983. *Que sait-on de l'amour en France au XIIIe siècle?* Oxford: Claredon Press.

———. 1994. *Mâle Moyen Age (Love and marriage in the Middle Ages),* translated by Jane Dunnett. Chicago: University of Chicago Press.

Dupâquier, J. 1988. *Histoire de la population Francaise.* Paris: Presses universitaires de France.

Ehrlich, P. 1968. *Population bomb.* New York: Ballantine-Sierra Club.

Flinn, M. W. 1981. *The European demographic system, 1500–1800.* Baltimore: The Johns Hopkins University Press.

Hareven, T. K., ed. 1978a. *Themes in the history of the family.* Worcester, Mass.: American Antiquarian Society.

———, ed. 1978b. *Transitions: The family and the life course in historical perspective.* New York: Academic Press.

———. 1982. *Family time and industrial time: The relationship between the family and*

James Z. Lee and Richard Steckel

work in a New England industrial community. Cambridge, N.Y.: Cambridge University Press.

———, ed. 1996. *Aging and generational relations over the life course: A historical and cross-cultural perspective.* Berlin, New York: W. de Gruyter.

———. 2000. *Families, history, and social change: Life course and cross-cultural perspectives.* Boulder: Westview Press.

Hareven, T. K., and Randolph Langenbach, eds. 1978. *Amoskeag: Life and work in an American factory-city.* New York: Pantheon Books.

Hareven, T. K., and Maris A. Vinovskis, eds. 1978. *Family and population in nineteenth-century America.* Princeton: Princeton University Press.

Knodel, J. E. 1974. *The decline of fertility in Germany, 1871–1939.* Princeton: Princeton University Press.

Laslett, P. 1971. *The world we have lost.* London: Methuen.

———. 1977. *Family life and illicit love in earlier generations.* Cambridge: Cambridge University Press.

Laslett, P., and R. Wall. 1972. *Household and family in past time.* Cambridge: Cambridge University Press.

Laslett, P., and D. Kertzer, eds. 1995. *Aging in the past: Demography, society and old age.* Berkeley: University of California Press.

Lee, J., and W. Feng. 1999. *One quarter of humanity: Malthusian mythology and Chinese realities, 1700–2000.* Cambridge, Mass.: Harvard University Press.

Lesthaeghe, R. J. 1977. *The decline of Belgian fertility, 1800–1970.* Princeton: Princeton University Press.

Livi-Bacci, M. 1971. *A century of Portuguese fertility.* Princeton: Princeton University Press.

———. 1977. *A history of Italian fertility during the last two centuries.* Princeton: Princeton University Press.

McDonald, T. J. 1996. *The historic turn in the human sciences.* Ann Arbor: University of Michigan Press.

McEvedy, C. 1978. *Atlas of world population history.* New York: Penguin Books.

Pomeranz, K. 2000. *The great divergence: China, Europe, and the making of the modern world economy.* Princeton: Princeton University Press

Rossi, A. S., J. Kagan, and T. K. Hareven, eds. 1978. *The family.* New York: Norton.

Ruggles, S. 1987. *Prolonged connections: The rise of the extended family in nineteenth-century England and America.* Madison: University of Wisconsin Press.

———. 1999. The limitations of English family reconstitution. *Continuity and Change* 14: 105–30.

Stone, L. 1977. *The family, sex, and marriage in England, 1500–1800.* New York: Harper and Row.

———. 1990. *Road to divorce: England 1530–1987.* New York: Oxford University Press.

———. 1993. *Broken lives: Separation and divorce in England, 1660–1857.* New York: Oxford University Press.

———. 1995. *Uncertain unions and broken lives: Marriage and divorce in England, 1660–1857.* Oxford, New York: Oxford University Press.

Van de Walle, E. 1974. *The female population of France in the nineteenth century*. Princeton: Princeton University Press.

Wall, R., J. Robin, and P. Laslett, ed. 1983. *Family forms in historic Europe*. Cambridge: Cambridge University Press.

Watkins, S. 1990. *From provinces in nations: Demographic integration in Western Europe, 1870–1960*. Princeton: Princeton University Press.

Wong, R. B. 1997. *China transformed: Historical change and the limits of the European experience*. Ithaca: Cornell University Press.

Wrigley, E. A. and R. S. Schofield. 1981. *The population history of England 1541-1871*. Cambridge: Cambridge University Press.

Wrigley. E. A., R. S. Davies, J. Oeppen, and R. S. Schofield. 1997. *English population history from family reconstitution, 1580–1837*. Cambridge: Cambridge University Press.

CHANGING CONCEPTIONS OF

RACE AND RACIAL INEQUALITY

MICHAEL K. BROWN

I

No terrain is more contested in the social sciences and history than the study of race. In many quarters, race is now seen as irrelevant, a noisome distraction that impedes rational discourse about economic and social inequalities. Other voices insist that race is far more fundamental to American history and contemporary social life than hitherto understood. Gunnar Myrdal assumed the problem of race in America turned on a conflict "in the heart of the Americans" between our credal beliefs in liberty and equality and the "valuations on specific planes of individual and group living, where personal and local interests; economic, social, and sexual jealousies; considerations of community prestige and conformity; group prejudice against particular persons or types of people . . . dominate" (1944, lxxi). Today, people think either that Myrdal's optimism in the capacity of Americans to change their hearts and minds has been vindicated or that he misunderstood the problem.

Many writers, both liberal and conservative, commonly express their desire to expunge race from our vocabulary. Biologists and geneticists think we should do away with the idea since the concept of race is biologically meaningless and utterly without scientific validity. Nor can race be rehabilitated as a social construction; it is too biologically encrusted. Since race always conjures up biology, Orlando Patterson insists we discard the term and replace it with ethnicity (1997, 72).

Other writers think race is irrelevant because racial prejudice has virtually disappeared—at least as measured by changes in racial attitudes over a fifty-year period. The civil rights movement eradicated legal segregation and made expressions of outward racial prejudice illegitimate. Neither political conflict over race nor persistent racial inequality can be explained, they think, by continued racial discrimination. Instead, cultural values—individual choices to work hard, stay in school, or where to live—account for differences in wages, income, and wealth between blacks and whites, or even residential segregation. Political conflict over affirmative action or any other racially motivated policy is not about who is for or against prejudice but about political principles—it is about conflict over the American creed itself (Thernstrom and Thernstrom 1997; Sniderman and Piazza 1993).[1]

There is a weariness among those writers searching for a way to banish race from our political lexicon. They believe, including certifiable left-wingers, that thinking of race only prolongs our common political agony. Yet, ironically, white weariness of race talk coincides with a wealth of new scholarship that peels away the layers of denial encasing race to reveal just how fundamental it is to United States history and life. Consider two examples, one from literature and one from political science.

Toni Morrison's extraordinary book *Playing in the Dark* is dedicated to the proposition that American writers as diverse as Poe and Hemingway are talking about race even when they appear to be talking about something else. American literature has been preoccupied with, indeed defined by, black slavery, the juxtaposition of slavery and freedom. All of the great themes of America's literature—individual freedom, the creation of a white identity in the New World, alienation, and fear—were formed by the construction of an American Africanism. This Africanism, Morrison writes, is "the vehicle by which the American self knows itself as not enslaved, but free; not repulsive, but desirable; not helpless, but licensed and powerful" (1993, 52).[2] In other words, the very identity of Americans is forged in the crucible of race.

Paul Frymer undermines the presumed virtues of competition between two political parties by introducing race. If there is a Holy Grail in modern political science, it is the idea that party competition promotes democratic accountability and responsiveness. Some think democracy is possible only when competitive political parties define alternative policy choices; others add that the absence of party competition leads to issueless, plutocratic politics (Schattschneider 1975, 137–38; Key 1984, 307–9). In his classic *Southern Politics in State and Nation*, V. O. Key Jr. assumed that dismantling Jim Crow and introducing real two party competition in the South would usher in a biracial coalition of low income voters and southern politics would henceforth be divided by social class (1984, 670–71). He was dead wrong. Although most southern elections today are highly competitive, party politics remains polarized by racial divisions. The problem, Frymer suggests, is that a competitive two-party system in a racially divided society legitimates "an agenda reflecting the preferences of white voters" and leaves black voters on the sideline (1999, 28).

The reason is that political leaders have powerful incentives in a political system with single member districts and plurality elections to

132

Michael K. Brown

appeal to the median voter, the large group of swing voters in the middle of the liberal-conservative continuum. If they are to win elections, politicians must aim for the middle, where most voters reside. Most political scientists assumed that once African Americans got the franchise, party competition would force politicians to appeal to them like any other voter. But Frymer points out that this is only true where there are no sharp divisions between a white majority and a black minority. In a racially divided society, the logic of party competition leads party leaders to appeal to the median white voter and ignore the interests of black voters since it costs them white swing votes (Frymer 1999, 32–33). Unable to switch parties and ignored by their own party, black voters become a captured minority in one party.[3]

As these two studies illustrate, the very problematic of race has changed. Race, and racial inequality, are no longer understood simply as a question of prejudicial beliefs. Instead, they are seen as a relationship of exclusion and domination underpinned by cultural practices and behavior that shape not just white beliefs about the inferiority of African Americans but the basic institutions of American society. Ironically, one reason our understanding of the concept of race and racial inequality has changed is because of the very success of the civil rights revolution. Civil rights leaders recognized at the time that their victory in bringing down legalized segregation and outlawing discrimination left them confronting a paradox: what good was it to desegregate restaurants if most blacks were too poor to pay for a meal? After the Watts revolt, Martin Luther King Jr. remarked, "I worked to get these people the right to eat hamburgers, and now I've got to do something . . . to help them get the money to buy [them]" (Garrow 1988, 439).

The failure to go beyond formal legal equality provoked a searching reassessment of the idea of race. Some thirty years after *Brown v. Board of Education* was decided, Judge Robert Carter, one of the NAACP lawyers who litigated the case, reflected that "It was not until *Brown I* was decided that blacks were able to understand that the fundamental vice was not legally enforced *racial segregation* itself; that this was a mere byproduct, a symptom of the greater and more pernicious disease—white supremacy. . . . It . . . remains the basic virus that has debilitated blacks' efforts to secure equality in this country" (Carter 1980, 23). Proponents of critical race theory drew a similar conclusion when they attacked a "formal equality [that] overlooks structural disadvantage and requires mere nondiscrimination or 'equal treatment'" (Harris 1995, 289).

How do we understand the ideas of race and racial inequality after the civil rights revolution and, importantly, the collapse of the prejudice model of racism? In unrelenting detail, a considerable body of survey research indicates the virtual disappearance of some of the most pernicious racial beliefs. For example, in the 1940s one out of every two whites believed blacks were intellectually inferior; by the 1990s only one out of eight did. Whites also widely endorse the principles of the civil rights movement, if not the policies needed to implement those principles. Although one can still find evidence that whites hold negative views of African Americans, it is more difficult to sustain the notion in light of these data that African Americans face widespread individual prejudice.

In this context, a politically odd assortment of conservatives, color-blind liberals, cultural radicals, and the political left, for whom social class is the bedrock of contemporary inequality, would do away with the idea of race altogether.[4] Some like Paul Gilroy suggest we simply act like race does not matter; others wish blacks would grow up and act like the middle class or working class people they really are; and yet others ascribe to African Americans a form of cultural inferiority because they have not followed in the footsteps of Irish and Italian immigrants and lag behind Asian Americans (see Gilroy 2000; Lind 1995; Thernstrom and Thernstrom 1997; D'Souza 1995). There is another alternative, however, one that follows Judge Carter's admonition to unravel white supremacy's various forms and bluntly confront the question of why racial inequality persists.

II

Hardly anyone today denies that race is a social construction. Yet if it is a cardinal sin to think otherwise, there is no agreement about what it means to go beyond the idea of individual prejudice as the defining model and describe how race is made and remade. Although racism, and various forms of racial oppression and exploitation, are the result of individual practices, by no means can the construction of race be understood simply as a matter of individual choice or attitudes. Rather, social distinctions based on race originate in political and economic struggles between groups or even social classes. Race is made, Thomas Holt writes, "not in individual pathologies but in social formations at specific historical moments that shape and make both self and other knowable" (1995, 10; see also Fredrickson 1997, 84–85).

Consider labor market discrimination. Economists usually regard any individual differences in wages or income that remain after individual traits such as education or experience have been taken into account as a "measure of discrimination," unequal rewards to otherwise identical workers. Yet as Ruth Milkman and Eleanor Townsley point out in their analysis of gender discrimination, this "approach . . . fails to capture the depth with which . . . discrimination and the norms associated with it are embedded in the economic order—in fact, they are embedded so deeply that a willful act of discrimination is not really necessary to maintain gender inequality" (1994, 611).

Labor market discrimination is better understood as an instance of what Charles Tilly calls "opportunity hoarding," the monopolization of valuable resources and privileges by members of a social group. Discrimination may be as simple as white workers using their position to benefit relatives or friends seeking employment. More commonly, though, white workers compete with blacks for good jobs and perks; racial invective or stereotypes, such as the myth that black workers are incapable of working with machines, are cultivated to exclude black workers from higher paying, more prestigious jobs (Tilly 1998; Lieberson 1980).

It does not make sense to see race as a transhistorical phenomenon, a "motor of history." One can speak of race as ever present, much as Toni Morrison does when she shows how race shapes literary imaginations. The meaning of race, either as an ideology or a specific set of social practices, changes with specific historical events and long-run changes in economic and social structures. "Racial privileges and identity form as a relationship between dominant and subordinate groups" in the struggle between ethnic groups and social classes over economic resources and political power (Brown 1999, 15; Fredrickson 1997, 85). The color line—a hierarchical relationship between racial groups based on segregation and subordination—is made and remade over time.[5] Just how, though, is a matter for empirical investigation.

This understanding of race and racial inequality stems from the revival of group-based conceptions of racism and reflects intellectual developments across the social sciences and history. Three separate but closely related bodies of research typify the evolving analysis of race. The first is the rehabilitation of Herbert Blumer's (1958) notion of "race prejudice as a sense of group position" by political scientists and social psychologists. Second, historians and historically minded social scientists are investigating race by elaborating the idea of white identity and privilege. Both of these approaches explore race from the vantage point of the subject, and in both race is constructed culturally and ideologically. Racial subordination and persistent racial inequality is explained by beliefs endemic to American culture and politics. The third approach, reflecting the new institutionalism in the social sciences, investigates how states make race. These do not exhaust alternative conceptions of race, but they do indicate some of the more interesting contemporary approaches in the social sciences and history.

Blumer argued that racial attitudes had little to do with individual prejudice. Instead, they were statements about relationships between racial groups. Racial attitudes entail claims of privilege based on one's racial status, a sense of superiority, and a belief that the subordinate group is alien—coupled with a palpable fear of that group. Measures of racial attitudes reflect beliefs of where "the two racial groups belong" (Blumer 1958, 5). Blumer thought that any analysis of the sense of group position ought to begin with recognition that relationships between racial groups are a historical product formed through a collective process of definition and redefinition.

Although Blumer published his theory over forty years ago, students of racist attitudes have turned to it only in the wake of the collapse of the prejudice model of racism. Lawrence Bobo, for example, has recently used Blumer's theory to explain the persistence of neighborhood segregation and opposition to any policies devised to diminish racial inequality, not just affirmative action. In a survey of whites, blacks, Latinos, and Asian Americans, Bobo found that blacks were the least preferred neighbors, even though of the four groups they were the most receptive to living in interracial neighborhoods. Many whites saw integration as diminishing their status or, more precisely, their sense of superiority over the other groups (Bobo and Zubrinsky 1996, 892–93, 905; see also Wellman 1993). Similarly, those whites strongly opposed to using welfare and antipoverty policies to fight black poverty believed these programs diminished their status and undermined their "psychic well being" (Warren 1976, 174).

In fact, survey data consistently reveal a large gap between the proportion of whites who express clear-cut support for principles of racial equality and the proportion who oppose government efforts to promote integration or diminish labor market discrimination. By the 1980s, for example, 93 percent of whites favored integrated schools while only 26 percent supported government efforts to do anything about it—a gap, I should add, that has grown larger since the 1960s (Bobo and Smith 1998, 194). One cannot explain the opposition to government-sponsored integration or even affirmative action by appealing to individual self-interest. However, one can understand such opposition in terms of a sense of group position. Donald Kinder and Lynn Sanders write, "insofar as interests figure prominently in white opinion on race, it is through the threats blacks appear to pose to whites' collective well-being, not their personal welfare" (1996, 85).

If the revival of Blumer's group theory of racial prejudice provides an

136

Michael K. Brown

alternative to the individual prejudice model, it does not help us understand either the development of the sense of group position or how it changes. For that one must explore the "effect of racist inflection on the subject," a task the recent literature on white identity and privilege undertakes (Morrison 1993, 11). Like those survey researchers seeking an alternative to the individual prejudice model, this research was inspired by the persistence of racial inequality in an era of formal, "color-blind," race neutrality. White supremacy and its latter-day form, white privilege, though, was intentionally devised as an alternative to the idea of racism. In his comparative history of race in the United States and South Africa, George Fredrickson focused on white supremacy rather than racism because the latter idea was too closely associated with genetic or biological interpretations of black inferiority. White supremacy put the spotlight on the "restriction of meaningful citizenship rights to a privileged group characterized by its light pigmentation. . . . It suggests systematic and self-conscious efforts to make race or color a qualification for membership in the civil community" (1981, xi).

Similarly, in rejecting the idea that racism or racial inequality could be understood as the result of "discrete acts of racial discrimination," critical race theorists identified their aim as understanding how the "subordination of people of color [has] been created and maintained in America" (Crenshaw et al. 1995, xiii). In an era when the idea of a color-blind constitution has superseded Jim Crow, they argue that racial subordination cannot be reduced to prejudice or even to expressions of white interest. Instead, they suggest that white privilege is embedded in the very structure of the law itself; racial subordination is produced "through myriad legal rules, many of them having nothing to do with rules against discrimination" or "racially biased decision-making," (Crenshaw et al. 1995, xxv). The civil rights movement may have taken down the "whites only" signs, but the "white norm" persists, Kimberle Crenshaw insists, "legitimating the continuing domination of those who do not meet it" (1995, 115).

Turning from simple models of prejudice to scrutiny of white privilege and white identity has enormous implications for the study of race. It erodes any distinction between race and ethnicity—one cannot see race and ethnicity in the same way after reading Matthew Jacobson's *Whiteness of a Different Color* (1998). It calls into question the very meaning of liberalism and republicanism in the United States. It changes our view of working-class formation. But it also leaves many questions unresolved.

Whiteness is a form of property, Cheryl Harris (1995) suggested in a seminal formulation, unacknowledged, indeed invisible mostly, but entitling all whites, rich or poor, to material advantages and sense of psychic worth. The idea is drawn from W. E. B. Du Bois's observation in *Black Reconstruction in America* that white workers compensated for their low wages and exploitation at the hands of employers through public recognition of their whiteness. They could associate with all classes of white people, they had the vote, and they were recognized members of the community—they were not black in other words (Du Bois 1992, 700–701).

In Du Bois's hands, the identification of white workers with their exploiters was an artifact of class conflict; white labor, he scathingly observed, was "betrayed into wars for profit based on color caste" (1992, 30). This old and recurring argument has some real bite to it—Edmund Morgan's brilliant account of the origins of slavery reveals how Virginia's economic elites reconciled discontented white freedmen to inequalities of power and status by distinguishing them from enslaved African Americans and cultivating an identification with their betters (Morgan 1975; see also Allen 1994). Yet it reduces racial oppression to a tale of ruling class manipulation and avoids questions about the significance of whiteness for the formation of a class identity among American workers and the emergence in Jacksonian America of a white republic governed by an ascendant coalition of yeoman farmers, urban workers, aspiring parvenus, and southern planters. In grappling with these issues, the new research on whiteness has taken two related paths. One approach focuses on what David Roediger called the "wages of whiteness," the economic and psychic benefits of white privilege. The other examines whiteness in relation to citizenship and the formation of national identity, virtually rewriting the history of political identity in the United States.

Exemplary of the first approach are Alexander Saxton's (1990) and David Roediger's (1991) studies of the emergence of white working class identity in Jacksonian America. Both reject narrow economic interpretations—racial labor market competition, for example—of whiteness. Saxton locates the origins of an ascendant white racial ideology in the protracted political struggles of early nineteenth-century America. White identity, emerging in opposition to Whig policies regarding territorial expansion and Native Americans, is the glue that held the Jacksonian political coalition together. Self-interest underpinned the motivations of planters, farmers, and workers, but white identity cannot be reduced to the crude calculations of self-interest. Saxton argues that whiteness had a moral basis in the ideology of a producer society arrayed against monopoly: "Jacksonian Democrats asserted the political, civil, and moral equality of white male citizens" (1990, 142).

Michael K. Brown

Saxton turns Du Bois on his head. Material benefits are not far removed to be sure—territorial expansion meant economic opportunity for each part of the coalition and entailed both the extermination of Native Americans and perpetuation of slavery—but Jacksonian Democrats idealized a white America of politically equal producers. Class conflict thus produced a social order in which white privilege was joined to the idea of a classless society.

David Roediger's explanation for the emergence of a white identity among northern workers is very different: "Whiteness was a way," he writes, "in which white workers responded to a fear of dependency on wage labor and to the necessity of capitalist work discipline." For white workers freedom came to mean the opposite of slavery; it was defined in opposition to race rather than independence from owners and bosses. Roediger calls this *Herrenvolk* Republicanism because it "read African Americans out of the ranks of the producers and then proved more able to concentrate its fire downward on to the dependent and Black than upward against the rich and powerful" (1991, 13, 60).

These ideas parallel Toni Morrison's (1993) ruminations about American Africanism in literature and Judith Shklar's insight that citizenship was defined by its relationship to free labor or, rather, in the shadow of its racial opposite, slavery (1991, 85–86).[6] Roediger adds a psychological dimension, arguing that white working class identity was solidified through a process of projection in which white workers "displaced anxieties within the white population onto Blacks" (1991, 100). White workers displaced to African Americans their fear of the discipline imposed by industrialization. Blacks symbolized a preindustrial past that white workers both missed and scorned. Accordingly, Roediger thinks that white workers' hostility toward free blacks, particularly the antiblack riots in 1830s Philadelphia, was not motivated by self-interest, but rather by a fear they would lose jobs to black workers (1991, 97, 106).

Roediger uses these ideas to explain the development of workers' consciousness of themselves as white workers by exploring minstrelsy and cultural changes in language—terms that go from white to black (coon, buck, Mose). Unlike Saxton, who thinks minstrelsy was an artifact of party politics and helped solidify the Democratic party coalition, Roediger argues that blackface was a way of harnessing racial invective and allowed white workers to displace their hostility toward owners to blacks. Minstrelsy, according to Roediger, becomes strongly antiblack; minstrels never crossed the color line and lent themselves to proslavery, antiblack policies. Minstrelsy derived from a nascent white working class consciousness and symbolized "a sense of popular whiteness among workers across lines of ethnicity, religion, and skill. It achieved a common symbolic language—a unity—that could not be realized by racist crowds, by political parties or by labor unions" (Roediger 1991, 127).

Although Saxton and Roediger both reject job competition in favor of cultural and ideological explanations for whiteness, both end up arguing that for white workers a white identity became the vehicle for labor solidarity in the late nineteenth century and the fulcrum of exclusionary labor market practices. American labor, as a Texas railroader put it in the 1890s, "would rather be absolute slaves of capital than to take the negro into our lodges as a equal and brother" (Arnesen 1994, 1629). Saxton observes that skilled white workers transformed the Jacksonian rhetoric of producers into a racial narrative that pitted (white) producers or workers against those who exploited producers by aligning themselves with blacks or, in the West, Mexican Americans (1990, 298). To be a member of a craft union was to be white, though of course the arrival of immigrants from south and eastern Europe in the late nineteenth century rendered the very meaning of whiteness ambiguous. What Roediger adds is an account of how the Irish, initially understood as an alien race, transform themselves into a white ethnic group. Tammany Hall was the vessel that incubated whiteness among Irish immigrants, inculcating in them Jacksonian notions of white supremacy along with a commitment to vote Democratic. New York City Irish quickly became aware of the advantages of whiteness and wielded it as a weapon in the fierce competition for jobs (Roediger 1991, 142–44, 148–49).

Saxton and Roediger deploy cultural analysis to explain the racial consciousness of white workers. Grace Hale uses a cultural framework to show how, after Reconstruction, southern identity was transformed into a white identity, partly to deal with the dislocation of civil war and reconstruction, but mainly to cope with the demise of slavery and an emerging black "middle class." Whiteness reproduced the white/black hierarchy of slavery while flattening, but not eliminating, class and gender divisions among whites—there is no suggestion of white (Jacksonian) equality (Hale 1999, 21, 46–48). Hale shows how lynching spectacles, as she refers to public lynchings, created a collective sense of whiteness—white southerners from all walks of life participated, either as perpetrators or spectators—and momentarily erased divisions of class and gender. "Lynching as the controlled inversion of segregation," she writes, "helped ease the class tensions within white supremacy. For poor whites, too, experienced a racial power that contradicted the inferiority of their class position" (1999, 236).

Hale suggests that white identity emerged in response to economic change. She links whiteness to consumption, arguing that southern

Michael K. Brown

white identity grew out of the anxieties of whites as the South modernized, penetrated by northern retail outlets. Color-coded consumption maintained the hierarchy of white over black in a market economy where economic transactions eroded social distinctions and brought whites and blacks into the same space. As she puts it, "segregation . . . became the foundation of southern society and the central metaphor of southern life because it balanced white demand for a racially figured power, the spread of the new national ways of buying and selling . . . and African Americans' insistence that freedom yield tangible benefits over slavery" (1999, 125).

Whatever one thinks of these studies, all share a common assumption: whiteness emerges from anxieties over economic change and dislocation and animosities generated by class conflict and class resentment. Whiteness and its attendant privileges mediate class conflict and changes in gender roles without eliminating them. These arguments also "democratize" the construction of whiteness, if you will; white economic elites are no longer understood as the sole creators of an ever-changing color line. Whiteness, though, is also a matter of political identity and emerges independently of economic conflicts.

American political identity is conventionally described as uniformly liberal, embodying a single creed enshrined in the Declaration of Independence and the Constitution. In his justly influential book *The Liberal Tradition in America*, Louis Hartz insisted that America was born liberal and remained so, lapsing into a static liberal tradition that he ironically characterized as a "kind of immobility" (1964, 3; see also Hartz 1955, 47–48). In *Civic Ideals*, Rogers Smith challenges Hartz's and Tocqueville's notion of America as a liberal society. Citizenship, he notes, was never defined simply as adherence to liberal or republican ideals; the law was riddled with exclusions that conflicted with the idea of America as a liberal society. Alexis de Tocqueville's account of the relative equality of white men (which is true) was "surrounded by an array of fixed, ascriptive hierarchies, all largely unchallenged by the leading American revolutionaries" (Smith 1998, 17). Hartz is simply wrong, Smith argues; American political development has been governed by three competing ideological traditions: liberal, republican, and ascriptive.

Smith's study focuses on citizenship laws, those "laws designating the criteria for membership in a political community and the key prerogatives that constitute membership" (1998, 30). These laws distribute power, assign status, define identities; they are constitutive, in other words, of the political identity of a community and are fundamental to the act of state building. Smith shows that these laws are better understood as the product of an ascriptive tradition that believes "'true' Americans are 'chosen' by God, history, or nature to possess superior moral and intellectual traits associated with their race, ethnicity, religion, gender, sexual orientation" (1998, 508). America was born white, not just liberal.

On this interpretation white supremacy was positively valued, and derived from "the presence in the nation's political culture of well-established arguments for the divine mission of the American people, the superiority of Anglo-Saxon civilization, patriarchal rule in the family and polity, and white racial supremacy" (Smith 1998, 167). Gone are the economic anxieties that supposedly explain white identity, replaced by the need to create a common identity in a new nation. Smith traces the origins of ascriptivism to the ethnic diversity of the early colonists and their thirst for land and labor. At the heart of ascriptivism in this account is conquest, pure and simple. The early colonists welcomed other Europeans to the new land but excluded Native Americans and African Americans who were impressed into slavery. The new Americans took a decidedly un-Lockean view of themselves as a "distinct people," the "sole bearers of the providentially favored Anglo-Saxon mission to build a realm of enlightenment and spiritual and political liberty" (Smith 1998, 74).

Ascriptivism flourishes in the thin soil of liberalism, its inability to forge common identities, and is nurtured by political elites who fashion "civic myths," noble lies that enable a people to live together while concealing rank exploitation. Tracing out the consequences of the ascriptive tradition for citizenship from the founding to the Progressive era, Smith goes way beyond economic or psychological explanations, finding the origins of white identity and racial oppression deeply embedded in American political culture and national identity.

Smith treats the ideological traditions he examines as separate but conflicting beliefs. Whether this is warranted is an open question. Other political accounts of whiteness argue that liberalism and republicanism were racially tinged ideologies from the outset. Charles Mills (1997) thinks that the classic social contract theorists presumed nonwhite inferiority. Matthew Jacobson takes aim at Republican ideology, suggesting that the test of fitness for citizenship in a republican government was whiteness. "With its abolition of monarchic power and its disruption of strict, top-down lines of political authority," Jacobson writes, "the new democratic order would require of its participants a remarkable degree of self-possession—condition already denied literally to Africans in slavery and figuratively to all 'nonwhite' or 'heathen' peoples." This relationship between whiteness and fitness for citizenship underlies the 1790 law that permitted naturalization only of whites and the ambiguous status of free blacks in northern states (Jacobson 1998, 26–30).

Michael K. Brown

The problem, Jacobson argues, is that this relationship was called into question with the surge of European immigration in the late nineteenth century. The "over-inclusiveness" of the 1790 definition of whiteness provoked a reassessment of who was white, while retaining the idea that fitness for citizenship depended on skin color. The tortured debate that followed made it clear that non-European immigrants, mainly Chinese railroad workers, were unfit, but left open the question of whether European immigrants were also unfit (Jacobson 1998, 41–42, 72–74).

Exploring the changing cultural and political meaning of whiteness, Jacobson shows how the new immigrants shed a racial identity and became white. To assimilate was to be white, any differences between Anglo-Saxons, Irish, Italian, Polish, Russian, Armenian immigrants evaporated, while whiteness was protected as a "bulwark against undesirable Others"—its value as property. A hard division between black and white replaced the ambiguity of whiteness (Jacobson 1998, 233, 236, 115–17). Jacobson attributes the consolidation of whiteness to several causes: the end of unlimited immigration in 1924, Jim Crow and the resulting black migration north, and court rulings that stretched the meaning of whiteness under the 1790 naturalization law to include virtually any and all European immigrants (see also Haney-Lopez 1996).

The details of Jacobson's study are less relevant than his argument that race, particularly whiteness, is imbued with political meaning, both as a criterion for citizenship and a marker of hierarchy, and is a contingent, ever-changing fabrication. Yet neither studies of working class identity nor national identity, including Jacobson's, treat whiteness as simply a cultural reflection of group tensions and conflicts; for all these writers whiteness does convey power, order social relationships, and determine the livelihoods of many people. Nonetheless, these studies raise as many questions as they answer. Much of the literature presumes that whiteness monolithically envelops all "white" people. Not every labor union was racially exclusive, however, and the interesting question may be how and why whiteness takes hold in some instances but not others (Arnesen 1998).[7] In this respect Neil Foley's (1997) revealing study of black, white, and Mexican American sharecroppers and farmworkers in Texas shows how whiteness constituted a matrix of power that relegated "poor white trash" to the nether world along with blacks and Mexicans.

No less important is the question of how and why white identity and privilege, or patterns of racial inequality, are perpetuated. Saxton, Roediger, and Jacobson all seek to understand how white political and social identity is reproduced in the nineteenth century after the social conflicts disappear that initially caused it. All leave open the question of whether it makes any sense to talk about whiteness after the civil rights movement discredited Jim Crow and the crude ideology of white supremacy that buttressed legal segregation in the South and violent discrimination in the North. In a pointed critique of Jacobson, Nathan Glazer admonished that whiteness "is being imposed as an explanatory variable upon a present in which its explanatory power is considerably reduced" (1998, 46).

One answer to this question is to look, as Lawrence Bobo and others do, at changes in racial beliefs. Biological racism, Bobo argues, has been replaced by a cultural racism that attributes continued racial inequality to blacks' warped cultural values. He calls this "laissez-faire" racism. "Many Americans," he points out, "have become comfortable with as much racial segregation and inequality as a putatively nondiscriminatory polity and free-market economy can produce" (Bobo and Smith 1998, 213). Put another way, white identity today is based on the ideology of a color-blind society, which accepts formal racial equality but tolerates pervasive inequality in status. Legally, race is rendered illegitimate, and the Supreme Court now willingly strikes down affirmative action programs as a violation of the equal protection clause of the Fourteenth Amendment but tolerates social inequities.[8]

With Bobo's articulation of laissez-faire racism we come full circle, back to the revival of Herbert Blumer's concept of racism as a sense of group position. Indeed, Blumer's idea that racial attitudes and beliefs are statements about the preferred relationship between groups suggests that today's pervasive cultural racism might be understood as the latest version of beliefs that go back to the founding of the country.

III

As important as it is, the cultural and ideological study of white identity has little to say about the origins of legal segregation and racial domination or how it is that white privileges are allocated, institutionalized, and maintained. Studies of cultural artifacts like Jacobson's illuminate the power of images but tell us little about how and why labor market discrimination, for example, arose and persists. Du Bois, who regarded race as a "cultural and sometimes historical" fact, pointed to a very different approach to understanding how racial distinctions were constructed and maintained than do students of white culture and ideology. When asked how one decided who was black and who was not if the biological conception of race was a myth, he pithily replied "the black man is a person who must ride 'Jim Crow' in Georgia" (1968, 153). In other words, states make race.

Michael K. Brown

Rather than analyzing the origins and persistence of white identity and whites' racial beliefs, institutionally centered studies of race explore the political and social origins of legalized racial domination or examine how otherwise "color-blind" public policies either create or reproduce racial distinctions. The wages of whiteness, one might say, are created by politics—legal rules that establish and maintain racial hierarchies and public policies that convey racial advantages or disadvantages. In either case, individual acts of discrimination or even prior beliefs in white supremacy are less important to the persistence of racial inequality than presence or absence of state-sponsored discrimination or racially biased policies. In fact, Anthony Marx (1998) boldly suggests that the congealing of racial identities is contingent on the emergence of legalized racial domination. However, as recent studies of the welfare state demonstrate, putatively "race-neutral" policies may reinforce racial divisions and white advantage even in the absence of explicit racial ideologies.

Anthony Marx's recent account of how states make race focuses on political and economic conflicts endemic to nation building. Like Rogers Smith, he argues that nation building is as much about the exclusion of social groups as inclusion. He asks why the emancipation of slaves led to publicly sanctioned discrimination in some cases—Jim Crow in the South and Apartheid in South Africa—but failed to do so in others, leaving only private, nonstate, discrimination as in Brazil. Marx insists that prior racial ideologies, slavery, colonial history, or religious beliefs cannot explain legalized racial discrimination in southern states and South Africa and its absence in Brazil. Rather, Jim Crow and Apartheid emerge from a violent internal struggle between opposing groups of whites over slavery and nation building. Faced with the task of reconciling whites and establishing the legitimacy of a national state, political and economic elites acted "to strike bargains, selling out blacks and reinforcing prior racial distinctions and ideology in order to unify whites. . . . 'To bind up the nation's wounds' among whites blacks were bound down." Where the process of nation building was more consensual, or at least lacked violent struggle as in Brazil, there was scant pressure to unify whites by state-sponsored racial domination (Marx 1998, 2).

Marx argues that deep divisions between an industrializing North and violent white southern nationalism after the Civil War threatened consolidation of the national state Republicans thought necessary for economic growth. Northern whites restored national unity by withdrawing from the South, allowing white southerners to erect a new form of racial domination and control. Similarly, in South Africa the British consolidated their hold on the society after the Boer War by aligning with the Afrikaners to oppress blacks—"racial prejudice came together with strategic advantage," Marx writes (1998, 91). In both cases, national unity was contingent on the acquiescence of the Republicans and the British to white Southerners' and Afrikaners' virulent nationalism and hostility to blacks.

The Brazilian case was very different. Pervasive racial discrimination never congealed into state-sanctioned racial oppression precisely because the state was not riven by deeply rooted internal antagonisms between whites. "With less pressure for intrawhite reconciliation, no racial domination was constructed" (Marx 1998, 179). Indeed, worried about incipient regional divisions and rebellious blacks, Brazilian elites were compelled to construct a form of nationalism premised on the inclusion of blacks.

The corollary to this argument is the suggestion that racial identity, and consequently black mobilization, depends on the presence or absence of state-sanctioned racial domination. Marx concludes that "When and where states enacted formal rules of domination according to racial distinctions, racism was reinforced, whites were unified as whites, challenges from those subordinated eventually emerged, and major racial conflict ensued. Where racial domination was not encoded by the state, issues and conflicts over race were diluted" (1998, 267).

Racial divisions would not persist in the United States, Marx argues, had it not been for Jim Crow, which created black identity. In Brazil, on the other hand, he suggests that the absence of state-sponsored racial domination meant that blacks were more likely to think they could advance by denying their racial identity (1998, 252).

Marx's interesting argument puts politics at the center of race, thus moving way beyond cultural studies and purely economic or psychological theories. Individual prejudice is subordinated to intentional political decisions to either exclude or include blacks in the nation. Whether these decisions adequately explain *de jure* segregation and racial oppression is another matter. Marx's analysis of nation building excludes obvious economic factors that mattered. For example, Jim Crow was less an intentional consequence of the compromise of 1877, than an effort by southern landowners to tie black farmers to the land and thwart an incipient alliance between black and white sharecroppers in the 1890s. Rather than unifying the nation, it would be more accurate to say that northerners consigned the South to the backwaters of industrialism once reconstruction had failed and acquiesced to Jim Crow.

When states make race they do more than physically segregate racial groups or politically exclude them; states also distribute racial privileges. Afrikaner-controlled governments made racial privileges a matter of law in order to advantage poor whites and solidify support for

Afrikaner rule. An official color bar in labor markets, for example, protected white employment and wages from black competitors by guaranteeing jobs and high wages (Fredrickson 1981, 228–29, 233).[9] In the United States, no formal color bar was enacted, but passage of draconian labor laws in southern states during Reconstruction, political disenfranchisement after 1890, and terror aided white exploitation of black labor and white advantage in the South. Like private employers, the federal government actively discriminated against black workers (King 1995).

Legalized racial domination is only one way states allocate racial privileges. Welfare states, conceived as institutions that minimize class distinctions in the name of equal citizenship, may also become bastions of white privilege. Because social policies provide collective benefits to individuals who may gain at the expense of others, welfare states often produce new forms of stratification (Marshall 1963, 110). Public policies can reinforce existing patterns of stratification or create new ones. Nowhere has this been more apparent than in the use of social polices from the Progressive era forward to construct and entrench white privileges.

Intentionally excluding racial groups from social programs is the most obvious way welfare states construct white privilege. Discrimination by design occurs because groups of whites were able to impose their will on legislation. For example, southern white Democrats, intent on preventing New Deal legislation from undermining Jim Crow, insisted on the exclusion of agricultural and domestic workers from the 1935 Social Security Act. As a result, about two-thirds of African American workers were denied access to national old-age insurance. African Americans were eligible for public assistance benefits under the Old Age Assistance and Aid to Dependent Children titles, but these locally controlled programs were riddled with discrimination (Quadagno 1988a, 1988b; Lieberman, 1998). In fact discrimination by design was characteristic of many New Deal programs—the Wagner Act not only excluded agricultural and domestic workers at the insistence of southern Democrats, but the American Federation of Labor successfully lobbied against an amendment barring racial discrimination by unions (Hill 1985, 104–6). In response to intense lobbying by real estate interests, the Federal Housing Administration issued discriminatory loan guidelines that led to the redlining of black neighborhoods (Jackson 1985).

None of these policies contained statutory color bars; all were statutorily "race-neutral." Yet whites reaped the advantages of discrimination by design: whites were favored over blacks in public assistance programs; white workers were not legally obligated to include blacks in their unions under the Wagner Act; and federal housing programs subsidized white home ownership. In fact, white southerners used federal social policies such as the 1946 Hill-Burton Act, which provided federal subsidies for hospital construction, to build a segregated system of health care and institutionalize Jim Crow at the expense of taxpayers (Brown 1999, 124–27, 132–33). Black taxpayers were forced to pay for their own subordination. Thus, either through implicit exclusions or administrative discrimination, these policies increased what George Lipsitz calls the "possessive investment in whiteness among European Americans" (1995, 372).

Seemingly race-neutral social policies also "make" race indirectly by amplifying the effects of private discrimination in labor and housing markets. Labor market discrimination produces higher unemployment and lower wages among African American workers. It therefore undermines their access to the welfare state and determines how and what kind of benefits they receive. Social insurance in the United States, for example, is based on wage-related eligibility and requires extended attachment to the labor force. Due to labor market discrimination black workers may be excluded from social insurance, particularly unemployment compensation, and receive lower benefits when they are included. It has also meant that poor African Americans are more likely to be beneficiaries of means-tested public assistance programs, with lower, stigmatized benefits, than social insurance (Brown 1999).

Putatively race-neutral policies, therefore, can produce racial advantages and disadvantages in a society with deeply entrenched patterns of discrimination. Indeed, one of the ways racial inequality is perpetuated over time is through the institutionalization of racial privilege in social policies. It is also the case of course that social policies may be used to undo the effects of past and present discrimination, but that requires acknowledging that racial inequality is not the result of individual acts of discrimination.

IV

Racial inequality and racial oppression cannot be understood simply as prejudice. Nor can race be dismissed as a political and intellectual distraction. The collapse of the prejudice model and the persistence of racial inequality after the civil rights revolution has inspired new approaches to the study of race over the last twenty-five years, substantially altering our understanding of racial inequality and subordination in America. Recent innovations in the study of race are

148

Michael K. Brown

not limited to the developments I have discussed—the revival of a group conception of race and racial inequality and its application to the study of contemporary racial discrimination, white beliefs and racial ideologies, and institutional forms of racial domination and advantage. All are motivated, nonetheless, by an effort to probe the depths of racial inequality, to understand how much of American social life and politics has been and continues to be shaped by what Toni Morrison calls an American Africanism.

To this discussion one should add two caveats. The study of race and racial inequality will undoubtedly benefit from comparison, both cross-nationally and between different racial groups within the same society (see, for example, Foley 1997). Second, one should be wary of the pitfalls to the group conception of race. It often loses sight of the internal tensions within groups and leaves social class and gender on the periphery. All of the recent work on whiteness and racial inequality underscores the complex ways race, class, and gender are interrelated, and it makes no sense to restrict analysis to one or the other. The most interesting confirmation of this point is found in recent studies of how African American politics is shaped not just by a common racial identity but by class, gender, and sexuality (for exemplary studies, see Cohen 1999; Lewis 1991). Indeed, these studies make clear, as do the studies discussed in this essay, just how little we really understand about the origins and persistence of racial inequality.

NOTES

1. There is no single American creed as Myrdal presumed. For an elaboration of this point see Smith 1998.
2. Similarly, Judith Shklar (1991) argues that the American conception of citizenship cannot be understood apart from the relationship between slavery and freedom.
3. This spatial model of party competition makes a number of assumptions many political scientists regard as dubious, for example, voters divide along a single-issue dimension. For a thorough critique of these models see Green and Shapiro 1994. Frymer's point, however, is that race is not usually considered an important division in electoral politics (Frymer 1999, 32).
4. I am indebted to Troy Duster for this insight.
5. St. Clair Drake and Horace Cayton formulated the classic definition of the color line in *Black Metropolis*. They define it as segregating blacks from whites and subordinating blacks "by denying them the right to compete, as individuals, on equal terms with white people for economic and political power" (1945, 101).

6. However, Shklar does not argue that the idea of citizenship in America acquired a white identity.

7. Eric Arensen (2001) also criticizes the concept as too vague to be of much use to historians and argues the evidence for it is thin (but see the rejoinders in Barrett 2001 and Hattam 2001). While the concept is often used imprecisely, Arnesen's critique elides the significance of whiteness for recent departures in the study of race and racial inequality. The problems with the literature have as much to do with limits to cultural approaches as with the idea of whiteness. For an elaboration of this point see Reed 2001.

8. This is the burden of Justice Sandra Day O'Connor's majority opinion in *City of Richmond v. J. A. Croson*, 488 U.S. 469 (1989). For a recent analysis of the Court's conservative turn see Siegel 1998.

9. South African Apartheid also proved to be a source of public employment reserved for whites—43 percent of the white labor force was employed by government by 1972, many of them working in the security apparatus (Marx 1998, 108).

REFERENCE LIST

Allen, T. W. 1994. *The invention of the white race: Racial oppression and social control.* New York, N.Y.: Verso.

Arnesen, E. 1994. "Like Bonquo's Ghost, it will not down": The race question and the American railroad brotherhoods, 1880–1920. *American Historical Review* 99: 1601–33.

———. 1998. Up from exclusion: Black and white workers, race, and the state of labor history. *Reviews in American History* 26: 146–74.

———. 2001. Whiteness and the historians' imagination. *International Labor and Working-Class History* 60: 3–32.

Barrett, J. R. 2001. Whiteness studies: Anything here for historians of the working class? *International Labor and Working-Class History* 60: 33–42.

Blumer, H. 1958. Race prejudice as a sense of group position. *Pacific Sociological Review* 1 (March): 3–7.

Bobo, L., and R. A. Smith. 1998. From Jim Crow to laissez-faire racism: The transformation of racial attitudes. In *Beyond pluralism: The conception of groups and group identities in America*, edited by Wendy F. Katkin, Ned Landsman, and Andrea Tyree. Urbana: University of Illinois Press.

Bobo, L., and C. L. Zubrinsky. 1996. Attitudes on residential integration: Perceived status differences, mere in-group preference, or racial prejudice. *Social Forces* 74 (March): 833–909.

Brown, M. K. 1999. *Race, money, and the American welfare state.* Ithaca, N.Y.: Cornell University Press.

Carter, R. L. 1980. A reassessment of *Brown v. Board.* In *Shades of brown: New perspectives on school desegregation*, edited by Derrick Bell. New York: Teachers College, Columbia University.

Michael K. Brown

Cohen, C. J. 1999. *The Boundaries of blackness: AIDS and the breakdown of black politics.* Chicago: University of Chicago Press.

Crenshaw, K. 1995. Race, reform and retrenchment: Transformation and legitimation in anti-discrimination law. In *Critical race theory,* edited by Kimberle Crenshaw et al. New York: The New Press.

Crenshaw, K. N., et al. 1995. *Critical race theory: The key writing that formed the movement.* New York: The New Press.

Drake, St. Clair, and H. R. Cayton. 1945. *Black metropolis: A study of negro life in a northern city.* New York: Harcourt, Brace and Co.

D'Souza, D. 1995. *The end of racism: Principles for a multicultural society.* New York: The Free Press.

Du Bois, W. E. B. 1968. *Dusk of dawn: An essay toward an autobiography of a race concept.* New York: Schocken Books.

———. 1992. *Black reconstruction in America, 1960–1880.* New York, NY: Atheneum.

Foley, N. 1997. *The white scourge: Mexicans, blacks, and poor whites in Texas cotton culture.* Berkeley: University of California Press.

Fredrickson, G. M. 1981. *White supremacy.* New York: Oxford University Press.

———. 1997. *The comparative imagination: On the history of racism, nationalism, and social movements.* Berkeley: University of California Press.

Frymer, P. 1999. *Uneasy alliances: Race and party competition in America.* Princeton: Princeton University Press.

Garrow, D. J. 1988. *Bearing the cross: Martin Luther King, Jr., and the Southern Christian Leadership Conference.* New York: Vintage Books.

Gilroy, P. 2000. *Against race: Imagining political culture beyond the color line.* Cambridge: Harvard University Press.

Glazer, N. 1998. White noise. *The New Republic,* 12 October, 43–46.

Green, D., and I. Shapiro. 1994. *Pathologies of rational choice theory: A critique of applications in political science.* New Haven: Yale University Press.

Hale, G. E. 1999. *Making whiteness: The culture of segregation in the South, 1890–1940.* New York: Vintage Books.

Haney-Lopez, I. F. 1996. *White by law: The legal construction of race.* New York: New York University Press.

Harris, C. 1995. Whiteness as property. In *Critical race theory,* edited by Kimberle Crenshaw et al. New York: New Press.

Hartz, L. 1955. *The liberal tradition in America.* New York: Harcourt, Brace & World, Inc.

———. 1964. *The founding of new societies.* New York: Harcourt, Brace & World, Inc.

Hattam, V. C. 2001. Whiteness: Theorizing race, eliding ethnicity. *International Labor and Working-Class History* 60: 61–68.

Hill, H. 1985. *Black labor and the American legal system: Race, work, and the law.* Madison: University of Wisconsin Press.

Holt, T. C. 1995. Marking: Race, race-making, and the writing of history. *American Historical Review* 100 (February): 1–20.

Jackson, K. T. 1985. *Crabgrass frontier.* New York: Oxford University Press.

Jacobson, M. F. 1998. *Whiteness of a different color: European immigrants and the alchemy of race.* Cambridge: Harvard University Press.

Key, V. O. 1984. *Southern politics in state and nation.* Knoxville: University of Tennessee Press.

Kinder, D., and L. M. Sanders. 1996. *Divided by color: Racial politics and democratic ideals.* Chicago: University of Chicago Press.

King, D. 1995. *Separate and unequal: Black Americans and the U.S. federal government.* New York: Oxford University Press.

Lewis, E. 1991. *In their own interests: Race, class, and power in twentieth-century Norfolk, Virginia.* Berkeley: University of California Press.

Lieberman, R. 1998. *Shifting the color line: Race and the American welfare state.* Cambridge: Harvard University Press.

Lieberson, S. 1980. *A piece of the pie: Blacks and white immigrants since 1880.* Berkeley: University of California Press.

Lind, M. 1995. *The next American nation: The new nationalism and the fourth American revolution.* New York: The Free Press.

Lipsitz, G. 1995. The possessive investment in whiteness: Racialized social democracy and the "white" problem in American studies. *American Quarterly* 47 (September): 369–87.

Marshall, T. 1963. *Class, citizenship, and social development.* Chicago: University of Chicago Press.

Marx, A. W. 1998. *Making race and nation: A comparison of the United States, South Africa, and Brazil.* New York: Cambridge University Press.

Milkman, R., and E. Townsley. 1994. Gender and the economy. In *Handbook of economic sociology,* edited by Neil J. Smelser and Richard Swedberg. Princeton: Princeton University Press.

Mills, C. W. 1997. *The racial contract.* Ithaca, N.Y.: Cornell University Press.

Morgan, E. S. 1975. *American slavery, American freedom: The ordeal of colonial Virginia.* New York: W. W. Norton and Company.

Morrison, T. 1993. *Playing in the dark: Whiteness and the literary imagination.* New York: Vintage Books.

Myrdal, G. 1944. *An American dilemma: The Negro problem and modern democracy.* New York: Harper and Row.

Patterson, O. 1997. *The ordeal of integration: Progress and resentment in America's racial crisis.* Washington, D.C.: Civitas/Counterpoint.

Quadagno, J. 1988a. From old-age assistance to supplemental security income: The political economy of relief in the South, 1935–1972. In *The politics of social policy in the United States,* edited by Margaret Weir, Ann Shola Orloff, and Theda Skocpol. Princeton: Princeton University Press.

———. 1988b. *The transformation of old age security: Class and politics in the American Welfare State.* Chicago: University of Chicago Press.

Reed, A. Jr. 2001. Response to Eric Arnesen. *International Labor and Working-Class History* 60: 69–80.

Roediger, D. 1991. *The wages of whiteness: Race and the making of the American working class.* New York: Verso.

152

Michael K. Brown

Saxton, A. 1990. *The rise and fall of the white republic: Class politics and mass culture in nineteenth-century America.* New York: Verso.

Schattschneider, E. 1975. *The semisovereign people: A realist's view of democracy in America.* New York: Harcourt, Brace, Jovanovich.

Shklar, J. N. 1991. *American citizenship: The quest for inclusion.* Cambridge: Harvard University Press.

Siegel, R. 1998. The racial rhetorics of colorblind constitutionalism: The case of Hopwood v. Texas. In *Race and representation: Affirmative action,* edited by Robert Post and Michael Rogin. New York: Zone Books.

Smith, R. M. 1998. *Civic ideals: Conflicting visions of citizenship of U.S. history.* New Haven: Yale University Press.

Sniderman, P., and T. Piazza. 1993. *The scar of race.* Cambridge: Harvard University Press.

Thernstrom, S., and A. Thernstrom. 1997. *America in black and white: One nation, indivisible.* New York: Simon and Schuster.

Tilly, C. 1998. *Durable inequality.* Berkeley: University of California Press.

Warren, D. I. 1976. *The radical center: Middle Americans and the politics of alienation.* Notre Dame, Ind.: University of Notre Dame Press.

Wellman, D. T. 1993. *Portraits of white racism.* 2d ed. New York: Cambridge University Press.

LITERACY AS SOCIAL

SCIENCE HISTORY

ITS PAST AND FUTURE—A

ROUNDTABLE

HARVEY J. GRAFF, CHAD GAFFIELD,

DAVID MITCH, ANDERS NILSSON,

DAVID VINCENT

Chairing the session, Harvey Graff opened with brief formal comments on the history and historiography of historical studies of literacy conceptualized as social science history. Previewing arguments he advanced the next day in his Presidential Address (see page 13–56), he commented:

"Firm connections between history and sociology have tended to occur only within substantive areas or within general approaches like Marxism or feminism," Andrew Abbott observed. The SSHA program comprises a roster of those "substantive areas." Prominent among those "substantive areas" is the study of literacy, which has been an established interest of social science historians across disciplines and a presence at SSHA meetings from the early years.

The history of literacy is an instructive example of social science history with respect to its founding and the course of its development. It followed a path common to social science histories. On the one hand, pioneering social science historians of the 1960s and 1970s confronted a diffuse historical literature that made easy (if poorly documented) generalizations about the distribution of literacy across populations and also (even though vaguely) the great significance of literacy's presence, absence, or degree of diffusion. On the other hand, they confronted a social science literature, some of it with theoretical aspirations, generally derived from modernization approaches that placed literacy squarely among the requisites for progress by individuals and by groups.

Critical of earlier work, the new literacy studies that emerged in the 1970s and 1980s questioned the received wisdom that tied literacy directly to individual and societal development, from social mobility (+) and criminal acts (-) to revolutions in industry (+), fertility (-), and democracy (+). Skeptical about modernization models and with at least some of the conclusions taken from aggregative data, researchers who come from an impressive number of nations, disciplines, and specializations were wary about imprecise formulations, levels of generalization, and their evidential basis. Critical and revisionist in intellectual orientation, a generation of scholars sought to test old and newer ideas, hypotheses, and theories with reliable and relevant data.

Earlier expectations (and theories) that literacy's contribution to shaping or changing nations, and the men and women within them, was universal, unmediated, independent, and powerful have been quashed. Literacy—that is, literacy by itself—is now seldom conceptualized as independently transformative. To the contrary, we now anticipate and recognize its impact to be shaped by specific historical circumstances as context-dependent, complicated rather than simple, incomplete or uneven, interactive rather than determinative, and mediated by a host of other intervening factors of a personal, structural, or cultural historical nature rather than universal. In other words, literacy is a historical variable, and it is historically variable.

The emergence of literacy as an interdisciplinary field for contemporary students opens the way for a richer exchange between social science historians and other researchers for the mutual reshaping of inquiry past, present, and future that is part of the promise of social science history. Historical studies of literacy, finally, contribute to public discourse, debate, and policy "talk" internationally. The many crucial points of intersection include the demonstration that no "golden age" for literacy ever existed, that there are multiple paths to literacy for individuals and societies, that quantitative measures of literacy do not translate easily to qualitative assessments, that the environment in which literacy is learned affects the usefulness of the skills, that the connections between literacy and inequality are many, and that the constructs of literacy (its learning and its uses) are usually conceived far too narrowly.

Chad Gaffield, David Mitch, Anders Nilsson, and David Vincent elaborate on these and other aspects of the historical study of literacy.

Literacy as Social Science History: Its Past and Future

Chad Gaffield

Who can read and write? Over the past four decades, this seemingly straightforward question has given rise to one of the most compelling, controversial, and confounding fields of socio-historical research. As periodically identified by one of its leading scholars, Harvey J. Graff, the historical study of literacy has gone through a series of conceptual and methodological phases in keeping with attempts by researchers to come to grips with the complex and often contradictory findings of their research projects. These findings have made clear that there is no easy answer to the question of literacy; rather, the ability to read and write is characteristically nested within a varying constellation of forces including those of class, gender, ethnicity, and historical context.

Less emphasized are the ways in which research on literacy has contributed to the larger rethinking of historical change that, quite unexpectedly, has occurred since the 1970s. Indeed, this contribution has been significant. Historians of literacy have consistently been at the forefront of the epistemological shifts that have moved the discipline since the days of "new social history." Similarly, relatively little attention has been paid to the ways in which the historical study of literacy has altered other subfields of socio-historical research. Beyond an enhanced knowledge of reading and writing's meaning in various times and places, research on literacy has significantly affected scholarly debate in other fields, most notably and obviously, the history of education but also areas such as historical demography.

In this context, the following discussion focuses on the role of literacy research in altering scholarly conceptions of historical change. Ten examples of these changing conceptions are used to illustrate the considerable diversity of this role. Then, attention is paid to the impact of literacy research on other socio-historical subfields by using the examples of the history of education and historical demography. This discussion provides a basis for concluding observations about certain promising ways of building upon the substantial research results of recent decades to further enhance our temporal understanding of literacy. Taken together, the consideration of literacy research in the context of general historical debate, in its relationship to other socio-historical fields, and in terms of future work is intended to help explain why the question of reading and writing has been, and promises to remain, one of the most active areas of historical research.

When historians began focusing on literacy during the 1960s and

Harvey J. Graff, Chad Gaffield, David Mitch, Anders Nilsson, David Vincent

early 1970s, they characteristically presented their work as a self-conscious contribution to the new social history, especially its expanded assumptions about agency. The attempt to identify societal patterns of literacy by systematically examining large-scale, routinely generated sources such as parish registers and censuses was usually aimed at explaining social change in terms of the experience and behavior of the "anonymous" as well as the famous and infamous. Over time, however, historical research on literacy helped move scholarly debate beyond the bottom-up/top-down debate to a wide variety of both conceptual and methodological issues that emerged from surprising and perplexing research results. The following ten examples do not do justice to the full range of these issues, but they do illustrate how literacy research has altered scholarly perspectives on historical change.

1. Historians of literacy have helped dismantle the single-variable interpretive framework that often implicitly and sometimes explicitly was associated with the new social history. Within this framework, it was considered important and meaningful in and of itself to compare specific characteristics across societies such as fertility levels, school attendance rates, or, in the case at hand, the proportion of adults who could read and write. Researchers soon emphasized, however, that such single-variable comparisons could often be highly misleading. The same overall literacy rate, for example, could have resulted from quite different dynamics. At the same time, diverse rates did not always have distinct consequences. As a result of these research findings, scholars of literacy have helped move the study of social change in the direction of multi-causal, contextually dependent analyses. Unlike the 1970s, few researchers now expect to find that any single characteristic or behavior, such as the ability to read and write, consistently and adequately explains any aspect of historical change.

2. Historians of literacy have contributed significantly to the increasingly interdisciplinary character of socio-historical research. In fact, literacy scholars have loomed large among those researchers who not only write about the advantages of integrating concepts, methods, and findings from various disciplines but who also practice what they preach. Since the 1960s, studies on historical literacy increasingly reflected the full breadth of the social sciences and humanities, and, to a lesser extent, began pointing to the potential ways in which the natural sciences, engineering, and the biomedical fields can contribute to historical research. Such interdisciplinarity provided influential examples of how historians can enhance their study of the past by drawing upon work in areas such as cognitive psychology and linguistics.

3. Historians of literacy have helped researchers learn to be much

more comfortable with ambiguities, contradictions, and inconsistencies both in historical evidence and interpretation. One unexpected result of the new social history was a heightened scholarly appreciation of the messiness of history. As a result of their work with documents such as the census, employment registers, and probate records, literacy historians encouraged researchers to be less prone to discount, or to see as a problem, evidence that does not "fit." In comparison to the work of several decades ago, historians are now much more likely to emphasize the often uneven and unintended character of historical change.

4. Historians of literacy have encouraged scholars to be more humble about their ability to explain the past. In the 1960s and 1970s, historians were generally still seeking Big Answers to the Big Questions—often at the nation-state level and sometimes even at the continental or Western Society level. However, the continual presentation of research findings that exposed the limits of each new major interpretation encouraged scholars to aim at lower levels of explanation. As a result, for example, intensive studies of certain places, which were initially undertaken in the pursuit of generalizable knowledge, often produced such inconsistent findings that scholars began recognizing that local context is crucial in determining the specific articulations of widespread change. In this increasing recognition, literacy historians played an important role especially in the overt debunking of "myths" that characteristically decontextualized the ability to read and write.

5. Historians of literacy have helped convince researchers to abandon the jigsaw metaphor of historical research. In this metaphor, researchers saw themselves as placing new pieces of knowledge to help complete an overall historical puzzle. During the 1960s and 1970s, the major missing pieces were seen to be the laboring or working classes, women, and minority ethnic groups, and thus literacy researchers (like their counterparts in other fields) strove to add knowledge about those who had previously been ignored by historians. Soon, however, it became clear that the "historical puzzle" was not composed of discrete pieces; indeed, the addition of each new "piece" seemed to change all the other pieces. Rather than resulting in a more complete picture of the past, research findings often raised new questions about previous conclusions. Studies of laboring groups called into question interpretations of elites. Research on women undermined earlier studies of men. And it became impossible to study minority ethnic groups without problematizing established views of the majority. In the same way, it became clear that better understandings of the history of reading and writing were rippling through many other aspects of historical interpretation. Research results were not simply additive; the jigsaw metaphor had to be abandoned.

Harvey J. Graff, Chad Gaffield, David Mitch, Anders Nilsson, David Vincent

6. Historians of literacy have moved researchers toward a greater appreciation of the different ways in which general phenomena have been articulated in specific contexts. At a macro level, literacy historians have documented the increasing ability of most people in many societies over centuries to read and write. However, this trend is not linear, consistent across time or space, or the result of similar developments in each setting. Learning (or not learning) to read and write occurred differently in different contexts and had diverse meanings for individuals in distinct settings. As a result, literacy scholars, like those studying other topics such as industrialization, now tend to perceive multiple historical paths rather than single trajectories of historical change.

7. Historians of literacy have helped push researchers to expand their chronological purview. The tendency among "new social historians" was to focus on a "modernizing" or "industrializing" period, especially the nineteenth century. Certainly, some researchers emphasized earlier settings such as colonial America or New France, but the general assumption was that the key developments took place after cities began growing rapidly, as factories were spreading, and as institutions were being established. By the 1980s, though, literacy historians were often both looking back into much earlier periods and were studying longer time periods. Their research results helped move the emphasis on urban, industrial change during key decades to a much broader conceptualization of uneven shifts in market economies linking town and country, and occurring over centuries.

8. Historians of literacy have helped expand the evidentiary foundation characteristic of scholarly research. This expansion occurred in two ways: initially, through the systematic use of a routinely generated source such as parish records and the census; and, subsequently, by the move away from primarily single-source studies to research involving disparate types of sources including those that permitted at least partial record linkage. Through the closing decades of the twentieth century, scholars tended to increase the research-intensiveness of their work at least partly in response to previous findings that emphasized the complexity of socio-historical change. In the case of literacy, researchers continued to rely on routinely generated sources, but they added a wide variety of other evidence in the pursuit of greater clarity and understanding of specific historical settings. Along with the findings of colleagues in other fields, their literacy studies demonstrated how a particular topic could be studied by way of many different sources.

9. Historians of literacy have contributed to fundamental reconceptualizations of historical topics. One prominent illustration was the widespread move from the singular to the plural in describing these top-

ics. As scholars began replacing "literacy" with "literacies," other historians started using, for example, "families" rather than "the family," and "identities" rather than "identity." A second illustration involves the shift from dichotomous thinking to continuous thinking, from either/or to "and" analyses. Rather than assuming any yes/no answers to historical questions, scholars began asking "to what extent?" in recognition of the characteristically partial quality of all associations.

10. Historians of literacy helped show how historical research could be seen to contribute to public policy debate. While all scholarship inevitably is linked to larger societal issues, both academics and decision-makers have tended to assume the dichotomy of pure and applied research. The example of literacy history suggests how this dichotomy does not describe the actual research process. As the demand for scholarly "relevance" grew stronger after the 1960s, literacy scholars became an example of how curiosity-driven research could also prove to be important to the media and to both private and public decision-makers.

Within the preceding ten examples of how literacy research contributed to key historiographical developments since the 1960s are many illustrations of the specific roles that this research has played in other fields of historical research. In other words, it should be emphasized that these examples do not imply that literacy research was limited to one of the "multiple paths" that historical research has traveled in recent decades. In fact, rather than parallel historiographical developments in different fields of socio-historical research, there has been considerable interrelationship and overlap as scholars themselves worked in different fields or as their own work was affected by research findings from other areas.

One illustration of the "horizontal" connections across scholarly subfields is the way that literacy research fueled the redefinition of educational history, and conversely, how educational historians have influenced literacy research. Most notably, perhaps, the frequent discovery of widespread literacy before compulsory school attendance encouraged educational historians to rethink the established research focus on formal schooling. As historians showed that many children and youth were learning to read and write before the introduction of mass education, educational researchers began enlarging their questions to include the history of childhood, family, institutions, and informal activities. In turn, educational historians were raising questions about the impact of formal instruction on literacy rates, such as the extent to which going to school resulted in the ability to read and write. Literacy historians thus made clear that educational change was not simply connected to the realm of formal instruction by specialists, while educational historians

Harvey J. Graff, Chad Gaffield, David Mitch, Anders Nilsson, David Vincent

showed that schooling was not consistently correlated with reading and writing.

A second illustration of the research interaction between literacy studies and other fields is provided by the stubborn question of fertility rates. Since the 1960s, researchers have documented the rise and fall of fertility rates over time and space. Their work has revealed considerable complexity behind overall changes in many societies even in the case of the so-called Western demographic transition of the later nineteenth and twentieth centuries. Historical demographers first emphasized that certain birth control efforts were well underway much earlier than previously assumed, and then they revealed how fertility declines were not always directly associated with major changes such as urban industrial development or mass schooling. The results of such research helped undermine the view that a constellation of forces interacted consistently to produce "modernity." For example, rising rates of literacy cannot be consistently correlated in a linear way with fertility declines; the ability to read and write has not always had the same meaning in terms of how individuals see themselves or their reproductive behavior. In this sense, historians of literacy research and those of historical demography have encouraged each other to move toward interpretations that address questions of context: under what conditions? in which setting? to what extent for different individuals and collectivities?

The diverse ways in which literacy research has contributed to the significant rethinking of historical change that characterized scholarly work during the closing decades of the twentieth century also point to the need for continued research on many key questions about reading and writing. One of the most urgent issues involves the roles of literacy in human development. Scholars may have successfully challenged the idea that literacy was clearly and consistently linked to any specific behavior, but some associations continue to appear so strong as to demand further attention—such as the historic and current finding that a high proportion of prison inmates are illiterate. Clearly, such strong associations are dependent on a variable host of other forces but, without reducing such complexity, literacy researchers may be able to make a special contribution to our understandings of certain institutionalized populations in terms of their human development.

Similarly, historians of literacy may be able to interact to a much greater extent with cognitive psychologists especially those who are neuroscientifically studying different methods of learning and the ways that different words are connected to different parts of the brain. By focusing on these questions, the ability to read and write becomes a central concern of the meaning of cognitive development for the ways that children grow up. The continuing need to confront the connections between literacy and human development is illustrated by Harvey Graff's major work on the history of childhood in the United States; the topic of literacy does not even appear in the index of this acclaimed book. Some of the key questions that could be addressed include the roles of literacy in influencing an individual's personal sense of power. Beyond its role as a "transactional technology," to what extent has literacy helped define an individual's perceived horizon of possibilities? How has the ability to read and write affected an individual's sense of self-expression? In what ways can we say that literacy has changed a child's sense of self and others?

Such questions are, of course, directly relevant to current public policy debate, and they point to the continuing need for literacy historians to meet the challenge of connecting their research results to nonspecialist debate. Indeed, literacy historians have failed miserably in convincing policy makers, the media, and even educators to abandon the "literacy myths" so convincingly debunked within the research community. Scholars could blame journalists, politicians, and teachers for not listening to the research findings, but a more promising approach would be for historians to develop more effective ways to communicate the central conclusions of the substantial research projects since the 1960s. At the moment, historians of literacy can indeed pride themselves on their significant role in the rethinking of historical change that occurred in recent decades; whether or not they can enhance public policy remains to be seen.

David Mitch
Retrospect and Prospect

The opportunity to consider the present and future as well as the past of an area of study provides justification for giving a relatively cursory summary of the latter. In the case of the use of social science approaches to studying the history of literacy over the last twenty-five years, one can concisely if cursorily summarize the contribution of this work by saying that it has shifted focus away from simplistic models of the causes and consequences of the rise of literacy in modern times to an appreciation of the complexity of forces at work involving literacy. The work of others on this panel, notably Harvey Graff's various works and David Vincent's recent survey, provide important examples. However, this summary position regarding the complex nature of literacy leads onto the issue of why continue to study the history of

Harvey J. Graff, Chad Gaffield, David Mitch, Anders Nilsson, David Vincent

literacy. After all, a null hypothesis of all-encompassing agnosticism, to borrow the phrase of Deirdre McCloskey, is hardly one to generate much energy or enthusiasm for pursuing a given research area, let alone garnering much grant support.

The Custodial Function of Continued Research on Literacy

However, if for no other reason, there is an important maintenance role that ongoing research into the history of literacy should contribute. Nonspecialists continue to put forward literacy as a fundamental variable in social and economic development. Daniel Lerner's work on modernization provides one important example in the dawning age of social science history. A recent example is provided by Jared Diamond's *Guns, Germs, and Steel*, a Pulitzer Prize–winning bestseller in which literacy is accorded a chapter of its own as a pivotal factor in the long-term development of the human species. And in my own field of economic history, I have been at a number of conferences just in the last year featuring papers in which literacy is assigned a key causal role in one or another process of economic development. Harvey Graff in a recent edition of his collection *Labyrinths of Literacy*, notes in his introduction that in an earlier edition, Shirley Brice Heath asserted that Graff's work should have laid to rest simplistic views regarding the primacy of literacy. Yet Graff also notes that such views continue to be expressed and by their very presence indicate that they have not been laid to rest.

A more basic maintenance task concerns cultivating and preserving a critical attitude toward the sources and evidence for the history of literacy, a concern central to the field of history in contrast to the social science side of the enterprise. Even a passing encounter with the history of literacy forces one to encounter the difficulties entailed in defining and measuring literacy. This is hardly an issue that has been solved or resolved, but ongoing work has continued to tease out new sources and measures and new perspectives on how literacy can be defined. This has entailed the discovery of alternative ways of making records, the unearthing and collation of diverse types of survey and examination evidence, and new appreciation of the complex ways in which literacy can be defined.

Such "janitorial" functions are important. Life in general becomes much less pleasant in the absence of someone to "clean up." But most historians, both social science and otherwise, aspire to be more than intellectual street sweepers.

The Future of the History of Literacy

Two important directions for further advances in the history of literacy come to mind. One concerns examining the role of local cultures and social communications networks. This should be done without getting enmeshed in too much particularism or too parochial a perspective.

a. This is required because of the complexity of the forces involved affecting literacy. Both individual-level and societal-level factors have an influence. Personal incentives to acquire literacy include impacts on employability, uses in economic transactions, and the desire to read texts for motives ranging from prurient entertainment to religious salvation. Parents, children, and adults seeking self-improvement guided by these personal motivations would have interacted with community and national-level agencies engaged in the provision of instruction, schooling, and related educational resources.

b. These factors interact at the local level. These interactions provide distinctive challenges for the practice of social science history. Previous practices of quantification, even as total history or collection of individual autobiographies, do not capture the interactions involving small groups of participants that influenced the development and practice of literacy at the local level.

c. The tools of the anthropologist and ethnographer requiring detailed description of individual interactions in local societies, as reflected in the development of the Culture Network in SSHA, provides one resource for pursuing this aspect.

The real million-dollar question with regard to the social and economic consequences of literacy is whether the acquisition of literacy changes the way people think. This question goes beyond whether literacy facilitates specific communications transactions to the more general issue of whether it changes general cognitive functioning. A central problem here is that social science history does not have much of a tradition of drawing on models from cognitive science and psychology. It is problematic whether psychology can be an historical social science given what it tends to presume about the constancy of human nature

and the human mind over time. The obvious recent exception to that has
been the boom of activity in the field of evolutionary psychology. But
this latter refers to a development over a much longer run in terms of
hundreds of centuries rather than the hundreds of years that is common
in SSHA. Would a new SSHA network in cognitive science and psychology be feasible?

In concluding, one can point to one example of a scholar who did
manage to blend the various concerns I have mentioned here in his work
on the history of literacy. Edward Stevens first made his mark in the field
with a landmark quantitative study of literacy in the United States with
coauthor Lee Soltow. He went on to pursue imaginative and creative
themes in his work on literacy and the law, and his notion of design literacy. His death a few years ago is certainly a major loss to the field but
his example also points the way forward. His approach to life and scholarship is exemplified by what I was told by one of his colleagues at Ohio
University: that he departed this world while sitting in his living room
reading a book. There can be few better ways for the serious historian of
literacy to go.

Anders Nilsson
Introduction

In 1969 Carlo Cipolla published a book that, although
small in format, came to exert a huge influence on our understanding of
the historical development of literacy in the nineteenth century. I refer,
of course, to *Literacy and Development in the West*. Cipolla demonstrated
that countries where high literacy levels prevailed in the nineteenth century experienced high rates of economic growth, and he suggested a
chain of causation: literacy approximated human capital, which was put
to productive use, hence high rates of economic growth.

Considerable progress has been made since the late 1960s as far as
measurement of historical economic growth is concerned. Angus Mad-
dison has published a series of, among other things, GDP estimates for
a large number of countries, which, in many cases, stretch back to the
early or mid-nineteenth century. Alternative estimates that try to take
purchasing power parity into account have been made by Leandros Pra-
dos. For a few countries there even exist historical national accounts,
which allow for more detailed research on disaggregated data. Thus,
empirical possibilities for much more sophisticated studies on the complex relationship between education, literacy, human capital, and long-
run economic growth are available. Unfortunately, much less effort has

been made to achieve good and internationally comparable measurements of literacy.

Theoretical Perspectives on the Use of Literacy as a Proxy for Human Capital

To a certain degree, the relative failure is due to differing interpretations of literacy as a form of human capital. Over the years, at least three approaches are discernible. In the first, literacy is considered as a—perhaps incomplete but nevertheless satisfactory—approximation of human capital in general, and the variable is treated analogous with physical capital. The concept is not problematized but taken more or less for granted. A common approach is to include human capital among other variables in growth equations and thus to estimate how much human capital has contributed to economic growth.

In the second approach, the equality between literacy and human capital is put in question. The proponents of the second approach—in Gabriel Tortella's terminology, "the reductionists"—maintain that it is necessary to demonstrate that literacy was put to productive use one way or the other. In particular, it has been questioned to what extent literacy was an asset in economic terms in traditional agriculture or during the early phases of industrialization in the late eighteenth and throughout the nineteenth century. The critics point out that there was little or no complementarity between the ability to read and write and the everyday doings in agriculture, such as plowing, sowing, and harvesting. There was also a very low degree of complementarity between the formation of physical capital and human capital. Practically all physical capital in agriculture was created by the use of manual, "raw" labor in, for example, digging ditches, building fences, raising barns, and so on (Sandberg 1982). A very limited number of literate people (a parson, notary, or ex-soldier) were sufficient to cope with the rare occasions when literacy was required, above all in contacts with officials of various kinds. Even in the most industrialized country in the nineteenth century, the United Kingdom, there existed a large number of occupations in which literacy was not an asset. Toward the end of the century, in 1891, 25 percent of the women and 37 percent of the men were engaged in occupations where literacy was unlikely to be useful (Mitch 1992).

The third approach is to regard literacy as a transaction technology, that is, literacy is considered, above all, as a device that helps to diminish transaction costs. The conception that transaction (as opposed to

Harvey J. Graff, Chad Gaffield, David Mitch, Anders Nilsson, David Vincent

production) costs are important has received renewed attention within neo-institutional theory, but it has in a less strict sense been present for a very long time. According to an accepted but not very precise definition, transaction costs consist of arranging a contract *ex ante* and monitoring and enforcing it *ex post* (Eggertsson 1990). Contracts can, of course, be oral as well as written, and being illiterate is not an insurmountable obstacle to engaging in various economic transactions. In many cases, it may not be an obstacle at all. The proponents of the third approach emphasize, however, that conditions changed markedly in connection with the transformation of agriculture in Europe from the mid- to late eighteenth century onward. Transformation included bureaucratic processes, above all in the redistribution of land in enclosure-like processes, increased market integration, information on new crops and farming techniques, and an increasing reliance on distant relationships in, for instance, credit facilities. In all these aspects literacy was an asset that permitted easier access to more reliable sources of information, enabled the literate person to verify exact wordings in contracts and agreements, and facilitated contacts with officials. It is also likely that by becoming literate, a person's perception of the world changed. In other words, the concept of literacy as a transaction technology not only implies that transaction costs were lowered to the literate, it also made him or her aware of new transaction possibilities.

Empirical Perspective—Measurements of Literacy

The early work by Cipolla (and others) stimulated research in several countries for measurements of literacy. A well-known study by Roger Schofield (published in 1973) exploited the existence of signatures of the spouses in marriage registers. Since then extensive use has been made of archives containing signatures. The measure has become *the* indicator of literacy. In the words of Schofield: "It is a universal, standard and direct measure." The approach raises two crucial questions—what do signatures signify in terms of literacy and in terms of human capital.

The basic problem stems from the fact that whereas literacy is a continuous variable, measures tend to become dichotomous. There is a world of difference in the potential use of the literacy of a person who laboriously forms the letters of his/her name and of a fluent reader and writer. In historical research, however, it is often not possible to distinguish between them. They would (probably) both be classified as "literate," in contrast to people who could neither read nor write, even though the difference between the "illiterates" and the person who laboriously forms the letters of his/her name could be negligible. Access to different sources could possibly change the classification of the first person, but that would not solve the basic problem. Any dichotomization of the literacy variable will be arbitrary. The arbitrariness becomes even more obvious in multilinguistic societies. István Toth has presented evidence from Hungary, where Latin was the official language until 1844 and where three, four, and perhaps even five different languages were in use in a single district. Here, the question of literacy relates not only to the degree of literacy but also to which language literacy refers to and what context literacy should be related to.

In international research signatures have, in spite of the various objections that could be raised, been accepted as a reasonable approximation of literacy. One important reason is that signatures are frequent in different source material and sometimes the only available indicator of literacy. It has also been widely accepted that signatures capture an ability between reading ability (only) and writing (and reading) ability. It is seldom noted, however, that this characterization is dependant on time and place. In eighteenth- and nineteenth-century Western Europe, children were taught to read and write in schools. In other parts of Europe, notably Scandinavia, most children were taught only to read, and only a minority of those proceeded with writing instruction. To what extent these children were able to read unknown texts or if they simply were able to recite well-known passages from the catechism is difficult to say. Undoubtedly, many of them were beyond the "reciting stage," but the percentage is totally unknown. Further, it is not possible to draw any conclusions of the extent of any writing ability from that material alone. Markings on reading ability in parish catechetical examination records is a different measurement of literacy than signatures, and they imply a different level of literacy. In consequence, the two measurements could also indicate different human capital.

It is an important research task to refine concepts and measurements of the different levels of literacy in the nineteenth century. New material and, above all, a better understanding of different levels or dimensions of literacy would form the basis for such a refinement. In addition, better use could be made of the different measurements or approximations that do exist. Rather than assuming that signatures, markings on reading (or writing) ability, notations in immigration records, and censuses all refer to the dichotomization literate/illiterate, each material could be assessed in terms of the degree of literacy it captures. Eventually, it seems possible to combine results from different studies to form some sort of a literacy index that would capture the different levels of literacy and, perhaps, provide researchers with a better approximation of human capital in the eighteenth and nineteenth centuries.

David Vincent
The Post

We can date the beginning of the era of mass literacy quite precisely. In 1874 the Treaty of Berne was signed, which led to the creation the following year of the Universal Postal Union (UPU).[1] The inhabitants of every country in Europe, together with Egypt and North America, were to be linked together in a common system of flat-rate postage, irrespective of geography or national boundary.[2] Manufacturer would be connected to customer, parent to child, lover to distant lover, through their common ability to read and to use a pen. For the local equivalent of a twenty-five centime stamp, thoughts, feelings, and information would be rapidly and securely conveyed along the dramatically improving communication networks of the modernizing world. In the words of the UPU's new journal, "there is scarcely a single individual, however wretched, in any civilized country who has not, at least once in his life, been put in communication with his fellow creatures by means of the post" (Universal Postal Union 1877, 16). The achievement was celebrated by contemporary commentators. As *The Times* wrote on 15 August 1891, "It is a literal truth that the Postal Union not only corresponds with the most advanced humanitarian spirit of the times, but is itself the most practical realization which human ingenuity has yet achieved of those floating aspirations towards universal brotherhood, regarded generally as of the nature of dreams, however decorative of the pages of poetic literature."[3]

In a way the UPU defines the dilemma that we now face. On the one hand, it was an event of genuine and still largely neglected importance. Together with the International Telegraph Union founded ten years earlier, it may be said to mark the beginning of global mass communication. It is not altogether surprising that its early history provoked such excitable rhetoric. But on the other hand, it was merely one more vehicle for the inflated claims for the potential of literacy, which have been so characteristic of the modern era. These claims are obvious targets. The little we know about correspondence suggests that in 1875 and for at least a couple of decades to come, letter writing was mainly confined to those with money to make and money to spend (Vincent 1989, 49). And as for the universal brotherhood, we have merely to note that the growth in European correspondence from three to twenty-five billion items a year between 1875 and 1913 did nothing to prevent the continent tearing itself apart thereafter. Only Switzerland, now established as the bureaucratic center of the world, escaped the coming conflict.

The Iconoclasts

The emergence of literacy as a discrete category of study in the sixties and seventies was fuelled by two perceptions: first, that this was a form of historical behavior that could be subjected to wide-scale, long-run quantification; second, that the move from an oral to a print culture had a transformative effect on individuals and societies. It was not long, however, before these convictions came into conflict. As the counting work became more sophisticated, the conversion claims appeared increasingly crude.

Harvey Graff's *Literacy Myth* of 1979 constituted a particularly effective demolition charge. His study, which was based on the 1861 Canadian census, attacked the generalized claims for literacy, especially in respect to the children who were beginning to spend increasing years locked up inside the classroom. The effect of their lessons had to be discovered in their later encounters with the patterns of class, ethnicity, and gender that would dominate their lives. Possession of the skills of reading and writing had no meaning outside the contexts in which they could be used. There was no necessary benefit from gaining a command of the written word, and a close examination of the economy of mid-nineteenth-century Hamilton, Ontario, suggested that there was no necessary loss in remaining illiterate. Literacy did not dissolve structural inequalities. While some men and fewer women might be launched into lives of intellectual discovery and occupational advance, "on the basic level of social and economic progress and those who determined it," as Graff wrote, "literacy was more valuable to the society's goals and needs than to those of most individuals within it" (1979, 33).

At the center of this critique, and that of other studies that followed it, was the assumed dichotomy between the spoken and the written. The notion of a discrete oral tradition became increasingly untenable, particularly as the qualitative techniques for studying literacy became more sophisticated. The concept of a folk culture defined by the absence of print was undermined, so also was that of a popular culture constituted by the absence of control over the means of production (Davis 1977, 9–12; Rose 1992, 58; Gildea 1976, 228). One by one the historiographical foundation stones were demolished. Roger Chartier stressed that there could be no necessary relationship between the printed word and the basic social or economic structures in which the literate lived and worked (1994, 7–16). The boundaries of cultural practice could not be determined by class or occupational status. It was argued that the notion of a distinct mass culture constituted by the capitalist production of consumer goods obscured more than it illuminated (Waites et al. 1982, 15).

The emphasis in the analysis of cultural practice moved from structure to flow. In the world from which the elementary schools took their pupils, poverty was never a passive condition. The less the command of material goods, the greater the impetus to borrow, share, and invent (Hall 1984, 5–14; Anderson 1991, 7). All forms of consumption depended on improvisation. Where outright ownership was difficult, other devices would be found to meet expanding demand. Possession became easier as innovations in production, distribution, and marketing brought down the cost of print, but appetite always outran the capacity to satisfy it. The traditional categories of print were everywhere subverted by the undisciplined energy of the newly literate. As with their stomachs, so with their minds poor readers were, to use de Certeau's term, life-long poachers (de Certeau 1998).

It remains necessary to count. Tables of signatures and postal flows, of print runs and prices, need to be calculated, but such activity supplies only the starting point for an analysis of what was read and written, by whom and with what effect. "Like writing," observed Daniel Roche, "reading is an act of mediation susceptible to infinite modulations, and nothing in notarial records tells us how to distinguish between fluent reading which presupposes the regular handling of books, the irregular, infrequent deciphering of print often linked with pictures, or reading aloud, shared among several people, which may have been an act of friendship, even love, or sociability" (1987, 215). The indeterminate nature of the use of literacy was captured by the notion of appropriation, which referred both to the annexation of objects and practices, and also to the derivation of meanings from the printed word (Chartier 1984, 2–35).

Life amid the Ruins

So as we stand amid the rubble of shattered images, what is the agenda for the third generation of literacy scholars? One answer is, in a sense, to return literacy to its original home. Before they emerged as discrete topics of study in the 1960s, reading and writing were seen as dependent factors in a range of cultural and material histories. Having undertaken the necessary task of theoretical, conceptual, and technical clarification, we can reinsert literacy into a diverse body of contextual histories deploying a wide variety of methodologies drawn from right across the humanities and social sciences (Graff 1995, 306). In my own recent work it has been an integral element in research on social mobility, the classroom, and privacy and secrecy, and the list can be extended almost without limit.

There are, however, a number of reasons for retaining literacy as an historical problem in its own right. The first of these has more to do with the present than the past. Much of the energy of Graff's *Literacy Myth* was derived from an engagement with the educational policies of the late 1970s. The book argued, with every justification, that the expectations invested in the contemporary school system required critical interrogation by historians as much as by other social scientists. And it has to be said that however great the impact of his work and that of other scholars of the 1980s and 1990s on the discipline of history, its effect on politicians and administrators appears negligible. The modern world keeps returning to literacy, reinventing the myths, and embodying them in yet more powerful institutional forms that are having profound effects on new generations of children, parents, and teachers. In Britain, the current government has introduced a new "National Literacy Strategy" that has led to the imposition of the so-called "Literacy Hour" in primary schools, a compulsory daily lesson, foregrounding basic skills and traditional methods at the expense of most of the rest of the curriculum in a move strongly reminiscent of the Revised Code of 1861. If history is to perform one of its key functions of interrogating the presentness of the present, then it is simply not permitted to abandon the critical study of literacy. An earlier onslaught by the governments of the early nineties devastated the history of education as a subdiscipline, erasing the subject from teacher-training programs and closing down posts across the university system. The new cohorts of schoolteachers know less about the past of their profession than any since the early nineteenth century, and their political masters care less. It has never been more necessary or more urgent to address the basic issue of what has happened in the classroom as children have been exposed to the rudiments of reading and writing.[4]

A second reason for retaining the topic is the sheer wealth of the material that has now been located and refined. We must of course retain a sharply critical stance toward transnational generalizations, toward the technical limitations of the quantitative data that inform them, and toward the monochromatic modernization theories, which so often drive them. But in the imperfect world that historians inhabit, where consistent data time-series rarely exist within, let alone across, national boundaries, we are in danger of losing sight of the untapped potential of literacy as a source for long-term comparative analysis. The point can be made by the Universal Postal Union. Correspondence fulfills the role demanded by so many scholars of constituting a measure not just of the possession but also of the use of literacy. From 1875 onward the tireless statisticians in Berne published detailed and largely consistent tables of postal flows, up to 1930, listing the per capita correspondence of what rapidly became the great majority of the world's population (Vincent 2000, 3–4). Categories of mail were separated, revealing, for instance, the early use by commercial firms of what we would now term junk mail. Modes of transport were specified, thus permitting a comparative analysis of the changing deployment of roads, trains, and water. And for the truly obsessive, it was possible to count the number of post-boxes per head of population from Austria to Vietnam. In the pursuit of comparative history, particularly as regards the interpenetration of the economic, political, and cultural spheres, the study of literacy retains a privileged position, and one that it should not readily vacate.

A third reason for retaining literacy as a broad, interdisciplinary topic of study in its own right stems from the consequences of the linguistic turn, which at one level has served to complete the iconoclastic work set in motion by the quantifiers. This has stressed that what the newly literate thought they were doing as they took up a book or a pen was not determined by the purposes designated by authors and educators. The iterations between the inscribed and prescribed significance of using literacy can be recaptured only by a patient historical identification of contexts and responses. This approach has been one of the means by which literacy has been reconstituted as an integral element of other subdisciplines, including the rapidly expanding "history of the book."

However, as the old dichotomies are reduced to ideological constructions, there remain problems of scope and causation. The diminishing emphasis on the determining role of class and other structures of inequality has reflected a growing preoccupation with certain aspects of the uses of literacy. The most striking recent work has focused on texts and how they were consumed. It has been alert to the ways in which material pressures shaped and constrained the formation of meanings and practices. There has been less concern with the reverse process, the ways in which ideologies of literacy may have influenced the development of basic structures of authority. "Too often," observed Bob Scribner, "the material conditions and the relationships that constitute the basis of human subsistence, have been ignored, possibly because they appear too mundane or perhaps for fear of falling into a reductive materialism"(1989, 181). There are dangers—not just in the implicit economic determinism of earlier treatments of popular culture but also in the conviction of many Victorian educators—that the world of books could constitute a protected sphere in which rich and poor could meet as equals.[5] The effort has to be made to understand the full range of interactions between literacy and the structural inequalities of Victorian capitalism, and in particular to clarify whether the relative autonomy of the meanings of literacy varied over time. The dissemination of mass literacy cannot be separated from the way in which ideological constructions of mass communication were entrenched in systems for reproducing the labor force. As Richard Biernacki has argued of this era, "culture exercised an influence *of its own* but not completely *by itself*. The power of culture arose from its inscription in material practice" (1997, 34–35).

The tendency for literacy to be reabsorbed into distinct disciplinary contexts needs to be countered by a continuing engagement with the breadth of issues implicated in the process of learning and using the skills of reading and writing. If we take the post as an example, we are faced with the most intense and protean form of communication, whose multiple possibilities for using and misusing written language have yet fully to be charted. The postcard for instance, which was the first truly popular form of correspondence, is only beginning to receive serious treatment.[6] We also have a complex transport history, an economic history of costs and of the internationalization of market transactions that fuelled much of the early expansion; we have a political history of the growth of national and international bureaucracy and regulation; we have a history of time as it became available to some sections of society and later to others; we have a history of privacy as sealing and opening the envelope became a prized extension of personal autonomy; and we have a history of secrecy as governments sought to interfere in the free flow of mail. All of these matters can be studied separately, but the challenge remains of fitting these histories together. The task is one of resisting the reductionism of engaging exclusively either with the material inequalities that shaped and were in turn reinforced by the use of the pen, or with the unpredictable outpourings of fact and imagination carried by the postman.

Historians of literacy must treat with equal respect the forces of anarchism and inertia inherent in the spread of written communication. Always there are children and parents subverting the intentions of the official curriculum, always there are readers taking ungovernable meanings from texts. Yet, as Harvey Graff argued twenty years ago, and the better studies have since confirmed, what so often emerges from analysis of mass literacy is the inability of the newly educated readers and

Harvey J. Graff, Chad Gaffield, David Mitch, Anders Nilsson, David Vincent

writers to use their skills to penetrate or dissolve the structures of material and social privilege. The only generalization to survive unscathed the era of iconoclasm has been a negative one, the widespread sense of waste and loss as generations of schoolchildren were equipped with tools of written communication too blunt to make an impression on the structures of inequality into which they were born.

NOTES

1. The organization was termed the General Postal Union at its foundation, but was renamed the Universal Postal Union at a second congress in Paris in 1878, and has retained this name to the present day (the official title was usually rendered in French—L'Union Générale des Postes, L'Union Postale Universelle).

2. Standard accounts of the organization are given in Codding 1964 and Menon 1965. On its foundation, see *A Brief Account of the Formation of the Universal Postal Union, Its Gradual Extension to the Various parts of the British Empire and the Reasons which have hitherto Deterred the Australasian and South African Colonies from Joining the Union* (London, 1886), 3–5, available at the Post Office Archive, POST 29/519, 326R/1891; "The History and Constitution of the Postal Union," *Times*, 15 August 1891; Baines 1895, 2: 159–60; Bennett 1912, 223–27; Robinson 1953, 190–91; Daunton 1985, 159–60.

3. On the contemporary association of the UPU with civilization, see Menon 1965, 3.

4. For a pioneering approach to this issue, see Grosvenor et al. 1999.

5. See, for instance, Craik 1830–31, 1: 418.

6. See Philips 2000.

REFERENCE LIST

A brief account of the formation of the Universal Postal Union, its gradual extension to the various parts of the British Empire and the reasons which have hitherto deterred the Australasian and South African colonies from joining the Union. London, 1886: 3–5, Post Office Archive, POST 29/519, 326R/1891.

Anderson, P. 1991. *The printed image and the transformation of popular culture 1790–1860.* Oxford: Clarendon Press.

Baines, F. E. 1895. *Forty years at the post office.* Vol. 2. London: R. Bentley & Son.

Bennett, E. 1912. *The post office and its story.* London: Seeley, Service & Co. Ltd.

Biernacki, R. 1997. *The fabrication of labour: Germany and Britain, 1640–1914.* Berkeley: University of California Press.

Chartier, R. 1984. Culture as appropriation: Popular cultural uses in early modern France. In *Understanding popular culture: Europe from the Middle Ages to the nineteenth century,* edited by Steven L. Kaplan. Berlin: Mouton.

———. 1994. *The order of books.* Cambridge, U.K.: Polity Press.

Codding, G. A. 1964. *The Universal Postal Union.* New York: New York University Press.

Craik, G. L. 1830–31. *The pursuit of knowledge under difficulties.* Vol. 1. London: C. Knight.

Daunton, M. J. 1985. *Royal mail.* London; Dover, N.H.: Athlone Press.

Davis, N. Z. 1977. The historian and popular culture. In *The wolf and the lamb: Popular culture in France from the Old Regime to the twentieth century,* edited by Jacques Beauroy, Marc Bertrand, and Edward T. Gargan. Saratoga, Calif.: Anma Libri.

de Certeau, M. 1998. *The practice of everyday life.* Berkeley: University of California Press.

Eggertsson, T. 1990. *Economic behavior and institutions.* Cambridge: Cambridge University Press.

Gildea, R. 1976. Education in nineteenth-century Brittany: Ille-et-Vilaine, 1800–1914. *Oxford Review of Education* 3 (2): 215–30.

Graff, H. J. 1979. *The literacy myth.* London: Academic Press.

———. 1995. *The labyrinths of literacy. Reflections on literacy past and present.* Rev. ed. Pittsburgh: Pittsburgh University Press.

Grosvenor, I., M. Lawn, and K. Rousmaniere, eds. 1999. *Silences and images: The social history of the classroom.* New York: P. Lang.

Hall, D. 1984. Introduction to *Understanding popular culture: Europe from the Middle Ages to the nineteenth century,* edited by Steven L. Kaplan. Berlin: Mouton.

Menon, M. A. K. 1965. *Universal Postal Union.* New York: Carnegie Endowment for International Peace.

Mitch, D. 1992. *The rise of popular literacy in Victorian England: The influence of private choice and public policy.* Philadelphia: University of Pennsylvania Press.

Philips, T. 2000. *The postcard century.* London: Thames and Hudson.

Robinson, H. 1953. *Britain's post office.* Oxford: Oxford University Press.

Roche, D. 1987. *The people of Paris.* Leamington Spa: Berg.

Rose, J. 1992. Rereading the English common reader: A preface to a history of audiences. *Journal of the History of Ideas* 53: 57–70.

Sandberg, Lars. 1982. The case of the impoverished sophisticate: Human capital and Swedish economic growth before World War I. *Journal of Economic History* 3: 225–41.

Schofield, R. 1973. Dimensions of illiteracy, 1750–1850. *Explorations in Economic History* 10: 437–54.

Scribner, R. W. 1989. Is a history of popular culture possible? *History of European Ideas* 10 (2): 175–91.

Universal Postal Union (UPU). 1877. Editorial comment. *Union Postale* 2 (January 1877): 16.

Vincent, D. 1989. *Literacy and popular culture: England 1750–1914.* Cambridge: Cambridge University Press.

———. 2000. *The rise of mass literacy. Reading and writing in modern Europe.* Cambridge, U.K.: Polity Press.

Waites, B., T. Bennett, and G. Martin, eds. 1982. *Popular culture: Past and present.* London: Croom Helm in association with the Open University Press.

Part Four

THE FUTURE OF

SOCIAL SCIENCE HISTORY

Within the context of the twenty-fifth anniversary theme of Looking Backward and Looking Forward, President Graff solicited special presidential panels anticipating future trajectories. In this spirit, two panels dedicated to expanding horizons were organized. The first, "Southern Perspectives on Historical Social Science," introduced some prominent postcolonial scholars and work that potentially "decenters" the normally European traditions that inform historical social science. This means not so much privileging voices from the global south, rather giving voice to research that challenges the conceptual apparatus of historical social science and presents new kinds of questions. Akhil Gupta interrogates the fashion of "globalization" studies by inverting perspective, subverting the conventions of the historical question of "why Europe?" and arguing for a more reflexive understanding of the colonial encounter. Fernando Coronil reconstructs the discourse of "globalization" around questions of difference (versus the universalizing themes associated with European expansion), suggesting that movements against global centralism will succeed to the extent that they reassert cultural difference. And Farshad Araghi identifies the vulnerability of the current form of globalism in its fundamentally exclusionary dynamic that undercuts the formation of a hegemonic ideology.

The second panel, "New Directions in Historical Social Science," brought together three scholars concerned with overcoming methodological limits in historical social scientific research. Thus Ann Stoler looks for convergences or commensurability between hitherto distinct historiographies of European and U.S. colonization projects in the management of race relations. Dale Tomich confronts the question of comparability, arguing for a historical method that collapses global/local, and universal/particular, dichotomies into mutually conditioning relationships. And Richard Biernacki, noting the recent overthrow of abstracted linear conceptions of time, argues for a similar transcendence of abstract notions of space by privileging place in historical investigation. Biernacki's paper is reproduced in full here, while the other papers (and discussion) are summarized from the session transcripts to provide the flavor of these special panels.

THE EVENT OF PLACE IN

HISTORICAL SOCIOLOGY

RICHARD BIERNACKI

For more than two decades now, historical investigators in the social sciences have endeavored to "unthink" the premises of the classical social theory they inherited from eighteenth- and nineteenth-century Europe (Wallerstein 1988, 185–91; Tilly 1987, 70–86). In their great house-cleaning, historians and sociologists have overturned the primary units of analysis, the substance of explanation, and the ground rules of temporality. They have jettisoned the nation-state as a self-evident unit of analysis; in its stead, they take as their basic units the webs of communication and social exchange that span local or global regions (Tilly 1988, 709). They have also dislodged the socio-economic setting as the pre-given foundation of development; in its stead, they examine figures of meaning and cultural legitimation that denominate periods in their own right. They have tried to divest themselves of the belief that time flows as a teleological unfolding of potentials, as had once been supposed by such grand theorists as Tocqueville and Marx.[1] My purpose here is to unshroud the career of an equally important supposition of classical social theory that has remained almost untouched—the treatment of spatial relations with the concept of "abstract space."

Encountering Space and Place

The concept of "abstract space" organized the key changes in the interpretation of evidence through which the social sciences took shape in the eighteenth century. The philosopher Alfred North Whitehead identified abstract space with a static, pre-given platform for process or action. It is featureless and purely extensional; it separates container from contained; and it defines an arena apart from its occupation by an embodied agent (Whitehead 1927, 67, 70–71, 74).[2] Mary Poovey has gone on to show more recently how administrative and intellectual elites used this kind of space to elucidate the movement of citizens in towns and of workers in factories. In the eighteenth century these new experts treated the scene of action as "isotropic (as everywhere the same) and as reducible (or already reduced) to a formal (that is, empty) schema or grid" (Poovey 1995, 17, 29). The concept helped theorists such as Smith, Marx, Durkheim, and Simmel construct an open, de-historicized platform for action; formalize basic "unit acts" of social interchange; and seal off the boundaries of interchange so that a system could cohere in a closed arena. Once abstract space was embedded in classical theory, it was naturalized by social scientists as an actuality rather than treated as a conventional "seeing as." It supported the notion of an autonomous domain of social exchange and indeed shaped the definition of knowledge itself. Yet as I will proceed to show, abstract space inevitably leads researchers to disturbingly faulty empirical results when they move from treating it as a mere metaphor to part of the essence of social processes.

A new constellation of historical analysts of cultural practice has initiated a momentous challenge to abstract space's primacy and verisimilitude by figuring spatial relations with the alternative concept of "place"—in brief, the configuration of the concrete setting to which we orient our bodies. These historical investigators of practice in place have set a unique emphasis on discerning the implicit assumptions that are built into agents' ways of using their spatial environments.[3] The keynote works of John Bender (1987), Norbert Elias (1969, esp. 68–101), Bill Hillier (1996), Patrick Joyce (forthcoming), Chandra Mukerji (1997), and Steven Shapin and Simon Schaffler (1985) hint at the disciplinary breadth of this shift to studies of culture as activities in place.[4] These historical investigators have revealed the spatial determinations of the self and literature; the rise of the modern state as an artifact of physical engineering as much as of social organization; and the dependencies of scientific knowledge on unique sites for using instruments and for witnessing the results. Even when they take "place" as a relatively small unit of observation, these researchers examine as well how local practices crystallize political-economic processes that have potentially larger spatial jurisdictions. "Not all social associations or forms of integration of people entail residential or habitation structures," Norbert Elias wrote in *Court Society*. "But they are all characterizable through particular kinds of spatial configuration" (1969, 70).

As opposed to abstract, geometrical space, the counter term "place" usefully marks the concept of spatial relations in the life-world that investigators are currently reclaiming after its eclipse in the early modern era (Casey 1997, 133–35).[5] With "place" the layout of relations is defined with respect to agents who are not located at a point in a grid, but who compose a setting and occupy it through the corporeal practices by which they relate their bodies to the environment. Lest this introductory declaration sound merely *au courant*, it is worth returning to the contrasts between space and place that the astringent academician Immanuel Kant hammered out. The specification of place in contrast to space was still at issue at the end of the eighteenth century among philosophers who were not wedded exclusively to the natural sciences. For example, Kant's essay of 1768 on how we orient ourselves to regions outside ourselves hearkens backward to premodern approaches to the spatial as well as forward to present-day concerns (Kant 1963a, 1:993–1000).[6] Kant viewed the categories of space and pure extension as intrinsic to the human mind, of course.[7] But having a sense of extension is very different from orienting oneself and other things in a setting. In contrast to abstract space's construction by the mind, the palpable regions of our human world, Kant said, were not just reliant upon our physical constitution, but logically organized by the order of our bodies. Perceptible regions ("over here" and "over there") and direction (up, forward, across) are conceivable and definable in practice based only on the prior orientation that the bilateral makeup of our body provides (Lakoff and Johnson 1999, 30–31, 34–35).[8] He reasoned that we can position for our mind a representation of "here" and "there," such as that of a map, only if we in some way "grasp" it in relation to our right and left hands or our front and back (Kant 1963a, 996). "Our most taken-for-granted knowledge of the position of places," Kant wrote in 1768, "would be of no help to us, unless we could also orientate the things thus ordered, as well as the entire system of their reciprocal positions, by arranging them as regions in relation to the sides of our body" (1963a, 996).[9] Sixteen years later Kant returned to the theme of spatial orientation in the world (seeking to develop analogies with the use of a spatial map to understand how we locate our selves in relation to our own thoughts). For spatial orientation, Kant said, "I entirely need the *feeling* of a difference on my own constitution, particularly of the right and left hand. I call it a feeling, because externally these two sides reveal on inspection no visible difference" (Kant 1963b). We cannot orient ourselves by intellectually interpreting our body as a marker, but have to begin by sensing its (or "our") relation to the setting (Smith 2000, 133–34). It is stunning that the cerebral Kant, who preferred to imagine we govern conduct by self-application of stringent rules, found through his analysis of place that our orientation, a premise of judgment and action, is granted by a "feeling." At this key moment in the exploration of how people "grasp" signs or maps for action—in brief, with the sighting of pragmatics—Kant called on the body and its emplacement.[10]

Kant has prepared us for appreciating how recent studies of the sites of cultural practice invoke a fundamentally different model of the spatial, not just one that is "micro" in its mensural scale. With place, the elements of the setting are made up of components of human practice: the dividers, apertures, connections, or protrusions of buildings and landscapes. This qualitative, historically specific configuration has a systematic relation to the bodies of the agents who participate in the creation of that place and whose actions extend through time. Whereas space designates extension, the concept of place signals the making of a relational process.[11]

Let me proceed now in three steps. First, I will review how the concept of abstract space constituted the theories of social relations in the eighteenth century and how it was carried into classical social theory. This is preparatory to showing how taking this category as a natural given leads to serious missteps in the interpretation of evidence and in how we warrant our knowledge as scientific. Finally, I sketch the promise of recent studies that emphasize how our practices and our knowledge take shape in place.

The Space of Modern "Social Relations"

We can trace three operations by which the uniquely modern experience of abstract space structured the classical theories of "social relations." First, theorists of eighteenth-century Britain and France reduced the practices that unfold through concrete sites of the life-world into generic "unit acts" that are merely formal and relational, and that are therefore inserted into space by what Whitehead termed "simple location" in a plane or shared arena.[12] Since the "unit acts" are not embedded in space by their material and corporeal features, they are rendered independent of the topography of any place (and therefore do not unfold processually in experience). By reducing practice to the *form* of communicative and commercial exchange, agents operate as intellectual mediators rather than as embodied persons whose actions unfold through occupying place. Smith, for example, takes the exchange of labor as the unit act and even reduces production itself to just a figure of exchange, that of labor for vendable goods (Smith 1976, 1:41, 112). He detaches the asset of "labor" from physical executions, because he recasts it as an unobservable, homogeneous element whose quantity is defined relationally, through circulation among networks of purveyors.[13] The labor metric of value establishes a purely human substance of exchange, independent of the contributions of nature and landscape.

Although we are inclined in our day to treat economists as purveyors of a theory of individual utilitarianism that depreciates the power of "social" relations, the eighteenth-century economists defended the autonomy of social relations in abstract space.[14] By installing socially interdependent labor as the regulator of development, Smith and the classical economists who followed him secured a pure social space of relations between producers detached from their relations to corporeal nature and place.[15] Smith's fashioning of labor and capital as entities of exchange presages a strategy among sociologists in our day, the incessant rediscovery of different kinds of cultural and social "capital" (Portes 1998, 1–24; Saint Martin 1989). The intellectual seed of this proliferation is that people's holdings have no stature by virtue of use in "place," only by institutional, human relations in space.[16] "Values are social commodities that have no significance of their own, but, like other commodities, exist only in the ever-changing relativity of social linkages and commerce," Hannah Arendt observed remorsefully (1963, 32). For Arendt, this historically novel kind of relational thinking signaled the melancholy "birth of the social sciences" (1963, 33).

In sum, the first move of the eighteenth-century inventors of "social relations" was to situate agents by ties of exchange in abstract space rather than by temporally unfolding practice at a place (Smith 1976, 1:1, 105). The altered horizon in popular consciousness to which these commentators lent expression is indicated by the evolving meaning of the term "market" in English. Through the early modern period, it designated a restricted locus in space and time, the square where bargainers met for designated hours or days as they used tumbril and weighing beam for trade (Markus 1993, 301). "Market" in the eighteenth century came to refer to an abstract foundation as the "basis" of observable action. Like the space it inhabited, it linked everyone, but it was implanted nowhere in particular (Agnew 1986, 55). In our day, the association of the market with the empty space in which we breath is unambiguous. "Euclidean space stands for the market, it is the framework in which interactions take place," an article in the senior journal of sociology in the Unites States recently declared, as if to state the obvious. "We model our entities as spatial objects with certain geometric properties that stand for sociological attributes" (Péli and Nooteboom 1999, 1133).

The second operation for which social theorists required the notion of abstract social space was that of imagining agents connecting to each other in an empty, transparent medium.[17] Since the synchronic relations among agents in theories of the social are formal and quantitative, such a blank platform is convenient for imagining how every unit act touches systematically upon all others. Space becomes a superficial conduit of exchange rather than a substantial, corporeal "place" for practice.[18] When social commentators in the eighteenth century began to assemble their new vision of networks of exchange, they disowned prior models of economic and social intercourse that had followed these contours of place and landscape. For example, the French economist Cantillon had focused on transportation routes in his country as the arteries of exchange, and he attended to how the use of farm lands depended on other enterprises in the immediate vicinity. In sum, he modeled the physical affordances of the landscape as a kind of irreducible patchwork that grounded economic processes. Cantillon's attention to spatial contours powerfully influenced Sir James Steuart, the most influential economist in Britain prior to Adam Smith. Smith, however, admitted location into his model only via transport costs, which varied by the type of good and were often offset by countervailing savings in wages. Smith thereby made location an abstractly convertible metric factor within the arena of the national market (Ekelund and Hébert 1999, 244–45).[19] He replaced Steuart's qualitatively differentiated landscape with his own economic space.[20]

Contemporary network theorists sometimes accentuate abstract space as a convention of their own analytic lens rather than as a real component given by historical development. In so doing, they not only confirm the link between abstract space and modern visions of the social,[21] but they also reveal a kind of unease with their model unless they can attach it to geographical territory. For instance, Bourdieu has underlined that his key framings of social relations—"a space of positions," "social topology," and "social field"—all depend upon prior identification of a multidimensional realm or lattice work by analogy with "geographic space."[22] The eminent sociologist Harrison White has proposed network analysts might in principle devise novel plans of "social space"—of the surfaces and possible kinds of locations that predetermine possible ties—by drawing on recent imaginative departures in the treatment of space in the physical sciences (White 1992, 309). New types of spatial contours could be used to preconfigure the possible positions of actors, including the exotic contours of coral reefs, White said in a spirit of creativity. Natural scientists who study ecological networks and spatial interaction among plants and animals are indeed exploring in detail the effects of positing different kinds of surface geometries and grids (Van Baalen 2000, 359–87). Yet in the social sciences, the network approach preserves its original cultural emphasis on the purely relational and autonomous character of social interchange by adhering to simple extensional space (White 1992, 308).[23] When the data of network analyses are merely aggregate statistics on frequencies of social ties, they initially may not appear to have a spatial grounding; but in interpreting the data, network theorists return to the base of abstract space (see, illustratively, Bearman 1993, fig. 2.2). They produce a verbal or graphical map of ties. The inventors of quantitative methods of network analysis in the 1930s touted the "visual display of group structure" as their most compelling accomplishment, and for many, methods for graphing networks remain an important specialty (Faust and Wasserman 1994, 2, 94–95).

This positioning of action on a platform is preliminary to the third operation for theorizing the social, cordoning off a platform as an analytically *closed* grid. Since the agents' acts are defined relationally, as sheer figures, a container must be sealed for the formal interconnections among them to cohere in an intelligible pattern. Only through closing off the boundaries of an abstract region can the relations take on their own dynamic and generate a providential or structured system, be it market equilibrium, social "order," structural differentiation, stable positional advantages, or some form of progress.[24] Establishing formal "social relations" therefore encouraged analysts to hypostatize a bounded arena with which they were already familiar. As it transpired, the nation state readily served that purpose in France and Britain.[25] Whereas we are apt to suppose that the emergence of the concept of a national "society" reflected the consolidation of the nation-state, history proceeded as much the other way around. What is more, attributing the emergence of the concept of a national society to the emergence of the nation-state does not clarify the historically more novel and analytically more precise concept of "social relations" that abstract space introduced.[26] The modern concept of social relations required (as much as it reflected) the reification of territories as general containers of systems. The force of that requirement for spatial closure has been carried forward into our day through the work of contemporary network theorists who wrestle with it as the "boundary problem" (Emirbayer 1997, 303–4). We also discern this need for closure in Bourdieu's premise that a system of social positions (such as that of professors in a university system) fits within the bounds of a nation (1988, 39). Or, moving nearer to the scenes of action, we see Bourdieu repeating that maneuver in his assumption the boundaries of "fields of play" are sealed and preconfigured.[27]

The notion of abstract space was therefore central to both halves of the enigma that made up the social scientific concept of society that first emerged in the eighteenth century: on the one hand, agents follow their own character or goals within the conventions of a setting; on the other, they do not singly or collectively command the pattern of interaction they themselves create.[28] For the first part of the enigma, abstract space was crucial for freeing conduct of compulsory tradition and corporate coercion. Separating individuals' conduct from the constraints and enablements of locally peculiar institutions and memories in "place" helped ensure it was "autonomous." The agents' conduct was not oriented toward a memory-bearing public, as are the enduring and theatrical "political" deeds that Hannah Arendt adopted as exemplars of genuinely human action by citizens. Instead agents followed impersonal logic intrinsic to any individual, exemplified by Smith's appeal to "the propensity to truck, barter, and exchange" (Smith 1976, 1:17). When network analysts today try to avoid simple economic reductionism, their problematic leads them to replace the search for economic gain with some other impersonal goal intrinsic to any individual, such as the search for "social capital." For instance, the network analysts Kenneth Frank and Jeffrey Yasumoto have written that "actors pursue a single resource, social capital, although through different mechanisms according to the social structure in which any given action is embedded" (1998, 643). Although motives are no longer "economic," they are still simplified, universal, and hatched internally in the agent.

For the second, paradoxical part of the modern view of society—the emergence of a collective pattern beyond human intervention—abstract space was also requisite. Locating human action in a pure, dehistoricized grid, above the limitations of place, enabled social theorists to conceive an emergent order of pure, impersonal reason, a bounded totality, more immaculate than corporeal individuals could themselves imagine or intend.[29] That emergent pattern, godly in its superiority, was sketched in the works of David Hume (1994, 132) and Adam Ferguson (1792, 2:313–14) and proclaimed most prominently in Adam Smith's *The Wealth of Nations* (1976 332), in which an "invisible hand" providentially distributed creative labors.[30]

It is inadequate to classify the abstract space of the social as a symptom only of a mathematical, Cartesian outlook. It was motivated as well by a liberal ethics of intercourse. The reification of abstract space enabled theorists of the social to refer to a virgin arena apart from the inherited religious divides, government encumbrances, and closed estates that had made up the experienced world of place. Allan Silver has traced in detail how the unprecedented model of nonexclusivistic "social space" served the moral goals of the classical liberals of the Scottish Enlightenment. As Silver has explained, these theorists endeavored to show how civil society could develop a diffuse, newly deinstitutionalized morality out of "the associations of private individuals meeting in a social space not shaped by institutional constraints" (1997, 55). The notion of individuals with simple location on a blank, dehistoricized platform established the independence and equality of individuals for liberal commerce.[31] Finally, a homogeneous platform for action enabled agents to imagine sharing an encompassing "common ground" with strangers. It enshrined the theoretical potential for each person in civil society to come into contact with and to engage sympathetically any other person—again, by setting themselves "in the other's position," as the new theorists of social relations liked to put it.[32]

Objectifying Space in the Nineteenth Century

Having suggested how abstract space was essential for the invention of the earliest theories that posited an autonomous realm of the "social," it remains to see how abstract space was carried into the theories that were central to the founding of the discipline of sociology. The work of Emile Durkheim powerfully illustrates how the three constitutive operations for creating the new object of social relations—formalizing unit acts, emptying a platform, and encircling a region—were carried into the classical sociological theory of the nineteenth century. In his well-known exposition in *The Division of Labor*, a requisite for generating the enigma of "the social" is absent from traditional communities, because the individuals merged in traditional communities do not conduct themselves autonomously. They act on shared prescriptions instinctively and, by aiming directly at cultural uniformity, they form a collective structure in a process that is completely manifest. Durkheim treated the spatial landscape in this era of traditional society as patchy and irregular, and he used metaphors of clumpy, sponge-like structures—such as that of an "alveolar system"—to characterize its spatial features. The corporate groups to which individuals belonged were concentrated around "small foci" and broken up by intervening "vacuums" of culturally empty territory. Within the settled sites, the environment was "essentially concrete" because individuals shared the same immediate contact with compelling landmarks such as rivers and noticeable foliage (Durkheim 1984, 229).[33] The development of the division of labor required a transformation of the character of space. When collective life is attached to place and topography, the spatial is defined by similarities in agents' ties to the idiosyncrasies of the landscape rather than by differences in agents' ties to each other. For the systematic principles of occupational differentiation and integration to come into play, the agents must be inserted into a large, homogeneous space in which agents' positions are defined by their formal relations to each other. Society, Durkheim summed up, had to become "general," and its morals had to "dominate more the space available." In his theory of history, Durkheim conjoins the modern emergence of "social relations" with the refashioning and domination of space as an abstract medium (1984, 230).[34]

For the first operation by which theorists call on abstract space to articulate the social—creating "unit acts"—Durkheim in *The Division of Labor* reduces action at the level of the individual to the creation and execution of responsibilities via contract (1984, 205). By depriving familial, business, scientific, and religious services of their specific organizations and disparate places of execution, Durkheim collates them as generic interactions. He accords them simple location on a plane and aggregates them to measure the total "density," "volume," "mass," and "condensation" of general social interaction (1984, 104). The prevalence of these metaphors of extension and mass signals the linkage between abstract space and his formalization of interaction.

For the remaining analytic operation—envisioning territory as an empty, transparent medium—Durkheim disengages the logic of social space from any qualities of the landscape. For example, he argues that variation in soil, climate, and other environmental endowments has no impact upon the processes of social and economic differentiation unless those natural features are culturally recognized and transformed by the autonomous moral principles of the division of labor (1984, 241). The division of labor attaches individuals to distant counterparts by formal interdependency in the social system. It is remarkable that Durkheim highlights the commodification of land in his notion of progress, whereas the creation of other commodities is peripheral to his theory. "So long as law and morals make the inalienable and indivisible nature of immovable property a strict obligation," he said, "the conditions necessary for the division of labour cannot yet exist." Most specifically, Durkheim argues that the sale of land and the transformation of sites from sacred places of collective tradition to indifferent, interchangeable media of action is requisite for the emergence of a social system (1984, 227). The disengagement of individuals from the qualitative or physical makeup of territory as "place" was the pivotal conceptual move for classical social theory, as it was for eighteenth-century political economy.[35]

For the step of invoking a closed container, Durkheim sanctifies the nation-state. The current borders between states strike him as elemental and indelible, since social interchange at any location within the nation exists only in relation to all other interchanges in the national system (1984, 207). From Smith through Durkheim to the contemporary network theorists, then, the relational qualities of networks are founded on their opposite, an imagined absolute, the naturalized base of abstract space. The notion that "social relations" could be separated from culture, historical process, and body was conjurable only by analogy with the notion that objects have "simple location" at a point in an abstract space. As Whitehead described in his history of classical physics, an object's "simple location" in abstract space is separable from all other qualities, and independent of process and experience; it is envisioned as a primary aspect of being, not as a more secondary trait of our perception. By this means abstract space lets theorists see social ties as enjoying an existence all their own, separate from the agent's beliefs, know-how, and emplacement, which may enter as secondary, contextual variables (Frank and Yasumoto 1998, 673).

Fallacies of Social Network Theory: An Intensive Case Analysis

Despite the intuitive plausibility of abstract space in our intellectual traditions, investigators who reason from social interaction in a grid of abstract space are led to faulty conclusions. Let me start with an intensive analysis of an exemplar to typify the misconstructions. Roger Gould's deservedly celebrated study of revolutionary Paris, *Insurgent Identities* (1995), has become, quite simply, a landmark for applying social network theory to the making of world-historical events. Gould compares the influence of the urban social networks on workers' insurgencies at two pivotal revolutionary moments, the June Days of Paris in 1848 and the Commune of 1871. For the 1848 and 1871 movements, Gould models Parisian arrondissements as blank platforms for social interchange and political action. Then he correlates the class "compositions" of the populations distributed in these spaces with participation in the insurgency. From the records of arrests of rebels in June 1848, for example, Gould reports that "workers on the whole were far more inclined to join the uprising than nonworkers; but workers who lived in the most exclusively working-class districts (above all, the eighth and twelfth arrondissements) were even more likely insurgents than workers in areas with mixed populations" (1995, 53). To explain this variation by neighborhood, Gould contends that higher densities of workers in areal space cause workers to form stronger and more homogeneous social networks. These networks sponsor interactions in which the category of worker provides the rationale for social cooperation and for which it becomes culturally salient. The networks also provide the social organization for channeling workers into concerted rebellion

(1995, 54–56). Gould reasons, in sum, from physical densities to networks and then to frequencies of revolutionary action.

In keeping with the logic of abstract space, however, revolutionary action has a simple location on a grid and does not extend though concrete places to unfold in time. Instead, analysis pivots on two static photographs: of the distribution of workers in linear space the instant before revolt contrasted with the distribution of arrestees at the revolt's end. Gould ignores the cultural repertoires and temporal flows of insurgency in 1848 as independent sources of variation in the intensity of battle. Gould's euphemism for combat in the cannon's mouth—"participation"—creates a generic "unit act" with simple location, in Whitehead's sense of the phrase. At the level of experience, however, the rebellion came to life through the techniques of organizing barricades in street intersections, squares, and thoroughfares. What were the repertoires for using space to erect and defend a barricade? How were those techniques passed on? In the hour of conflict, how was the process of recruiting individuals to barricades enacted through the neighborhood? Each of the three fallacies I outline here ensues from giving human action simple location in abstract space rather than acknowledging how practice is constituted through its historical qualities in place.

The Fallacy of Space as a Blank Platform

The assumption that variation in participation reflects the current physical distribution of persons in an empty medium assumes that concrete sites do not contain differential pockets of history. Yet the uneven saturation of blocks, corners, and intersections with remembered history varied individuals' capacities to engage in revolutionary practice. After the revolt of 1830, memory of the precise locations of barricades in past Parisian insurrections served as a script for reconstructing them in renewed political crisis to mark the sovereignty of the common people. Residents erected barricades in places that were important in local revolutionary memory but that sometimes were disadvantaged from the instrumental viewpoint of lines of fire and communication. Since barricades were frequently constructed by residents living adjacent to the sites, memory of how they were built and how they connected to nearby passageways facilitated their reappearance in the identical place "as if by magic" over successive revolts after 1830 (Traugott 1997, 74).

Independent of the intensity of everyday working-class social interaction, therefore, the disproportionate engagement of those in skilled working-class neighborhoods in 1830 transmitted a spatially skewed distribution of cultural resources for building barriers to the active eighth and twelfth arrondissements in 1848. The proximity of residences to past battle sites in those districts facilitated the neighbors' transmission of lore about barricade tactics and heroism (Blanqui 2000). Memoirs from June 1848 recount recruitment for barricade building by spontaneous groupings of residents from within particular apartment buildings (Clavier and Hincker 1997, 212). To be sure, the "place" made up of domiciles and plazas does not transmit local memories on its own. But "place" helps to define and accredit collective lore, and the physically anchored culture of buildings and arteries contributes a resource of its own to the emergence and crystallization of webs of association. Attributing the key correlation for 1848 (that between the composition of districts that were historically commanded by workers and the rates of worker participation) to networks alone is not only spurious reasoning, but a logical error built into the concept of abstract space: the concept installs a tabula rasa by reducing the long unfolding of what Whitehead termed a "total event" to simple locations in the immediate, physically measured present.

The Fallacy of Action Having "Simple Location" in Space

Just as important, the effective maintenance and defense of barricades in 1848 depended on the balance of power in whole neighborhood blocks and the relative contiguity of blocks to others successful in the uprising (Tocqueville 1970, 140). That relational process prevents the analyst from reading the lower arrest rates of workers who lived in districts with low proportions of workers as indicators of these workers' fainter social ties with other workers and weaker commitment to the revolutionary cause. In the early hours of the June uprising, it was unclear whether insurgents would succeed in assembling their battle walls through all of Paris. Isolated barricades that were erected in relatively nonworking-class areas or in working-class islands, however, were quickly surrounded and dismantled before the process of converting and mobilizing local defenders could proceed (Clavier and Hincker 1997, 210). In his graphic memoirs of 1848, Tocqueville described the means by which workers used the barricades as a tool for creating affiliation, not just for marking it. In heavily working-class areas, pedestrians who encountered barricades were required by insurgents to add paving stones or other materials to the barrier before receiving permission to continue on their way (Tocqueville 1970, 139). In this fluid testing of will, a passerby who carried out this intermediary level of engagement got to try out the role of the insurgent (Clavier and Hincker 1997, 213). The proximity to barricades, and therefore the ability to "discover" greater commitment to the cause during the days of revolution, varied by location independently of the intensity of individuals' prior attachments to the identity of worker and independently of the "underlying," prerevolutionary structure of worker networks. A misleading liberal model of politics based on independent individuals expressing their "voting" preferences platonically in abstract space authorized this neglect of the embodiment and physical organization of action.[36] Independent of commitment to the "participation identity," isolated workers were less *able* to join up due to the spatial preconditions of revolutionary practice. Gould's explanation alerts us to a tie between concepts of the spatial and of human action that we will encounter again; to read the action as reflecting the "will" and "identity" of the agent, the affordances and constraints of the spatial environment have to be neutralized by treating them as constants or by erasing them in abstract space.

The Fallacy of Assuming the Priority of Social Relations

In the problematic of classical social theory, the properties of relations in the social system crystallize people's interests, capacities, and identities. This social infrastructure subsequently finds expression in collective actions that have simple location in abstract space. The techniques for engaging in this action are only a convenient *means* determined by the goals of the underlying social associations. Thus does Gould interpret the workers' service on strictly local barricades in 1871 as a mirror of the scale of motivating social solidarities—strictly municipal. Alternatively, however, since urban insurgency must take place through the occupation of territory—it is not an individual "vote" like a ballot—the cultural repertoire for occupying blocks may direct the mobilization of social associations as much as social association fuels the enactment of the repertoire. If building a barricade is the way to occupy a city, and that practice necessarily relies on and evokes local know-how and knowledge about passageways, then the repertoire tilts the mobilization toward the level of local neighborhoods.[37] Instead, the cultural techniques for using place, and thus for staging revolt, may limit and select the *social* associations that can come to light in the annals of urban insurgency.[38]

Explaining variation in conduct in 1848 in terms of the concept of place is methodologically more promising for several positive reasons, not just for avoiding the fallacies of abstract space. The approach of place better accounts for the specific sites of barricades, the nuts and bolts of the uprising, as invocations of memory. Above all, explanations based on place have greater causal immediacy. They are constitutively linked to the execution of insurrectionary practices, whereas social networks in space represent a chronologically and situationally more remote background condition. Paradoxically, Gould's study of 1848 suggests that that structural remove makes sociologists more accepting of explanations that postulate social connections even when those connections are unsighted and unmeasured.

Since each of the three evidentiary fallacies follows from the reductions of abstract space, they have become recurrent in quantitative analyses of urban life. A stimulating example comes from Douglas Massey's and Nancy Denton's remarkable *American Apartheid,* their study of residential segregation by race in the United States (1993, 163). Massey and Denton draw a compelling portrait of the consequences of increasing segregation of black Americans in mono-racial neighborhoods. One of Massey and Denton's striking arguments is that spatial segregation promotes growing divergence in black versus white speech patterns by reducing interracial linguistic contact. In so reasoning, the authors reduce cultural practice to a generic act—"communication"—among individuals who have simple location in areal regions, the census tracts (Labov 1991, 38; Labov and Harris 1986, 20).[39] The fallacies of treating space as a blank platform and of explaining change by physically independent interactions that have only "simple location" become clear from evidence about individual-level variation in formats of speech. Linguists who identify the characteristic profiles of whites who are leading the gradual changes in pronunciation and grammar within the major cities find that the setting matters principally as it is imbued with a history of claims-making. William Labov and Wendell Harris found that it was not social interaction in space that influenced language use, but strategies for marking status in a particular locale. Whites who are concerned to maintain claims to privilege or advantage through locally based networks— such as bank employees, craft workers, teachers, and community leaders—are most likely to lead the development of locally distinctive pronunciations.[40] Place matters due to the tacit history of struggles for territorial authority and for city resources, and speech styles implicitly invoke those collective memories at the site of communication. Collective relations of power in historically imbued place, Labov and Harris found, not quantitative frequencies of "communication" in space, shape the geography of speech.[41]

The last fallacy of abstract space, the misleading priority of the social relations, also follows from Massey's and Denton's model of interaction in abstract space. If rates of social interaction explained speech patterns, the increasing intercity communication among whites would progressively lead to linguistic homogeneity. Yet Massey and Denton alert us to the opposite: the speech of whites, linguists find, is becoming more distinctive to each city of the United States. The structure of white dialect in each city establishes different morphological opportunities for contrasting dominant white with subordinate black speech. Since whites modify their speech to accentuate local belonging and locally based authority, whites implicitly strategize within those local linguistic frameworks. That is, language structure—or "culture"—defines agents' opportunities and guides linguistic differentiation between cities. Just as indicative, a model granting priority to *rates* of social interaction (over place and accompanying cultural qualities of speech) is not equipped to explain why the speech of blacks, unlike that of whites, is becoming increasingly homogeneous across cities.

Space and the Making of Knowledge

The notion of abstract space has not only skewed our use of evidence, but our means of warranting what we do with the evidence. It has papered over crucial epistemic problems in the adventure of Western philosophy. To appreciate the issues that are reopened by questioning abstract space, let us examine space's problem-solving function in Kant's (1994) brief, extraordinary essay of 1784 addressing the question "What Is Enlightenment?" Kant portrays intellectual advance as a process of becoming an adult who relinquishes childish comfort to reason independently. But no individual can go it alone. Only an entire public together can move beyond accustomed habits of deferring to the ready advice of appointed authorities. Only the united public can undertake to "disseminate the spirit of rational respect of one's self-worth and of the calling of all men to think for themselves" (Kant 1990, 7, Axi). In *The Critique of Pure Reason*, of course, Kant appealed to this public as a kind of "law tribunal" that would correct the steps of inquiry. In that work, Kant undermined the natural self-sufficiency and transparency of individual reason for the sake of critiquing reason. He discarded the foremost premodern trope for reasoning, that of a lonely thinker's hushed communion with God (Arendt 1954, 15–16; Kant 1990,

687–88, A751–52). Once Kant corroded any preestablished authority, he had to find a new warrant for his reconstruction of genuine knowledge. Rather than calling on the rhetoric of introspection and autobiography, as Descartes did, Kant described the investigation of the grounds of reason as an essentially collective judicial process (1990, 687–88, A751–52). To interrogate reason, Kant said, he aimed "to install a court of law" (1990, 7, Axi). The advance of comprehension, no longer secured by individual meditation, became public and social. It developed, Kant said, through "the evaluative know-how of an epoch."[42]

We can sight this fateful transition to the "public" construal of reason across all fields of inquiry in Europe. Steven Shapin and Simon Schaffler have shown how it played out in the natural sciences. Scientific inquiries in the course of the seventeenth century came to depend less upon universal experience and deductive reasoning, both of which had been verifiable by the solitary individual. Instead, inquiry relied upon collectively managed experiments sequestered in specially equipped laboratories or offices. To warrant the legitimacy of novel experimental observations for building knowledge, scientists developed conventions for "virtual witnessing." That is, they developed institutions for depicting and publishing information that enabled remote scholars to accept the laboratory trials as first-hand facts even if the trials were not personally glimpsed or replicated. "Virtual witnessing acted to ensure that witnesses to matters of fact could effectively be mobilized in abstract space, while securing adequate policing of the physical space occupied by local experimental communities" (Shapin and Schaffler 1985, 336). Knowledge became authentic through transmission in an ideal social domain (Kant 1994, 57–58).[43] In many specializations, the enduring commitment to experimental methods that were simple and accessible testified to the notion that science was a venture of the public sphere (Golinski 1992, 286).

But if genuine knowledge is transcendent and timeless, how can it depend upon contingent, worldly assemblages of publics? If it is social and historical, assembled by a contingent intersection of ideas, how can it be general and objective? Kant illustrates how Western philosophers negotiated this problem with abstract space as a crutch. In Kant's view, autonomous action and intellectual circumspection cannot take place in any earthly place of collective assemblage: neither in lecture hall nor church, neither in the tutor's house nor municipal office (Kant 1994, 58). In these tangible locales, individuals act as subservient members of authority-bearing institutions. By contrast, a person who "speaks as a scholar through his writings to his actual public, namely the world at large . . . enjoys an unlimited freedom to exercise his reason and to speak in his own person" (1994, 57, 58). To envision genuinely free agents, Kant divests them of locale and installs them in an abstract "public sphere" of the written and published word. The exercise of reason via printed communications is absolutely free and self-determining because the corporeal makeup and physical locations of author and reader appear extraneous to communication and revelation of self. The world of print seems to remove authors from desks, readers from chairs, and everyone from corporation and state. The withdrawal of the reading audience from any historical or geographical context is conspicuous in Kant's vocabulary. An author addresses simply "the world at large," Kant says, or "the reading world"—not a community or historical nation (1994, 58).

Indeed, Kant uses the independence of print from the limitations of place to reverse the usual application of the terms private and public. He classifies as domestic or private any gathering of people in place, even in municipal or community meetings. By contrast, solitary writers reflecting at home are in the public, because they are within an abstract space, an empty medium of exchange. The principal German term for the public, "die Öffentlichkeit," facilitated Kant's inversion of meanings, because it lacks the Anglo-Saxon connotations of a civic body bounded by a territory. The German term indexes merely that which is open or accessible. The divide Kant drew in his social analysis between mechanically compulsory relations in the face-to-face life-world (where agents encounter each other in physical settings) versus free intellectual agency (when insulated authors create and communicate outside the limitations of place) parallels *The Critique of Reason,* in which Kant contrasts the compulsory relations in the experienced physical setting versus the autonomy of self-contained intellects (Kant 1990, 525–27, A536–37).

The creation of abstract public space solved the epistemological puzzle of imagining that genuine knowledge was both social and transcendent. It enabled Kant to conceive a social infrastructure for reason that was not contaminated by the particularity of place or by the wishes of our bodies and governments. Once it shifted toward a public conception of reason, however, Western philosophy and science were bound to the model of modern "social relations." To be sure, Kant sketched only an abstract space for a public, not a well-defined system of social relations. But classical sociology called more immediately on that model to elaborate the objective conditions under which the warranting public came into its own. To cite a well-known elaboration, Durkheim posited a divide similar to Kant's between place and space. Traditional, indeliberate action proceeds in place (mechanical solidarity), where thinking is bound by local, particular categories. Modern, autonomous action proceeds in space (organic solidarity), where thinking calls upon universal, general categories. "Religious beliefs in less advanced societies carry the imprint of the soil upon which they are formed," Durkheim wrote with a graphic accent on the spatial anchor. "Today, the truths of science are independent of any local setting" (Durkheim 1900, 3:557).[44] This developmental progression suggested that objective knowledge was not only possible but ordained, as people were detached from place and oriented purely by function toward their counterparts in abstract space.

One of the chief ironies in the development of European self-understandings, then, has been obscured by the career of abstract space. In our day many are apt to believe that recognizing the "social" warranting of knowledge is a recent innovation of critics who want to subvert objectivity. Instead, modern philosophers had long recognized socially constituted processes of examination and evaluation as part and parcel of the justification of knowledge. But they hid the contingencies and perils of that social process by the epistemic maneuver of abstract space. As Durkheim's theory showed, the vision of social relations that abstract space invoked—stripped-down, impersonal, liberated from emplacement at concrete sites—made the normative ideal of objectivity appear as an inbuilt endpoint of the socio-historical development, since that process culminated in "modern" society. Western philosophers of dispassionate knowledge used abstract space to permit themselves to "go social," so to speak, a very long while ago.

The classical social theorists who parted with positivist vindications of knowledge had all the more cause to carry out the epistemic maneuver of abstract space. Georg Simmel did so by disparaging people who were enamored of the concrete features of place as intellectually "primitive." They suffered, he said, from a childish inability to distinguish between self and environment, as well as between the meaningful and the tangible (Simmel 1903a, 48).[45] By contrast, persons located in complex social networks, especially in impersonal cities, "accustomed themselves to incessant abstractions, to indifference toward physical neighbors and to a close relation to spatially very distanced persons" (1903a, 49). As social development liberates interpersonal relations from the concreteness of place, Simmel claimed, it detaches individuals from the bodily passions. It frees them to cultivate the advanced intellectual traits of "stability, precision, dispassionateness."[46] Simmel not only invoked the successively more neutral and formal makeup of social relations to underwrite the superiority of modern knowledge, he also postulated that scientific dialogue advanced when it took place in an "empty space" where no one felt at home. That modern trope of disengagement from place remains a key for philosophers who make knowledge relative to

its creators, as Thomas Nagel did in *The View from Nowhere*. Nagel rec-
ommends that we develop a theory of how "institutions" can follow "a
single set of principles" to help one achieve "transcendence of one's time
and place" (1986, 187–88). People can warrant their knowledge when
they are placed in sanitized relations of abstract space that release them
from local context.

Two Strategies for Connecting
Knowledge to Place

Against this inherited trajectory of reasoning, refocusing
on the simple hypothesis that knowledge-making is transacted by corporeal agents in concrete locales becomes terribly consequential (Lakoff and
Johnson 1999).[47] In a landmark review of inquiry into local knowledge,
Adi Opher and Steven Shapin (1991) have shown how this elementary insight is driving departures across so many subdisciplines, it is almost
welding together a revolution from below. Knowledge is constituted by
spatial arrangements not only because concepts acquire clarity, reference,
and influence through the design of the local setting in which they are
used. In addition, we think by manipulating and veritably handling public symbols—concrete implements, if you will—that are embedded in
place. Clifford Geertz insisted therefore that the pundit's desk, the football
field, the judge's bench, and the auto seat are not background settings for
individuals to think but are themselves the genuine sites of thought (1973,
83). Cultural investigators have followed two strategies to show how
knowledge-making that seems to emerge from cogitation in an abstracted
realm (projected by the analyst) actually depends upon and unfolds
through the concrete designs of place.

With the first strategy, investigators use the blueprints of buildings or
settlements as evidence for the enactment of beliefs—as a kind of men-
tal design, Lévi-Strauss said, only "in an exteriorized and, let us say,
crystallized form" (1958, 321).[48] In a case that seemed ready-made for
testing the independent influence of spatial configuration, Lévi-Strauss
showed that the religious doctrines of the Bororo in Brazil were so intri-
cate, the beliefs' transmission was contingent on the daily practices that
flowed from the layout of Bororo villages as circles. Europeans who
sought to disrupt the transmission of religious belief found that the most
effective intervention was to break up the circular arrangement and introduce rows of parallel dwellings.[49] The comparative evidence from
this enacted experiment is telling, because it shows that place does not
merely support the most elementary or semantically blunt ideas; the de-

sign of place can sustain more complex effloresces of ideas than can verbal expression alone.

Rather than viewing this physical dependency of ideas as a quaint indicator of primitive cogitation, therefore, cultural historians of practice have gone on to show how the most generic and widespread categories of our own age are similarly anchored by the design of place. To draw an example from the regime of economics, the reification of labor as an abstract measure of value defined the uniqueness of the modern era not only for Marx, but for the eighteenth-century theorists of "social relations." "Everything in the world," David Hume summed up, "is purchased by labour" (1994, 99).[50] In his renowned parable of the fetishizing of labor products into carriers of abstract value, Marx portrayed the sphere of exchange as one in which independent commodity producers who labored in private met to exchange their products in abstract space (1980, 1:73). Marx knew that in actuality producers labored neither in privacy nor independence; that they cooperated and united in the process of manufacture; and that dependent proletarians peddled their "labor" rather than marketed their products. Marx emphasized further that workers conveyed their "labor" through practice at a tangible site, the factory. He even asserted that it was historically inconceivable for labor to be commodified among a society of independent petty commodity producers, because the subordination of workers stripped of assets was a requisite of the commodification of labor rather than a result (Marx 1953, 1:183). Why then in his theory of the fetishization of commodities, the central theme of Western Marxism, did Marx invoke a model so contrary to essential fact that it was not intended to serve even as an ideal type? By invoking such a model, Marx secured the advantage of deducing the most general truth of the capitalist life-world—the appearance of human labor in the guise of abstract value—from the purely formal features of human commerce. In his tale of the fetishizing of commodities, even if the "private" realm of individual production was an aspect of place, the ghostly social pattern took shape through exchange in an abstract space where everyone's action was interconnected and public.

Although Marx's tale offers rich hypotheses for investigation, pursuing them requires us to move from space to the configurations of place. Comparative analysis of nineteenth-century German and British factory layouts suggests more plausibly that definitions of labor as an abstract substance were defined and transmitted through the spatial configuration of the workplace (Biernacki 1995, part 1). Prior research has shown, for instance, that British textile mills used fortress-like cordons to lock workers out who arrived late to work. This accent on the perimeter of the

Richard Biernacki

owner's space defined the start of employment by the workers' location on the property rather than by the workers' setting of labor power into motion. The design encoded workers' responsibility to the owner as the timely delivery of products by contractors. In Germany, where mill design highlighted authority over the use of labor power, floor plans laid priority less on reinforcing the building's perimeter than on sequestering workers within the room where they actually put their bodies to task. Factory design in Germany thereby defined the conveyance of labor power and, in Britain, of labor concretized in products (Biernacki 1995, 128–43). The minutia of architecture reveal how a general, putatively objective category of capitalist thought—labor as an abstract substance—assumed its shape in contrasting fashion through local differences in spatially organized practices. Geertz was prescient in his insistence that schemas of thought are lodged as much in collectively shared place as in private minds.

In this first general approach to connecting knowledge to the design of place, the configuration of place can support implicit beliefs in several different ways. For instance, if the design of stone and mortar serves as "an iconographic index to the mind," as Carl Schorske put it, the holdings of the mind may deceive people about their own social organization (1979, 17). The relation between belief and the principles by which the society fits together and reproduces itself as an institution may be diabolically opaque, as Lévi-Straus found for the Bororo (Lévi-Strauss 1958, 176). More fundamentally, with this approach there are opposing means for defining a place's form. The investigator can decompose the overall morphology of a place, as with city street plans or architectural blueprints. As an alternative to this kind of static photograph from above, however, it is possible to view the configuration from the visual standpoint of a pedestrian or driver who is moving on the ground. Bill Hillier analyzed the successive visual frames that a pedestrian on the ground would have of a journey in London, so as to show how the pedestrian would develop an overall image of the city.[51] Although the conventions of depiction in our era encourage us to imagine the form of place from a stationary frame of reference, there is much evidence from cognitive science that orientation and the perception of contours depend on a person's co-awareness of self and environment in the process of movement (Gibson 1979, 199–200). What these methods for analyzing place share, however, is the premise that the buildings are not just diagrams or scenes of realized human action, but that they concretize the generative schemas, the generic abstractions, by which societies reproduce themselves. If place is the very seat of thought, then society reproduces itself through these figures of earth and stone as much as through normative tradition or institutional convention.

Historians of science have taken up that notion of the reproduction of action by the resources of place in their study of scientific continuities. Experiments and protocols that are envisaged as governed by goals of inquiry and by theories—both properties of the minds of scientists—turn out to depend upon architecture and implicit know-how in place. A striking illustration of place as a holding tank for schemata of action comes from Myles Jackson's study of Joseph von Fraunhofer's laboratory for diffraction gratings in Napoleonic Bavaria. Von Fraunhofer purchased a Benedictine cloister for his research site and, to his fortuitous advantage, found that his lab procedures took on features of the layout and contemplative rituals of the cloister (Jackson 1999, 141–63). Compared to Foucault's dark accent on place as a site of domination, the more fine-grained, case-specific studies of historians of science have underscored how configurations of place shape knowledge by fostering legitimacy and trust.[52] But the loss of the ground of an abstract public space remains profound: reconstructing scientific observation and claims-making gives us a context for their historic shifts, but does not restore a public warranting of reason.

The second broad strategy for connecting knowledge and place establishes an ironic and contradictory relation between knowledge and place. The surreptitious design of influential places may not parallel the canons of science and philosophy, implicit or explicit; they may actually contravene doctrine and yet specify and sustain it. In *Discipline and Punish* Foucault contends that noisy Enlightenment discourse, with its emphasis on contractual, juridical, and equalitarian relations among political subjects, derived both its concepts and its credibility from insidious practices that constituted human subjects in a new mode. As is known, "place" for Foucault is made up of visual fields and implements that turn individuals' bodies into media of control. Knowledge-bearing elites use the configurations of place—workplaces, prisons, schools, and hospitals—to impose power relations that are asymmetrical, scrutinizing, and ultimately coercive. These "emplaced" apparatuses, by targeting a calculable "interior" for each individual, also made real the concept of an individual rational soul. In so doing, the practices did not merely violate in silent practice the noisy Enlightenment discourses of freedom and social contract: they made convincing the cognitive premises of liberal discourse. "The disciplines, real and corporeal," Foucault announced with irony, "constituted the foundation of the liberties, formal and juridical" (1975, 224).

The principle that ideals rest on contrary practices, an earnestly platitudinous conclusion, is not what lends Foucault his methodological spark. He has provoked a surge of research into the environment of place because he illustrates how chaste ideals of enlightened liberalism are not just historically, but intrinsically dependent on their squalid opposites.[53] Foucault suggests that the human subject, though viewed as essentially autonomous, is constructed by and inseparable from oppressive implements of place; that concepts of equalitarian intellectual intercourse are embedded in local sites of surveillance and domination; that space, an *a priori* of pristine analyses, is the dirty product of place; and that universalistic philosophy remains dependent for its very meaning on the material particulars of locale. In this approach, what matters is not that the ideas held to be self-sufficient and self-defining depend on something of a different nature; the distinguishing feature of Foucault's analysis is that explicit beliefs are expounded and understood through contrary practices "in place" and are not just circumstantially dependent upon such practices.

Above all, Foucault suggests that place is not a particular instantiation of monolithic, *a priori* space. He shows that it is the efficient cause of space. The architectural plan of public and service buildings of all kinds is based on seriality and interchangeability: lines of cells, columns of desks, formally equivalent positions. The effect, Foucault concluded, is the production of "segmented, immobile, frozen space" (1975, 198). Foucault inverts all the claims about place and space on which classical sociological theory was founded: the abstract social space of modernity arises from a new fixity in place, not from mobility; from intensified surveillance, not from the relaxation of collective scrutiny or the latitude of urban anonymity; from the imbrication of people with the material contours of place, not from their insertion into the self-determining networks of social relations.[54] Both for liberal political economy's labor as a quantifiable substance of value and for enlightenment discourses of consent and contract, a focus on place upsets the "ground" premise of liberalism's explanations, that of an abstract plane on which agents meet as equals.

Recurrent Issues in Socio-Historical Inquiry

To assess the implications of a return to place, let us return now to controversial problems in socio-historical inquiry that have become increasingly prominent in the past decade: the status of the "social," the concept of a cultural system, and the choice of spatial units for analysis.

The Crisis of "the Social"

The cultural turn in historical analysis since the 1980s has not only deprived the social of its automatic explanatory power. It also raised difficult questions about the referent of "the social" in social theory. If the social is no longer identified with a self-evidently real socioeconomic base, what is it? At the very least, as a recent book title suggests, most of us have put "the social in question" (Joyce 2001). A sophisticated but dismissive answer to the status of the social is that it is principally a discursive construction of a particular epoch, destined to fade upon the ascent of new epistemes (Joyce 1995).[55] Sociologists have by and large embraced a less unsettling alternative, the view that the social resides in networks of interaction. The eminent sociologist Harrison White said these formal ties comprise "the purely social" (1992, 14). For social theorists, the strictly relational quality of networks was attractive for rethinking "the social" because it avoided positing essential or material grounds of identity and action.[56] In my view, however, this renewal of interest in the network approach returns us more clearly to the disconcerting founding moment of the modern social sciences two centuries ago.

As a social theory, the network approach is not merely partial; in its application to historical cases, it is not merely incomplete. Through intensive consideration of selected examples I have endeavored to establish more radically that the constructions of network theory, accepted on their own terms, are misspecified and nonexplanatory. I have argued, then, for the explanatory priority of place over space on several levels: that of method, by showing abstract space misconstrues evidence; on the level of intellectual history, by recalling the brevity, oddity, and ideological mainsprings of abstract space's reign; on the level of explanatory integrity, by arguing that temporal process is tied to place rather than to space; on the level of efficient causes, by proposing that abstract space emerges out of our orientation to the appurtenances of place; and on the level of epistemology, by contending that abstract space served as a farfetched crutch for Western objectivity, whereas we behold the riddles of our own knowledge-making if we examine practice in place.[57]

In view of the problematic ground of theories of social networks, it is tempting to jettison reference to networks altogether. But the imagery of networks is rhetorically so influential, a rigid censure of the concept would be of little avail. Further, the imagery of social networks denominates an intuitively appealing approach to the enigma of social relations,

Richard Biernacki

that of autonomous action by individuals and of emergent linking patterns among individuals. It is not surprising that social theorists are trying to rethink how networks operate from the perspective of the configured relations of place.

Bruno Latour has faced that challenge by examining changes in the character of associations based on the enactment of rituals in the place of the laboratory. In *The Pasteurization of France,* Latour has overturned the notion that social exchanges have fixed properties and dynamics of their own. What varies historically with changes in biotechnology and scientific claims-making is more than the quantity or distribution of social ties, and more than what people happen to exchange. The very grounds of ties shift as laboratory procedures invent new "agents," such as microbes, that reshape the materials of action and the possibilities of association. For example, Pasteur's certified techniques were requisite for colonial administration in the tropics and for the meeting of armies in contaminated battlefields; in France, they set up new associations for hygiene and agriculture (Latour 1988, 138, 142). Pasteur thereby used the laboratory, like Archimedes' lever, to "displace" society itself—shifting it, literally, to a different environment. The ritualized "place" of the controlled experiment was crucial for identifying the microbes in a standardized guise. Yet, conversely, it was Pasteur's mobilization of the networks of believers in his demonstrations that lent his manipulative experimental results the influential status of transportable science.[58] Latour's narratives show how the site of demonstration in place and the networks of believing accomplices are dependent on each other for their historical significance. He thereby forsakes the classical premise of a separate space of interaction that is distinctively "social," along with its predictive principles. Sociology, Latour declared, "thinks it knows *what* society is made up *of.* . . . The few sociological explanations are feeble compared with the strictly sociological master stroke of the Pasteurians and their hygienist allies, who simply redefined the social link by including the action of the microbes in it" (1988, 38). Yet, after critiquing our ontology of social space, Latour leaves us with a sharpened description of a process rather than a specification of the distinctive contributions of elements to that process. In what respects would changes in the shape the medical demonstration assumed in place, or changes in the structure of the receptive networks of potential accomplices, have modified the historical outcome?

To explore such counterfactual questions of explanation, it is useful to adopt a comparative design that varies aspects of practices in place while treating the broader networks of social exchange and communication as generic constants. That, in fact, was the approximate plan of research on nineteenth-century factory practices at the site of production in *The Fabrication of Labor.* In the countries of Western Europe the schemas for coordinating the conveyance of labor in the "place" of the shopfloor structured correspondingly different patterns of technological investment and rhythms of development at the level of the national economy (Biernacki 2001, 194–97). Sociologists have tried to show how the very establishment of ties of exchange, not just their rhythm of use, depends on practices in place. The early history of "market places" as privileged sites segregated from the rest of social life, often placed under the tutelage of a potentate, hints at that dependency of "free" exchange on forms of command and legitimacy. Viviana Zelizer (1994) has complemented this emphasis on power in place with a cultural perspective. Her examination of nineteenth- and twentieth-century America has demonstrated how cultural distinctions between different sources of funds inside the household structured networks of exchange with outside "markets." The earmarking of a wife's self-generated "pin money" created, in effect, a separate currency. It was physically segregated in its own jars and bowls, and applied only for specific treats, such as tickets for a concert. Its dollars were not compared with or traded against family monies for other, more pedestrian items (Zelizer 1994, 62–63). Exchange was organized by the cultural encoding of productive activity in the "place" of the family household. As sociologists and cultural historians seek to "embed" the market in its conditioning institutions, they increasingly shift their lens from abstract space as a medium of exchange to place as a site of enacted practice.[59] Their fresh attempts to link place to systems of exchange diverge in an important respect from the earlier attempts of Marx and Bourdieu. In Bourdieu's model an abstracted status system defines the relevant features of body hexis in place; and in Marx's model, the categories of exchange value define the relevant features of corporeal work in place. For both, place illustrates the reproduction of a predefined system. In the work of the new sociologists and cultural historians, however, the concepts used in the system of exchange emerge and vary contingently with forms of emplacement.

The Concept of Culture

The processes of place threaten some forms of cultural explanation as much as the conceits of economic reductionism. The principal figure of culture that prevailed in the cultural turn—that of a system of interrelated signs—has hidden affinities with theories of social networks. Culture as an overarching sign system presents culture as

Richard Biernacki

a property of a "semiotic community"—a group of symbol readers adept at interpreting signs, but whose use of signs is detached from any location or type of site in the world. As with modern network theory, the formality and ideality of this figure of culture is compatible with the assumption that the logic of human action becomes intelligible by separating it from embodiments in place. As with network theory, the elements that enter into the portrayal of a particular culture relate to each other strictly by the principles of their own internal relations. As with network theory, reifying a sealed boundary to the system is requisite for inducing those relations. These models of social networks and of culture are affiliated matches, so theorists are able to isolate either of them—culture or social networks—as the main object of analysis while imagining the other serves as a contextual background.[60]

When we put culture back in place, therefore, we do not merely insert culture into an embodied context: we transform what we mean by culture. Instead of imagining symbols relating to each other by a purely semiotic logic of contrasts, we see that they *exist* through their relations to place—they are not merely exemplified *by* place. Our thinking about the world is oriented by the relations of our hands and legs to it; those relations have a corporeal order that is irreducible to the semiotic logic of a sign system or to the intellectual processing of visual markers.[61] The process of orienting ourselves to a sign and grasping it as such operates through the body's emplacements (Schwartz and Black 1999, 116–36).

The Choice of Spatial Units

As historical sociologists dismantled the nation state as a privileged unit of analysis, they sought to demarcate other system-like social networks at the level of the city, province, transnational region, and global economy. The dazzling controversies that resulted—over supranational governance, global cities, and regional trading blocks—have pivoted on how these units of analysis intersect with each other.[62] In my view, however, it is important to see how sociologists and other analysts sustained these debates with the standard operations that constitute the social. They imagined generic kinds of exchanges in parceled and abstract spaces and then debated the privileged coherence of several of those spaces over others—usually based on predominant scales either for the regulation and reproduction of capital or for the circulation of cultural artifacts and signs (Sahlins 1989, 107–15). Many theories of globalization merely transfer the notion of abstract "social space" to the largest spatial domain and call on the rhetorical presumption that the boundaries of that domain (earth) are those given most "naturally."

Can the concept of place be used to sort out these debates? Is place in effect limited to face-to-face interactions or can it encompass "larger" domains? As a mode of human emplacement, events of place are not tied to a particular geographical scale, and the interconnections of places can unite different "levels" of analysis. Analysts usually assign observations involving short "distances" to local "place" and greater ones to global "space," as if the extension of each were gauged with a yardstick. In a word, both members of the pair are interpreted relative to abstract space.

Place, however, is defined not by metric distance, only by the qualitative configurations in which embodied agents situate themselves.[63] An exemplar for approaching expansive distance from the perspective of place is Fernand Braudel's (1995) magisterial study of the Mediterranean. In the introduction to *The Mediterranean and the Mediterranean World in the Age of Philip II*, Braudel anticipates that his readers may have a sense of incongruity when they encounter a narrative of "a stretch of water," a history that figures the sea, as much as any human traverser, as an agent. Yet Braudel embraces that ambiguity to suggest how human enterprises are constructed out of the powers of place: the channels, inlets, straits, cordilleras, and precipices in which action is "emplaced." To present the Mediterranean as a stretch of configured locales rather than as a space, he tours it as a "complex of seas" (Braudel 1995, 1:18). Further, since a defining characteristic of place in contrast to space is that it is never sealed, always defined in part by how it opens upon a broader living environment, Braudel surveys the Mediterranean's passageways to surrounding areas (Heidegger 1954). He sculpts the object of his history not by analytic boundary-drawing, not by reifying an interrelated system, but by specifying the modes of access and dispatch between his places and others. How people act through the contours of seas and peninsulas sponsors cultural affiliations, circuits of trade, and advances in shipbuilding and technical lore. To shield his entity from the reductive tools of space, he reminds us that the Mediterranean "cannot be contained within our measurements and classifications" (Braudel 1995, 1:18). Accordingly, Braudel does not define region or process by mensural distance. By defending the integrity of places and their connections—by contiguity and by the nesting of the local configuration in the regional—Braudel defines a coherent object that is not, however, a totalized "system." Above all, Braudel shows that place does not designate just the local level in the current state of play; it designates a theoretical object that can vary in its geographical reach.[64]

208

Richard Biernacki

Although he initiated a place-based history, Braudel's division of time
scales prevented him from carrying through on his experiment. He associated place with physical geography, and for the sake of presentation,
assigned the undertakings tied to place a temporal cadence separate
from the identifiable episodes of social change and politics. The techniques for cultivating lands and crossing seas comprised "geographical
time," a ponderous, virtually "timeless history, the story of man's contact
with the inanimate" (1995, 1:20). Braudel thereby made it appear that
social groupings and politics, in which the passage of time and the exer-
tions of agency are more striking, relate to place only at a remove, via the
circumstance that economic resources have to be wrested from the natural environment (1995, 2:1242). A fully realized history of place would
consider how the other two levels of Braudel's narrative, the intermedi-
ate level of social interaction, as well as the frothy upper level of political decisions of diplomats and statesmen, called as much as did the
slow agricultural and trading systems on schemas of practice that were
lodged in place. For actions at the other "levels," as Braudel termed
them, namely those of social institutions and of eventful politics, are
equally graspable as procedures for displaying body and self in relation to locale (1995, 2:1242). These operations of place, since they depend
in turn on the configuration of buildings, roads, and canals in relation
to the landscape, are inseparable from the physical environment that
Braudel sketched so aptly.

Exactly that kind of integrated strategy missing from Braudel is exemplified in Chandra Mukerji's studies of the crafting of the natural environment to create the authority of the centralizing French state. In *Territorial Ambitions*, Mukerji (1997) shows how the state in the seventeenth
century defined itself through its relation to the French lands. It remade
the earth with fortresses and aquaducts, and in the massive engineering
of the Versailles gardens it demonstrated its ability to "root" the social
order in the harmonious subordination of nature. "The France that was
produced this way was not a political concept, a title for a regime, or the
product of an imagined history. It was a *place*," Mukerji summed up. "It
lay *in* the land and the peculiarities of its ordering" (1997, 324; emphasis
added). From my view, what is most significant about Mukerji's strategy
is how the figures of places welded together Braudel's levels of the economy, society, and politics. Consider the production of politics through
the landscape at Versailles. The layout and statuary of the gardens
looked out upon, and incorporated, the engineering works that crossed
the face of the land at large. When the nobles promenaded in alignment
with the gardens' geometry, the cultivation of nature at Versailles became a model for the noble's orientation to their own bodies and for the

presentation of a new kind of disciplined self in social rites. Thus does Mukerji connect the "inanimate" landscape to Braudel's level of the social. The nobles' silent conformity with the order of the gardens defined, truly, "earthly" subordination to the king, and thus the kind of authority the king could exercise (Mukerji 1997, 247). Forms of bodily emplacement in the landscape thereby composed Braudel's third level, that of conjunctural political acts. In the gardens of Versailles, Mukerji shows how Braudel might have used interconnecting configurations of place to explain how the longue durée of economy and society connects to the quick events of politics, how both locales and national landscapes fall under the qualitative configurations of place.[65]

In *Science and the Modern World,* Alfred North Whitehead (1927) criticized our concept of abstract space as a stunning exemplar of "the fallacy of misplaced concreteness" (Sewell 1980, 144). In a similarly wry spirit, Harrison White, perhaps the preeminent sociologist of networks, has observed that just as our concept of space structures our concept of social interchange, so conversely does our concept of social interchange structure that of space. This, he concluded, inaugurates the "chicken-and-egg conundrum" of theory (White 1992, 310–11).[66] By treating this conundrum not as merely analytic but as a real problem, agents address through their actions in place the new historians of cultural practice promise to fulfill Whitehead's and White's intuitions. They encourage us to pursue the tantalizing hypothesis that spatial relations are neither a fiction nor a fact of nature, neither an inner experience nor an external given, only an emergent, explicable quality of events of human practice. Processes of emplacement intersect local, regional, and global levels of analysis.[67]

NOTES

1. On the nation as the unit of analysis, see McMichael 1992; on political culture as an independent constituent, see Somers 1995, 113–44; on temporal progression, see Sewell 1996, 247.

2. As a shorthand, I talk here of *"the"* concept of space for what actually comprises a cluster of concepts with family resemblances. Abstract space can be invoked when positions in the grid are absolute or relative to orienting points, for instance. Erwin Panofsky called it "systematic space" to highlight its quality of being defined purely by mathematical features of extension, independent of its relation to the physiology of the human agent, and to highlight the way that reciprocal relations among envisioned axes systematize the positions and appearances of all objects in its domain (Panosfsky 1991, 29–30, 43). Merleau-Ponty defined it, similarly, as "geometrical" space in contrast to "anthropological" space

Richard Biernacki

(1976, 324–44). Henri Bergson discussed the paradoxes of defining space as "a reality with no quality" (1916, 95).

3. For discussion of a shift to study embodied forms of culture in reaction to the questioning of the category of "the social," see Victoria Bonnell's and Lynn Hunt's Introduction to their edited volume *Beyond the Cultural Turn* (1999, 11 and n. 31). A pithy account of how the study of the schemata of practice has revived the salience of the concrete locale of practice can be found in David Livingstone introductory remarks to his essay "Science and Religion: Foreword to the Historical Geography of an Encounter" (1994, esp. 368–71).

4. Other examples of the new cultural history of practices in place include Mark Traugott's (1997, 71–81) analysis of the repertoires of barricade building and Oleg Kharkhordin's (1999) analysis of spatial arrangements in the construction of the self in Soviet collectives. Even Simon Schama's work on landscape and memory does not merely trace literary beliefs about woodlands and estates: it shows how those beliefs were inscribed and retained in the face of the earth (1995, 15, 343).

5. For bibliographical references that develop the distinction between place and space, see Maplas 1999, 21ff. For sources on the revival of place since Heidegger explored the distinction, see Casey 1993, 316.

6. The distinction between place and space also formed part of Hegel's ontology, as Lukács showed with greater clarity than Hegel himself (Lukács 1984, 1:497).

7. For an outstanding essay that distinguishes among the respects in which Kant can be said to derive space from mind, see Warren 1998. In my view, it is characteristic of the modern age that Kant thinks the representation of objects as spatially related presupposes the representation of a general space those objects occupy.

8. Foucault makes an analogous distinction between space, defined by the objectifying viewpoint of linear perspective, versus place, defined by how regions relate to the stance of our bodies (1986, 107).

9. The quote links adjacent sentences in the original.

10. Kant's prescient insight that our orientation in the place-world and application of signs is not based only on the mind and its reading of sign contrasts, but is governed by the experienced order of the body and has been independently duplicated by contemporary geographers and cognitive scientists (Franklin and Henkel 1995, 406).

11. For an argument that places are neither objectively given nor a subjective construction, only a relation and process of engagement between people and their setting, see Lang 1997, 189. The inability of concrete partitions to create places on their own is illustrated in ethnographies of life in office buildings. The walls of buildings act as constraints in part because they are recognized as such through conventions, such as norms against eavesdropping.

12. For discussions of how Adam Smith models production as acquisition by exchange, see Biernacki 1995, 239 n. 125, 253.

13. On Smith's identification of "capital" with the liquid money of an enterprise, rather than with equipment used at a site, see Cannan 1921. For the parallel

logic in France, where Condorcet saw "value" in exchange as the key to social relations between autonomous individuals, see Condorcet 1976, 196.

14. For a discussion of how early political economy created the "society" as an ontological category, see Heller 1967, 25.

15. For evidence that labor was adopted as the measure of value to secure the autonomy of social interdependency, see Meek 1967, 204.

16. "Social capital is defined in terms of resources that actors may access through social ties" (Frank and Yasumoto 1998, 645).

17. See, for example, Durkheim 1984, 201. To create this empty medium, analysts sometimes disconnect social space from any geographical platform, treating "distance" as only a social metric. Alternatively they assimilate social space to geography by treating physical space as a blank areal unit for social interaction. It is possible for analysts to switch between these two spatial constructions of the social. For a fascinating but largely forgotten illustration of the ambiguity, see Feldman and Tilly 1960, 877–84.

18. The new theorists of "social relations" recast agricultural production, once viewed as action tied to the "place" of the land, as only another instantiation of exchange of labor for harvest (Smith 1976, 10; Hume 1994 99).

19. For a neglected study that seeks to "unthink" political economy's neglect of the locations of activity since the eighteenth century, see Ponsard 1954.

20. French political economy in the eighteenth century went through a similar process of replacing a theory of singular places with one based on homogeneous "Cartesian" space. See Markovits 1986, 291. What Smith accomplished in theory had already become part of common practice, however. Travelers had become accustomed to drawing geometric circles around major towns, independent of actual arteries, to trace differences in zones of abstract space in the prices of staples and in wages. Arthur Young remarked upon viewing such tables that national variations in the cost of offering foodstuffs in the market towns were so regular, rising proportionately with distance from nearest major market, that distance comprised a metric for determining the value of produce (Young 1770, 62–64).

21. On continuities between the eighteenth-century theorists of the social and the sociologists of networks today, see Silver 1997, 67 n. 63.

22. Bourdieu underscores how the resort to geographic analogy follows from his "relational mode of thinking" (1989, 16); see also Bourdieu 1985 723–25.

23. Blank Euclidean space, if not a logically necessary geometric figure, may be congenial to network analysts because of its cultural affinity with the modern gesture of "wiping the slate clean" of prior assumptions about actors' possibilities of sighting, discovering, contacting, or exchanging positions. For a recent example of theorizing about contacts among firms as geometric figures in N-dimensional Euclidean space, see Péli and Nooteboom 1999.

24. For an analysis that suggests an interesting role for "spatial models" in political scientists' search for equilibria among collective interests, see Green and Shapiro 1994, 147–54.

25. On the "presumption of homogeneous and equivalent spaces" in theory that takes nation-states as units of analysis, see Gulbenkian Commission 1996, 84.

Richard Biernacki

26. "Society" and the sense of "social relations" have partially contrasting provenances and senses. The term "society" traded on distinctions between the tangible associations of "civil society" and another substantial organization—the state (Arendt 1954, 33, 38, 43, 56). Concepts of society, unlike that of the social, did not necessarily include a perspective on individual behavior. When they did, they sometimes saw society menacing and subordinating individual action (see, illustratively, the sources cited by Pitkin 1998, 188). Therefore recognizing "society" in the guise of group pressures or law-like changes in institutions does not on its own yield a theory of "social relations" as I define it here. In my terms, for example, Marx articulated his vision of "the social" only when he descended to the level of individual exchange in his earliest philosophical writings and in *Das Kapital*. Marx tried to show in his late work how agents' own fruitful labor and formally free intercourse conjures the properties of a system: the reified forms of exchange value and circuits of capital accumulation. Or, to adduce an example of a theory of the social beyond political economy, Durkheim imagined that agents in contemporary society who adapted to competition by narrowing the scope of their activity in the division of labor not only reinforced the ideal of individuality, they also deepened interdependencies among producers and unintentionally produced more intensive collective integration. "In reality," Durkheim said of this induced pattern, "the duties of the individual to himself are duties to society" (1984, 332).

27. See Lamont's substantive critique of Bourdieu's enclosures (1992, 183).

28. For examples of the development of this problematic in eighteenth-century Britain, see Ferguson 1819, 221–22, and Smith 1976, 440. Michel Foucault's historical analysis of governmentality as the indirect sponsorship of self-regulating individuals and of productive exchange offers further evidence of the new problematic of the social (1991, 100; 1984, 243).

29. For an overview of how European thinkers transferred metaphors of a divine totality from theology into the social sciences, see Sahlins 1996, 407.

30. For overviews, see Hamowy 1987 and Hill 1996, esp. 207–9.

31. The base of abstract space made each individual emotionally equal with all others in the sense that they could conceivably exchange "positions" in their undivided arena. The expressions of "exchanging positions" and "taking the position" of another for sympathetic fellow feeling had a well-crafted underpinning.

32. This brief paragraph develops the spatial metaphors in Allan Silver's excellent discussion (1997, 52–56).

33. To maintain the dimension of individual autonomy in the problematic of the social, Durkheim set out radical conditions for genuinely voluntary and contractual intercourse (1984, 317).

34. Apart from the division of labor in space, of course, Durkheim believes that modern solidarity still calls upon the periodic reaffirming of religious sentiments through face-to-face reunions. But in his account of these assemblies, Durkheim describes only the spiritual contacts among persons and collective use of the site to mark social feelings, not the relation between embodied persons and the environment that creates the event of place (1968, 610).

35. On the experience of "real and mobile property" in the formation of Smith's views of society as interchange, see Pocock 1985, esp. 122–23.

36. On the relative absence of circulation of workers between districts, see Clavier and Hincker 1997, 212.

37. The form that mobilization takes does not mirror the spatial scale of the agent's political identities' and demands: the emphasis on action by local neighborhoods reflected belief in ground-up popular association for change, not a denial of the need for a radically interventionist state as well. Envisioning the concrete topography in which insurgent practices unfold through time uncovers the logical error of treating the social and the structural as the basic matrix of history.

38. Raymond Grew's study of Italy in the period of the French Revolution suggests that the cultural lore and know-how embedded in urban place—interaction in the piazzas—configured the social ties that could be mobilized in politics (1999, 407–33).

39. Labov and Harris conclude that "social networks have little explanatory value for individual differences in linguistic systems" (1986, 21). For a network analysis that clarifies the relatively weak influence of social ties by comparison with the historically acquired characteristics of individuals that shape their personal strategies, see Fischer 1977, 137.

40. For accounts of the continuing centrality of Kant's essay, see the collection of twentieth-century responses in Schmidt 1996.

41. Similarly, see Suttles 1968, 65, 145.

42. Kant's phrase is "Urteilskraft des Zeitalters" (1990, 7, Axi). Michel Foucault credited Kant with assigning to philosophy the goal of investigating the socio-historical conditions for the deemed truth of knowledge (1993, 18). In Britain Thomas Carlyle recognized this new "public" manner of warranting knowledge sardonically: "Has any man, or any society of men, a truth to speak, a piece of spiritual work to do; they can nowise proceed at once and with the mere natural organs, but must first call a public meeting, appoint committees, issue prospectuses, eat a public dinner; in a word, construct or borrow machinery, wherewith to speak it and do it" (1971, 65).

43. For an analysis of how the architecture of the sites for lab experiments supported the credibility of the results, see Gooday 1998, 216–45. In a word, Gooday shows how the use of place structured debates in the abstract space of the public sphere.

44. I am indebted to Steven Shapin for calling attention to this obscure passage.

45. Simmel also correlates the detachment of thought from place with improvements in "abstracting ability" (1903b, 297). Simmel's disparagement of views other than those based on abstract space has endured in many treatments of spatial relations. Neither the child nor the "untutored adult," Robert David Sack has written, makes a "high degree of conceptual separation between subjective and objective and space and substance" (1980, 121).

46. Habermas continues this separation of knowledge from the social dynamics of place with his notion of "autonomous public spheres" for reflective discussion in rationalized cultures. See, illustratively, Habermas 1990, 325, 365.

Richard Biernacki

For a contrasting example of an analyst who insists there can be no public sphere apart from the concrete sites of the agora or the forum, see Arendt 1954, 38.

47. For a fascinating account of the corporeal reorganization of reading practices between the eighteenth and nineteenth centuries, as well as their effect on cognitive processes, see Schön 1993.

48. Examples of this procedure are legion in anthropology. See, illustratively, Sahlins 1976, 34, 40.

49. Lévi-Strauss's dissection of the ground plan of Bororo villages is especially compelling because of comparative evidence isolating the effect of the circular configuration of place. The religious system was so complex, Lévi-Strauss concluded, it could live only through "the schema made patent in the lay-out of the village" (1955, 250).

50. For other references to the reification of labor as a quantifiable substance in eighteenth-century Britain, see Biernacki 1995, 236–39, 477 n. 6. For a fascinating comparison of the recognition of labor as a measure of value in the United States versus Britain, see Dippel 1981, 210–14.

51. See discussion of Hillier above, {000}.

52. For a survey, see Shapin 1998, 5–12. My presentation of the dependence of knowledge on place relies on Shapin's lead.

53. See, illustratively, Sennett 1994. Charles Rosenberg contended that the experience of nineteenth-century hospital architecture, not experiment, subtly manufactured belief in atmospheric notions of infection (1987, 138–39). For a more scholarly survey of the architectural designs that Foucault only glossed, see Markus 1982.

54. On the creation of "collective, homogeneous space," see Foucault 1963, 198.

55. "The meaning of the 'social,'" Bruno Latour has written, "continually shrinks" (1988, 205).

56. Margaret Somers offers an elegant statement of this view (1996, 199). See also Emirbayer 1997.

57. For an empirical defense of the local dependencies of knowledge, see Opher and Shapin 1991.

58. "A theater of proof, like the ordinary theater, needs all its accessories. . . . They [the Pasteurians] need the safety of long networks for the 'truth' they declare to be made indisputable on all points" (Latour 1988, 93).

59. As John Lie has emphasized through his fecund concept of a "mode of exchange," trade between places does not grow spontaneously into a fluid market. It is structured by the elites who dominate place, as was easy to see in the manorial mode of exchange in medieval Europe. In that setting, agrarian elites used their control of land to tax and regulate the development of translocal exchanges. Likewise, different forms of putting-out networks rose in the countryside of proto-industrial Europe, depending on how elites were able to club together at inns to organize and control nodes of communication (Lie 1992).

60. One of the inherited encodings of "abstract space" is that of an underlying frame of reference that constitutes the sum total of all places. Contesting the primacy and taken-for-granted reality of abstract space in social science is eas-

ily interpreted as a denial of any such inclusive frame of reference. After the cultural turn, it is all too common to read a history of the constructedness of a putatively objective category as an endorsement of multiple frames of reference made to order for incomparable places. In my view, the relevant issue is only that of the methodological usefulness of a concept for our socio-historical inquiries.

61. See Sayeki 1997, 91–98. Many examples of the effect of that corporeal order on the use of signs comes from experiments into the effects of suppressing body movement during speech. Speakers who are prevented from gesturing prove to be handicapped in describing happenings that have spatial analogies or referents. The speakers need the participation of their bodies to retrieve the spatial concepts and corresponding words, as if language use is a skill of dexterity (Rauscher, Robert, and Chen 1996, 229).

62. For an incisive survey of the debates to which I refer, see Brenner 1999a. Brenner vividly amplifies the metaphors of abstract space on which these debates depend. See in particular Brenner 1999b.

63. Abstract space, conversely, is defined by how it defines location independently of process and other attributes. Obviously it can be applied to face-to-face groups.

64. Conversely, some analysts of micro-level, face-to-face interaction empty place of its spatial qualities and treat it as a blank background for people to read action and speech as "signs." For an example of a study theorizing the micro as a setting in which individuals engage in the "thick" reading of signs, see Boden and Molotch 1994.

65. For another example of how the architecture of a residence articulates with the surrounding regional landscape as part of the shared configuration of place, see Bentmann and Müller 1992, 33–34.

66. For a simple example of the dependency of space on features of network ties, see Specter and Rivizzigno 1982, esp. 75.

67. For a scintillating study of emplacement in large regions, see Schivelbusch 1986.

REFERENCE LIST

Agnew, J.-C. 1986. *Worlds apart: The market and the theater in Anglo-American thought, 1550–1750.* Cambridge: Cambridge University Press.
Arendt, H. 1954. *The human condition.* Chicago: University of Chicago Press.
———. 1963. *Between past and future: Six exercises in political thought.* New York: Meridian Books.
Bearman, P. 1993. *Relations into rhetorics: Local elite social structure in Norfolk.* New Brunswick, N.J.: Rutgers University Press.
Bender, J. 1987. *Imagining the penitentiary: Fiction and the architecture of mind in eighteenth-century England.* Chicago: University of Chicago Press.
Bentmann, R., and M. Müller. 1992. *The villa as hegemonic architecture.* Atlantic Highlands, N.J.: Humanities Press.

Bergson, H. 1916. *Time and free will*. London: George Allen & Co.

Biernacki, R. 1995. *The fabrication of labor: Germany and Britain, 1640–1914*. Berkeley: University of California Press.

———. 2001. Labor as an imagined commodity. *Politics and Society* 29 (2): 173–206.

Blanqui, A. 2000. Les Barricades. Exposition La Commune Musee D'Orsay [museum exhibit].

Boden, D., and H. L. Molotch. 1994. The compulsion of proximity. In *NowHere space, time and modernity*, edited by Roger Friedland and Deirdre Boden. Berkeley: University of California Press.

Bonnell, V., and Lynn Hunt. 1999. *Beyond the cultural turn*. Berkeley: University of California Press.

Bourdieu, P. 1985. The social space and the genesis of groups. *Theory and Society* 14 (6) 1985: 723–44.

———. 1988. *Homo academicus*. Stanford: Stanford University Press.

———. 1989. Social space and symbolic power. *Sociological Theory* 7 (1): 14–25.

Braudel, F. 1995. *The Mediterranean and the Mediterranean world in the age of Philip II*. 2 vols. Berkeley and Los Angeles: University of California Press.

Brenner, N. 1999a. Beyond state-centrism? Space, territoriality and geographical scale in globalization studies. *Theory and Society* 28 (2): 39–78.

———. 1999b. Globalisation as reterritorialisation: The re-scaling of urban governance in the European Union. *Urban Studies* 36 (3): 431–51.

Cannan, E. 1921. Early history of the term capital. *Quarterly Journal of Economics* 35 (May): 468–81.

Carlyle, T. 1971. Signs of the times. In *Selected Writings*. Harmondsworth: Penguin Books.

Casey, E. S. 1993. *Getting back into place: Toward a renewed understanding of the place-world*. Bloomington: Indiana University Press.

———. 1997. *The fate of place*. Berkeley: University of California Press.

Clavier, L., and L. Hincker. 1997. La Barricade de Juin 1848: Une construction politique. In *La Barricade: Actes du colloque organisé les 17, 18, et 19 mai 1995*. Paris: Publications de la Sorbonne.

Condorcet, J.-A.-N. 1976. A general view of the science of social mathematics. In *Condorcet: Selected writings*, edited by Keith Michael Baker. Indianapolis: Bobbs-Merrill Company.

Dippel, H. 1981. *Individuum und Gesellschaft: Soziales Denken zwischen Tradition und Revolution: Smith—Condorcet—Franklin*. Göttingen: Vandenhoeck & Ruprecht.

Durkheim, E. 1900. Morphologie sociale. *L'année sociologique 1898–1899*, vol. 3. Paris: G. Baillière.

———. 1968. *Les formes élémentaires de la vie religieuse*. Paris: Presses universitaires de France.

———. 1984. *The division of labor in society*. New York: Free Press.

Ekelund, R. B., and R. F. Hébert. 1999. *Secret origins of modern microeconomics*. Chicago: University of Chicago Press.

Elias, N. 1969. *Die höfische Gesellschaft. Untersuchungen zur Soziologie des Königtums* und der höfische Aristokratie mit einer Einleitung: Soziologie und Geschichtswissenschaft. Darmstadt: Hermann Luchterhand.

Emirbayer, M. 1997. Manifestor for a relational sociology. *American Journal of Sociology* 103 (2): 281–317.

Faust, K., and S. Wasserman. 1994. *Social network analysis.* Cambridge: Cambridge University Press.

Feldman, S., and C. Tilly. 1960. The interaction of social and physical space. *American Sociological Review* 25 (6): 877–84.

Ferguson, A. 1792. *Principles of moral and political science.* Vol. 2. Edinburgh: A. Strahan and T. Cadell.

———. 1819. *An essay on the history of civil society.* 8th ed. Philadelphia: A. Finley.

Fischer, C. S. 1977. *Networks and places: Social relations in the urban setting.* New York: Free Press.

Foucault, M. 1963. *Naissance de la clinique: Une archéologie du regard médical.* Paris: Presses universitaires de France.

———. 1975. *Surveiller et punir: Naissance de la prison.* Paris: Éditions Gallimard.

———. 1984. Space, knowledge, and power. In *The Foucault reader,* edited by Paul Rabinow. New York: Pantheon Books.

———. 1986. *Death and the labyrinth: The world of Raymond Roussel.* London: Athlone Press.

———. 1991. Governmentality. In *The Foucault effect: Studies in governmentality,* edited by Graham Burchell, Colin Gordon, and Peter Miller. Chicago: University of Chicago Press.

———. 1993. Kant on Enlightenment and revolution. Reprinted in *Foucault's new domains,* edited by Mike Gane and Terry Johnson. London: Routledge.

Frank, K. A., and J. Y. Yasumoto. 1998. Linking action to social structure within a system: Social capital within and between subgroups. *American Journal of Sociology* 104 (3): 642–86.

Franklin, N., and L. A. Henkel. 1995. Parsing surrounding space into regions. *Memory and Cognition* 23 (4): 397–407.

Geertz, C. 1973. *The interpretation of cultures.* New York: Basic Books.

Gibson, J. J. 1979. *The ecological approach to visual perception.* Boston: Houghton Mifflin.

Golinski, J. 1992. *Science as public culture: Chemistry and Enlightenment in Britain, 1760–1820.* Cambridge: Cambridge University Press.

Gooday, G. 1998. The premisses of premises: Spatial issues in the historical construction of laboratory credibility. In *Making space for science: Territorial themes in the shaping of knowledge,* edited by Crosbie Smith and Jon Agar. New York: St. Martin's Press.

Gould, R. 1995. *Insurgent identities: Class, community, and protest in Paris from 1848 to the Commune.* Chicago: University of Chicago Press.

Gulbenkian Commission on the Restructuring of the Social Sciences. 1996. *Open the social sciences.* Stanford: Stanford University Press.

Green, D. P., and I. Shapiro. 1994. *Pathologies of rational choice theory: A critique of applications in political science.* New Haven: Yale University Press.

Grew, R. 1999. Finding social capital: The French Revolution in Italy. *Journal of Interdisiplinary History* 29 (3): 407–33.

Habermas, J. 1990. *The philosophical discourse of modernity: Twelve lectures.* Cambridge, Mass.: MIT Press.

Hamowy, R. 1987. *The Scottish enlightenment and the theory of spontaneous order.* Carbondale: Southern Illinois University Press.

Heidegger, M. 1954. *Vorträge und Aufsätze.* Pfullingen: G. Neske.

Heller, A. 1967. *Renaissance man.* London: Routledge & Kegan Paul.

Hill, L. 1996. Anticipations of nineteenth- and twentieth-century social thought in the world of Adam Ferguson. *Archives Européennes de Sociologie* 37 (1): 203–28.

Hillier, B. 1996. *Space is the machine: A configurational theory of architecture.* Cambridge: Cambridge University Press.

Hume, D. 1994. *Political essays,* edited by Knud Haakanssen. Cambridge: Cambridge University Press.

Jackson, M. W. 1999. Illuminating the opacity of achromatic lens production: Joseph von Fraunhofer's use of monastic architecture and space as a laboratory. In *The architecture of science,* edited by Peter Galison and Emily Thompson. Cambridge, Mass.: MIT Press.

Joyce, P. 1995. The end of social history? *Social History* 20 (1): 73–92.

———, ed. 2001. *The social in question.* London: Routledge.

———. 2003. *The rule of freedom: Liberalism and the modern city.* London: Verso.

Kant, I. 1900. Morphologie sociale. In *L'année sociologique 1898–1899.* Vol. 3. Paris: G. Baillière.

———. 1963a. Von dem ersten Grunde des Unterschiedes der Gegenden in Raume. In *Vorkritische Schriften bis 1768.* Vol. 1. Darmstadt: Wissenschaftliche Buchgesellschaft.

———. 1963b. Was heisst sich im denken orientieren? In *Vorkritische Schriften bis 1768.* Vol. 3. Darmstadt: Wissenschaftliche Buchgesellschaft.

———. 1990. *Kritik der reinen Vernunft.* Hamburg: Felix Meiner.

———. 1994. Beantwortung der Frage: Was ist Aufklärung? In *Was ist Aufklärung? Aufsätze zur Geschichte und Philosophie.* Göttingen: Vandenhoeck & Ruprecht.

Kharkhordin, O. 1999. *The collective and the individual in Russia: A study of practices.* Berkeley: University of California Press.

Labov, W. 1991. The three dialects of English. In *New ways of analyzing sound change,* edited by Penelope Eckert. San Diego: Academic Press.

Labov, W., and W. A. Harris. 1986. De facto segregation of black and white vernaculars. In *Diversity and diachrony,* edited by David Sankoff. Amsterdam: John Benjamins.

Lakoff, G., and M. Johnson. 1999. *Philosophy in the flesh: The embodied mind and its challenge to Western thought.* New York: Basic Books.

Lamont, M. 1992. *Money, morals and manners: The culture of the French and American upper-middle class.* Chicago: University of Chicago Press.

Lang, A. 1997. Non-Cartesian artifacts in dwelling activities: Steps towards a semiotic ecology. In *Mind, culture, and activity,* edited by Michael Cole,

Yrjo Engestrom, and Olga Vasquez. Cambridge: Cambridge University Press.

Latour, B. 1988. *The pasteurization of France.* Cambridge, Mass.: Harvard University Press.

Lévi-Strauss, C. 1955. *Tristes tropiques.* Paris: Plon.

———. 1958. *Anthropologie structurale.* Paris: Plon.

Lie, J. 1992. The concept of mode of exchange. *American Sociological Review* 57 (4): 508–23.

Livingstone, D. 1994. Science and religion: Foreword to the historical geography of an encounter. *Journal of Historical Geography* 20 (4): 367–83.

Lukács, G. 1984. *Zur Ontologie des gesellschaftlichen Seins.* Vol. 1. Darmstadt: Hermann Luchterhand.

Maplas, J. E. 1999. *Place and experience: A philosophical topography.* Cambridge: Cambridge University Press.

Markovits, F. 1986. *L'ordre des échanges: Philosophie de l'économie et économie du discours au XIII siècle en France.* Paris: Presses universitaires de France.

Markus, T. 1982. Buildings for the sad, the bad and the mad in urban Scotland, 1780–1830. In *Order in space and society: Architectural form and its context in the Scottish Enlightenment,* edited by Thomas Markus. Edinburgh: Mainstream Publishing.

———. 1993. *Buildings and power: Freedom and control in the origin of modern building types.* London: Routledge.

Marx, K. 1953. Fragment des Urtextes von *Zur Kritik der politischen Ökonomie. Grundrisse der Kritik der politische Ökonomie.* Berlin: Dietz.

———. 1980. *Das Kapital.* Vol. 1. Berlin: Dietz Verlag.

Massey, D., and N. Denton. 1993. *American apartheid: Segregation and the making of an underclass.* Cambridge, Mass.: Harvard University Press.

McMichael, P. 1992. Rethinking comparative analysis in a post-developmentalist context. *International Social Science Journal* 133: 351–65.

Meek, R. 1967. *Economics and ideology and other essays.* London: Chapman and Hall.

Merleau-Ponty, M. 1976. *Phénoménologie de la perception.* Paris: Gallimard Tel.

Mukerji, C. 1997. *Territorial ambitions and the gardens of Versailles.* Cambridge: Cambridge University Press.

Nagel, T. 1986. *The view from nowhere.* Oxford: Oxford University Press.

Opher, A., and S. Shapin. 1991. The place of knowledge: A methodological survey. *Science in Context* 4 (1): 3–21.

Panofsky, E. 1991. *Perspective as symbolic form.* New York: Zone Books.

Péli, G., and B. Nooteboom. 1999. Market partitioning and the geometry of the resources space. *American Journal of Sociology* 104 (4): 1132–53.

Pitkin, H. F. 1998. *The attack of the blob: Hannah Arendt's concept of the social.* Chicago: University of Chicago Press.

Pocock, J. G. A. 1985. The mobility of property and the rise of eighteenth-century sociology. In *Virtue, commerce, and history: Essays on political thought and history, chiefly in the eighteenth century.* Cambridge: Cambridge University Press.

Ponsard, C. 1954. *Économie et espace: Essai d'intégration du facteur spatial dans l'analyse économique*. Paris: Sedes.

Poovey, M. 1995. *Making a social body: British cultural formation 1830–1864*. Chicago: University of Chicago Press.

Portes, A. 1998. Social capital: Its origins and applicability in modern sociology. *Annual Review of Sociology* 24: 1–24.

Rauscher, F., R. Krauss, and Y. Chen. 1996. Gesture, speech, and lexical access. *Psychological Science* 7 (4): 226–31.

Rosenberg, C. 1987. *The care of strangers: The rise of America's hospital system*. New York: Basic Books.

Sack, R. 1980. *Conceptions of space in social thought: A geographic perspective*. Minneapolis: University of Minnesota Press.

Sahlins, M. 1976. *Culture and practical reason*. Chicago: University of Chicago Press.

———. 1989. *Boundaries: The making of France and Spain in the Pyrenees*. Berkeley: University of California Press.

———. 1996. The sadness of sweetness: The native anthropology of Western cosmology. *Current Anthropology* 37 (3): 395–428.

Saint Martin, M. 1989. Structure du capital, différenciation selon les sexes et 'vocation' intellectuelle. *Sociologie et sociétés* 21 (2): 9–25.

Sayeki, Y. 1997. "Body analogy" and the cognition of rotated figures. In *Mind, culture, and activity*, edited by Michael Cole, Yrjo Engestrom, Olga Vasquez. Cambridge: Cambridge University Press.

Schama, S. 1995. *Landscape and memory*. New York: Alfred A. Knopf.

Schivelbusch, W. 1986. *The railway journey*. Berkeley: University of California Press.

Schmidt, J., ed. 1996. *What is enlightenment? Eighteenth-century answers and twentieth-century questions*. Berkeley: University of California Press.

Schön, E. 1993. *Der Verlust der Sinnlichkeit oder die Verwandlungen des Lesers: Mentalitätswandel um 1800*. Stuttgart: Klett-Cotta.

Schorske, C. E. 1979. *Fin-de-siècle Vienna: Politics and culture*. New York: Knopf.

Schwartz, D., and T. Black. 1999. Inferences through imagined actions: Knowing by simulated doing. *Journal of Experimental Psychology; Learning, Memory, and Cognition* 25: 116–36.

Sennett, R. 1994. *Flesh and stone: The body and the city in Western civilization*. New York: W. W. Norton and Company.

Sewell, W. H. Jr. 1980. *Work and revolution in France*. Cambridge: Cambridge University Press.

———. 1996. Three temporalities: Toward an eventful sociology. In *The historic turn in the human sciences*, edited by Terrence McDonald. Ann Arbor: University of Michigan Press.

Shapin, S. 1998. Placing the view from nowhere: Historical and sociological problems in the location of science. In *Transactions of the Institute of British Geographers*. Vol. 23. London: G. Philip.

Shapin, S., and S. Schaffler. 1985. *Leviathan and the air pump: Hobbes, Boyle and the experimental life*. Princeton: Princeton University Press.

Silver, A. 1997. "Two different sorts of commerce"—friendship and strangership in civil society. In *Public and private in thought and practice*, edited by Jeff Weintraub and Krishan Kumar. Chicago: University of Chicago Press.

Simmel, G. 1903a. Soziologie des Raumes. *Jahrbuch für Gesetzgebung, Verwaltung und Volkswirtschaft* 27: 27–71.

———. 1903b. Ueber räumliche Projektionen socialer Formen. *Zeitschrift für Socialwissenschaft* 6: 287–302.

Smith, A. 1976. *An Inquiry into the nature and causes of the wealth of nations.* Vol. 1. Chicago: University of Chicago Press.

———. 2000. Spatial cognition without spatial concepts. In *Spatial cognition: Foundations and applications*, edited by Sean O Nuallain. Amsterdam: John Benjamins.

Somers, M. 1995. What's political or cultural about political culture and the public sphere—toward an historical sociology of concept formation. *Sociological Theory* 13 (2): 113–44.

———. 1996. A second look at a classic. *Archives Europennes de Sociologie* 37 (1): 180–202.

Specter, A. N., and V. L. Rivizzigno. 1982. Sampling designs and recovering cognitive representations of an urban area. In *Proximity and preference*, edited by Reginald G. Golledge and John N. Rayner. Minneapolis: University of Minnesota Press.

Suttles, G. D. 1968. *The social order of the slum: Ethnicity and territory in the inner city.* Chicago: University of Chicago Press.

Tilly, C. 1987. Shrugging off the nineteenth-century incubus. In *Beyond progress and development: Macro-political and macro-societal change*, edited by Jan Berting and Wim Blockmans. Aldershot: Avebury.

———. 1988. Future history. *Theory and Society* 17 (5): 703–12.

Tocqueville, A. 1970. *Recollections.* Garden City, N.J.: Doubleday and Company.

Traugott, M. 1997. Les barricades dans les insurrections parisiennes: Rôles sociaux et modes de fonctionnement. In *La Barricade: Actes du colloque organisé les 17, 18, et 19 mai 1995.* Paris: Publications de la Sorbonne.

Van Baalen, M. 2000. Pair approximations for different spatial geometries. In *The geometry of ecological interactions: Simplifying spatial complexity*, edited by Ulf Dieckmann, Richard Law, and Johan A. J. Metz. Cambridge: Cambridge University Press.

Wallerstein, I. 1988. Should we unthink the nineteenth century? In *Rethinking the nineteenth century: Contradictions and movements*, edited by Francisco O. Ramirez. New York: Greenwood.

Warren, D. 1998. Kant and the apriority of space. *The Philosophical Review* 107 (2): 179–224.

White, H. 1992. *Identity and control: A structural theory of social action.* Princeton: Princeton University Press.

Whitehead, A. N. 1927. *Science and the modern world.* Harmondswroth: Penguin Books.

Young, A. 1770. *The farmer's guide in hiring and stocking farms.* London: W. Straham.

Zelizer, V. 1994. *The social meaning of money: Pin money, paychecks, poor relief, and other currencies.* New York: Basic Books.

SOUTHERN PERSPECTIVES ON

HISTORICAL SOCIAL SCIENCE

SUMMARIES OF PRESENTATIONS

AND DISCUSSION

Akhil Gupta (Stanford)

Gupta offered an iconoclastic analysis of globalization, arguing not only that it is not new, but that the historical verdict will show that the twentieth century reversed globalization via the elaboration of systems of territorial states and the maturation of parochial nationalisms. In addition, he argued that globalization is neither singular nor unitary—having quite different forms and meanings across time and space. If some understand globalization as intensified flows of finances and images, others view it as the erection of laws against mobility of people and intellectual property. Further, positioning in class, racial, gender, and sexual hierarchies yields different experiences of globalization. From the Western perspective, globalization might be seen to have been interrupted by the protectionism of the nation-state, whereas from the postcolonial subaltern perspective, globalization was a continuing feature of the era of developmentalism corresponding to the Western social-democratic interlude. Through an accounting for the movements of foodstuffs like spices and then crops over the past several centuries, Gupta emphasized that the construction of regional/ cultural cuisines stemmed from differentiated global processes—such that in the early modern period sugar was central to the Atlantic circuit, while pepper defined the Pacific circuit. This gave rise to the final observation that those who fixate on the historical question of "why Europe?" are often unable to reflect on the proposition that Europe, understood as a fictional self-representation, was just as likely to have been shaped by the ideas, technologies, and resources of the non-European world.

Fernando Coronil (Michigan)

Coronil viewed dominant globalization discourses as concealing differences between the West and its Others, constituting cultural difference around subalternity rather than alterity. Within this subaltern perspective, such "global centralism" projects the potential equality and uniformity of all peoples and cultures. This is reflected in the privileging of the capital/labor relation in capitalist discourses, which discount nature and culture, subordinating them to the market. Coronil argued that nature is here discounted as constitutive of the modern world, occluding the role of the colonies in the formation of capitalism as a global, rather than a Western, phenomenon. Contemporary neoliberal globalization compels subaltern nations to intensify nature-dependent activities at the expense of state projects of economic diversification. And, given the financialized and cybernetic character of contemporary globalization, all wealth is reduced to capital and speculative opportunity (that is, risk) via financial derivatives. Opposition to global centralism involves the reassertion of cultural difference and the deconstruction of the homogenizing operations of financialized capital.

Farshad Araghi (Florida Atlantic)

Araghi specified globalization through periodization into "three colonialisms of historical capitalism" in order to reveal continuities and discontinuities. The first colonialism, providing the preconditions of industrial capitalism, involved military conquest and force in extracting African and Indian labor and resources in the non-European world. The second colonialism used state power to reorganize colonial labor forces to extract food and industrial raw materials to subsidize burgeoning industrial classes. Anticolonial movements ended this period of colonialism as the west incorporated their demands via development discourse. The third colonialism, following the decline of the Cold War, sees transnational corporations and their agencies (the IMF, the World Bank, the WTO) reorganizing the global division of labor around the reproductive needs of transnational capitalism, through the invisible hand of debt and the global market. The transition between the second and third colonialism involved a variety of discursive interventions via the theme of developmentalism. The first, right-wing developmentalism, countered socialism and promoted nationalism within internationalism via modernization theory. Its critique,

Akhil Gupta, Fernando Coronil, Farshad Araghi

left-wing developmentalism, shared the assumptions of evolutionism, nationalism, and industrialism. Each of these versions incorporated Third World demands, and in that sense represented the hegemony of developmentalism. In the third colonialism, globalism (unlike developmentalism) has as yet to develop an ideology (in the Gramscian sense) as its discourse has been based on an exclusionary agenda that only conceals superficially a highly unstable and increasingly unequal form of globalization, which is unable and unwilling to meet universal needs. The rise and strengthening of a broad antiglobalization movement today is linked with this fundamental weakness (despite appearances) of the neoliberal globalism of our times.

Discussion

Discussion revolved around the various perspectives on globalization proposed by the panelists—noting that each differentiated globalization across time and space but not necessarily in the same way. Araghi, for example, saw the nationalist interregnum in the mid-twentieth century as a more substantial (than Gupta's view) response to subaltern demands in the colonial and postcolonial world, providing an opportunity for a hegemonic, developmentalist ideology quite distinct from globalist ideology of today. Panel debate centered on the question of who defines/represents the world and in what terms as a way of understanding globalization as a discursive instrument of rule and/or of organizing the world.

NEW DIRECTIONS IN

HISTORICAL SOCIAL SCIENCE

SUMMARIES OF PRESENTATIONS

AND DISCUSSION

Ann Stoler (Michigan)

Stoler addressed the role of sex, domestic arrangements, and child rearing in the making of racial categories as part of the management of imperial rule. Her concern was twofold: to juxtapose imperial projects to compare how they attended, respectively, to relations of intimacy; and to question the use of separate conceptual frames in the construction of the historiography of European imperialism and U.S. colonization. Her point was that the monitoring of the "intimate frontier," however particularistic in the various colonial state projects, drew on commensurable political and social concerns in managing race relations in domestic settings. Colonial authorities investigated, debated, and tried to identify the psychological and affective coordinates of race as part of the process of developing technologies of rule. In the Indies, the French colonies, and the American colonies, similar concerns with demarcating race, on the one hand, and with social reform as a complementary civilizing mission on the other, marked the parallel history of these imperial projects. Stoler's point is that comparison across these distinct historiographical traditions is fruitful since they implicitly and explicitly address shared categories and processes of rule of nonwhites by whites. Such comparison also renders national/colonial archives part of a world-historical context expressed in circuits of knowledge. Furthermore, she argued that the rule-makers implicitly and explicitly compared their technologies of rule, rendering comparison very much part of the politics of empire and expressed, for example, in international conferences on the subject of race relations and reform.

Dale Tomich (Binghamton)

Tomich addressed the unit of analysis problem via a critique of the use of the global/local dichotomy. He characterized the latter as informing the standoff between the globalism (universalism) of Wallerstein's world-system analysis and the localism (particularism) of poststructural analyses. The way beyond this impasse is through the comparative method, and in particular that form of comparison that "internalizes" the global/local distinction as one that is both ontologically impossible and mutually conditioning. Tilly's "encompassing comparison" comes close but continues to distinguish unit cases as locations within, and as subordinated to, a larger world structure. Alternatively, McMichael's "incorporated comparison" views cases as instances or outcomes of historically integrated processes, conceived relationally in order to reconstruct the historical complex to which they contribute, and from which they derive. Tomich used the *falta de brazos* (labor problem) in the Latin coffee cultures to illustrate his point, arguing that the *falta de brazos* is routinely taken as a national given (production relation) in coffee culture histories, rather than as a facet of the ensemble of world coffee relations as a whole. Tomich shifts the focus/question to understanding nationally located sites as particular instances of coffee production in global commodity circuits. The *falta de brazos* is, therefore, mutually conditioned by immediate environmental, labor, spatial, and political relations, and by the competitive political-economic relations of the commodity circuits among these sites. In this alternative method, the global and the local are outcomes of our theoretical and historical reconstruction of the *falta de brazos* and not its empirical, and seemingly self-evident, presuppositions.

Discussion

Led by Catherine LeGrand (McGill), discussion centered on the question of the unit of analysis—that is whether and to what extent places are real sites of knowledge production, or abstract insofar as they are not situated within broader, historical relations—in which case place becomes a site/unit of observation rather than units of analysis in their own right. Both Tomich and Stoler, in distinctive ways, were viewed as contributing to a concretization of place as incorporating circuits of exchange relations and/or knowledge, respectively.

These concerns, linked with Biernacki's insistence on the importance of cultural practice/meaning as part of the understanding of place, addressed the other two issues debated: namely, how to integrate the economic and the cultural, and the epistemological status of categories, such as place, global, and local.

APPENDIXES

CONTRIBUTORS

APPENDIX A

SSHA PRESIDENTIAL ADDRESSES, 1976–2000

Dates are to the published editions, although the addresses were made one or two years earlier.

Benson, Lee (1976–77) Changing social science to change the world. *Social Science History* 2 (1978): 427–41.

Bogue, Allan G. (1977–78) Data dilemmas: Quantitative data and the Social Science History Association. *Social Science History* 3 (1979): 204–26.

Miller, Warren E. (1978–79)

Aydelotte, William O. (1979–80) The search for ideas in historical investigation. *Social Science History* 5 (1981): 371–92.

Fogel, Robert W. (1980–81)

Tilly, Louise A. (1981–82) People's history and social science history. *Social Science History* 7 (1983): 457–74.

Flanigan, William H. (1982–83) The conduct of inquiry in social science history. *Social Science History* 8 (1984): 323–39.

Clubb, Jerome M. (1983–84) Computer technology and the source materials of social science history. *Social Science History* 10 (1986): 97–114.

Schwartz, Mildred A. (1984–85) Historical sociology in the history of American sociology. *Social Science History* 11 (1987): 1–16.

Alexander, Thomas B. (1985–86) Ex parte county aggregates et cetera. *Social Science History* 11 (1987): 449–62.

Clausen, Aage R. (1986–87.) Social science history: Citation record, 1976–1985. *Social Science History* 12 (1988): 197–215.

Smith, Daniel Scott. (1987–88)

McCloskey, Donald [Deirdre] N. (1988–89) Ancients and moderns. *Social Science History* 14 (1990): 289–303.

Hanawalt, Barbara A. (1989–90) The voices and audiences of social history records. *Social Science History* 15 (1991): 159–75.

Laslett, Barbara (1990–91) Gender in/and social science history. *Social Science History* 16 (1992): 177–95.

Engerman, Stanley L. (1991–92) Chicken Little, Anna Karenina, and the economics of slavery: Two reflections on historical analysis, with examples drawn mostly from the study of slavery. *Social Science History* 17 (1993): 161–71.

Monkkonen, Eric H. (1992–93) Lessons of social science history. *Social Science History* 18 (1994): 161–68.

231

Watkins, Susan Cotts (1993–94) Social networks and social science history. *Social Science History* 19 (1995): 295–311.

Hareven, Tamara K. (1994–95) What difference does it make? *Social Science History* 20 (1996): 317–44.

Skocpol, Theda (1995–96) The Tocqueville problem: Civic engagement in American democracy. *Social Science History* 21 (1997): 455–79.

Schofield, Roger (1996–97) Through a glass darkly. *Social Science History* 22 (1998): 117–30.

Katznelson, Ira (1997–98) DuBois's century. *Social Science History* 23 (1999): 459–74.

Haines, Michael R. (1998–99) The great modern mortality transition.

Graff, Harvey J. (1999–2000) The shock of the "'new' (histories)": Social science histories and historical literacies. *Social Science History* 25 (2001): 483–534.

APPENDIX B

SOCIAL SCIENCE HISTORY

MISSION STATEMENTS

Objectives in the Constitution of the SSHA

The major purpose of the Social Science History Association is to improve the quality of historical explanation in every manner possible, but particularly by encouraging the selective use and adaptation in historical teaching and research of relevant theories and methods from related disciplines, particularly the social sciences.

The Association will seek to achieve this purpose by:

Developing a publication program that will encourage and disseminate social science history of high quality devoted to substantive research, to methodological concerns, and to curricular development.

Organizing conferences, both regional and national, to bring together like-minded historians and other social scientists with interdisciplinary interests. In this respect members of the Association will endeavor to foster those research areas in which work is particularly experimental or pathbreaking in nature as well as those that have already attracted considerable numbers of adherents.

Encouraging the introduction of the materials of the new social, political, and economic history into the undergraduate curriculum, with appropriate concern for the development of teaching methods appropriate to the new course content, at all curricular levels but particularly in college and university introductory sources and in the offerings of junior and community colleges. We are particularly concerned that ways be devised to carry the challenge and exhilaration of the research process into the classroom.

Sponsoring or assisting in the development of summer institutes or other training programs to enable historians and other social scientists to learn skills necessary for the various types of interdisciplinary historical research and their presentation in the classroom.

Fostering the retrieval and archiving of quantitative historical data for general scholarly use and its processing in data series of wide applicability as well as assisting in the dissemination of such materials for both research and classroom use.

Enabling history and the other social sciences to respond better to the growing interest in the historical dimension in various social science disciplines by promoting the evaluation of historical research proposals by fund granting agencies on the basis of the substance of the research problem rather than in terms of the departmental or disciplinary affiliation of the applicants.

Working to achieve maximum freedom of access for scholars to data of particular interest to social science historians.

Preparing and submitting grant proposals where appropriate to enable the executive officers and council members of the Association to realize the major and subordinate objectives of the Association.

Taking any other appropriate action, which the members of the Association may believe necessary to achieve the above objectives.

Editors' Foreword to *Social Science History*, volume 1, no. 1 (fall 1976)

Social Science History is the journal of the Social Science History Association. This organization was formed in 1974 for the purpose of improving the quality of historical explanation by encouraging the selective use and adaptation in teaching and in research in relevant theories and methods from the social science disciplines. The Association's Organizing Committee includes scholars from a wide range of disciplines interested in developing a common enterprise within which historians seeking a more rigorous and consciously theoretical orientation in their discipline might join forces with other social scientists interested in longitudinal analysis. *Social Science History* will constitute one of the most important avenues through which the Association hopes to implement its goals of encouraging substantive research, fostering appropriate curricular development, and stimulating theoretical, methodological, and data-gathering activities relating to these objectives.

The editors of *Social Science History* will encourage and provide a forum for research that attempts generalizations of some breadth verified by systematic examination of the relevant evidence and supported by quantitative analysis when appropriate. Research efforts involving comparisons across time between individuals and groups within a single population and between different and properly comparable populations across space and over time will be particularly welcome. We shall also welcome contributions to the development of theory and techniques, which, although firmly centered in particular social science disciplines, can provide a genuine interdisciplinary focus in approaching the historical dimension. We shall, of course, be particularly receptive to research of a path-breaking or experimental nature, but we also accord a high priority to significant research advances in the more highly developed areas of social science history. Within the general framework delineated by these guidelines, the Editors declare their interest in case studies of an innovative nature and in interpretive inquiries into the "state of the art." To this end, we plan to inaugurate a series of "retrospective" reviews that will attempt to assess the significance and impact of some of the major writings in the areas that share common concerns with social science history.

Additionally, the editors hope to stimulate the development of social science history courses in college and university curricula by publishing articles, which aim at developing teaching methods that will carry the challenge and exhilaration of the research process into the classroom. In pursuit of this goal, we shall disseminate information on cross-disciplinary or program-oriented course experiments that have innovative promise and that are judged to deserve a wide audience. Also, on a selective basis, *Social Science History* will inform its readers about new developments in social science data archives, research funding agencies, training programs and summer institutes, and significant new publications in the history and social science disciplines.

In conclusion, the editors affirm their total commitment to the position that systematic contact and interchange of ideas between kindred spirits in history and in the social sciences will be immensely beneficial to all concerned. We believe that the study of social theory within an empirical historical context can make a uniquely valuable contribution to our understanding of societies, past and present, and we intend that *Social Science History* should be an important means by which that contribution will be transmitted throughout the scholarly community.

Front Matter Description to *Social Science History*, volume 23, no. 3 (fall 1999)

Social Science History is the journal of the Social Science History Association and exists to publish material directed to improving the quality of historical explanation in teaching and research of relevant theories and methods from the social science disciplines. It is aimed at social scientists interested in longitudinal analysis and historians seeking a more rigorous and consciously theoretical orientation. The editors encourage and provide a forum for research that attempts generalizations of some breadth verified by systematic examination of the relevant evidence and support by quantitative analysis when appropriate. Research efforts involving comparisons across time between individuals and groups within a single population and between different and properly comparable populations across space and over time will be particularly welcome. The editors welcome contributions to the development of theory and techniques that, although firmly centered in particular social science disciplines, can provide a genuine interdisciplinary focus in approaching the historical dimension. The Social Science History Association will also inform its members about new developments in social science data archives, research funding agencies, training programs and summer institutes, and significant new publications in history and the social science disciplines through its newsletter.

CONTRIBUTORS

Harvey J. Graff (English & History, Ohio State University)
Leslie Page Moch (History, Michigan State University)
Philip McMichael (Rural Sociology, Cornell University)

Andrew Abbott (Sociology, University of Chicago)
Richard Biernacki (Sociology, University of California, San Diego)
Allan Bogue (History, University of Wisconsin, Madison)
Michael Brown (Political Science, University of California, Santa Cruz)
William Flanigan (Political Science, University of Minnesota)
Chad Gaffield (History & Institute of Canadian Studies, University of Ottawa)
Barbara Hanawalt (History, Ohio State University)
Ira Katznelson (Political Science & History, Columbia University)
James Lee (History, California Institute of Technology)
Mary Jo Maynes (History, University of Minnesota)
David Mitch (Economics, University of Maryland Baltimore County)
Anders Nilsson (Economic History, Lund University, Sweden)
Daniel Segal (Anthropology, Pitzer College)
William Sewell Jr. (History & Political Science, University of Chicago)
Daniel Scott Smith (History, University of Illinois at Chicago)
Richard Steckel (Economics, Ohio State University)
David Vincent (History, The Open University, England)